D1244603

REVOLUTIONARY ENIGMA

MARTIN H. BUSH

REVOLUTIONARY ENIGMA

A Re-appraisal of
GENERAL PHILIP SCHUYLER
of
NEW YORK

Port Washington, N.Y.
IRA J. FRIEDMAN, INC.
1969

EMPIRE STATE HISTORICAL PUBLICATIONS SERIES No. 80

Manufactured by
Taylor Publishing Company
Dallas, Texas

For my wife

Elinor Seward Bush

CONTENTS

PREFACE

Philip Schuyler was initially drawn into the controversy with Great Britain because he sought to preserve and maintain America's economic and social privileges and not because he wanted to break away from the mother country. He did not wish for independence, nor did he fight for it. Rather, he fought to get Britain to cede its power of taxation to the American colonies without any thought of promoting democratic ideals, since he preferred to keep New York under British rule and in the hands of aristocrats of wealth and power.

During the war, Schuyler performed valuable services for America in the Continental Congress and in the Continental Army. He struggled to invade Canada in 1775, support the army before Quebec that winter, delay Sir Guy Carleton's invasion in 1776, and defeat "Gentleman" Johnny Burgoyne in 1777; but the absence of workmen, the shortage of money, bad weather, inadequate numbers of troops, New England's hostility toward him, and conflicts with members of Congress brought about his ultimate downfall. Throughout it all, he remained an outspoken critic of Congress because he thought it could not govern the nation. Therefore, he dedicated himself to bringing about a reconciliation with the mother country until the conclusion of the war.

Because Philip Schuyler's role in the American Revolution has generally been misunderstood, the mere mention of his name usually brings to mind the picture of an overcautious general who was suspected of treasonable communication with the enemy. One might also recall that General Richard

Montgomery gave the order to invade Canada immediately after Schuyler left for an Indian conference in late August, 1775, ostensibly because of Schuyler's reluctance to act. Then, after rejoining his army, Schuyler fell ill and returned to Fort Ticonderoga just as his troops attacked Fort St. John's.

Two years later during the Burgoyne campaign, Schuyler was dismissed from his command under a cloud of suspicion and discontent because he had not been at Fort Ticonderoga when it was evacuated without a fight. Since the general was also an extremely unpopular officer, especially among the New England troops, his image suffered badly throughout the war. As a result of these ignorant and often jealous misrepresentations, Schuyler remains an enigma, still suspected of having secretly been a Tory, or, at best, an incompetent aristocrat. But what of the real Schuyler? What kind of a man was he? Was he a coward and a traitor to his country, or a general whose reputation has been unfairly maligned by distortions and myths?

It is safe to say that Philip Schuyler was neither a hero nor a traitor. In the following pages, one can sense the complicated character of a man who was drawn into a struggle he did not approve of even though he served his country with great courage and devotion. He was obstinate, fiercely proud, and impatient to the point of arrogance, yet he had high moral standards and the capacity to forgive those who honestly opposed him. Unfortunately Schuyler was also suspicious by nature, and extraordinarily sensitive. This is why he was deeply disturbed by the harassment of New Englanders when he headed the Northern Department, particularly in his command controversy with General Horatio Gates. In the end, therefore, he preferred to remain on the sidelines as an observer rather than a participant as America moved toward independence in 1783.

In this volume I attempted to go to primary sources whenever possible in writing about the war years. No attempt was

made, however, to do a great deal of research in the years
prior to 1775, since Schuyler's activities in this period were
well covered by Don R. Gerlach in an excellent book entitled: *Philip Schuyler and the American Revolution in New
York, 1733-1777.*

Gerlach's emphasis is on politics and he has traced in
admirable fashion Schuyler's family history, business activities, and political career. He has uncovered much new information about Schuyler's background for which I am indebted
to him, but, to avoid needless duplication, I have not drawn
upon his book at length.

I have acquired many obligations in the course of writing
this book, and these few words represent a most inadequate
acknowledgement. Most of all I want to express my gratitude
to O. Theodore Barck for his patient and helpful reading of
the manuscript; to Frank P. Piskor and Ronald Rader for
the help and encouragement they gave me to finish it; to
Harvey Chalmers who read the manuscript and saved me
from many errors; and to the late Albert Corey, for his
assistance in making it possible for me to use many rare
manuscript collections.

Most of the research for this book was done in two fine
libraries, the Syracuse University Library, and the New York
State Library in Albany, in both of which I was accorded
the wholehearted help of the staffs, and special assistance
from Donald Anthony and Charles Bruns. To my secretaries,
Martha Holt, Elaine Kenyon, and Candace DeSilvey, I
am grateful for having wrestled with my handwriting and
revisions.

Finally, my thanks go to my wife, Elinor Seward Bush,
who bore the writing of this book with unusual tolerance
and support.

Martin H. Bush

Syracuse, New York
October 2, 1968

INTRODUCTION

by
Ira M. Leonard

Martin H. Bush's book, *Revolutionary Enigma*...is a welcome addition to the historical literature on New York and the role of New Yorkers during the War for American Independence. This is a carefully conceived, very well researched, crisply written narrative of Philip Schuyler's activities during the Revolutionary War. However, the author's basic purpose is to vindicate Schuyler of the onus of responsibility, while Commanding General of the Northern Department, for the abortive Canadian Campaign in the Winter of 1775 and the loss of Fort Ticonderoga to the British in July 1777. I think Bush succeeds admirably in establishing Schuyler's lack of guilt in these episodes. Indeed, Schuyler emerges from these pages as an energetic, practically tireless, and determined officer in the Revolutionary War effort, although Bush is careful to point out, repeatedly, that Schuyler was not a devoted Patriot and doubted that the struggle would result in a victory for the American cause.

In 1964 Professor Don R. Gerlach published the first of a projected two volume life of Philip Schuyler *Philip Schuyler and the American Revolution in New York, 1733-1777* (Lincoln: University of Nebraska Press) , and, though there are significant differences between the two studies, some discussion of the basic features of each work seems in order.

Gerlach has written a political biography of Schuyler and his times. In admirable fashion, and with extensive documentation, he traces Schuyler's family background, business activities (especially land business), and political career to

1777 when he was defeated by George Clinton for the governorship in New York's first state elections. Beyond writing a life of Schuyler, Gerlach was principally interested in challenging Carl Becker's long accepted interpretation of politics in pre-Revolutionary New York as a class conflict between a privileged aristocracy and an unprivileged lower social order over "who shall rule at home." Thus Gerlach's basic emphasis was upon politics in New York, and his biography largely given over to a discussion of the colony's political structure on the eve of the Revolutionary crisis and its reaction to English imperial policies and to an analysis of the important New York Assembly contests of 1768-1769. In this context the author not only tests the Becker Thesis but also tries to suggest Schuyler's role in the political rivalries within New York's ruling elite between the lower Hudson De Lanceys and upper Hudson Livingstons.

Because of this focus upon politics, Gerlach for the most part slights the military side of the Revolutionary struggle, and thus does not provide a satisfactorily detailed account of Schuyler's role in the war. Though he gives little credence to the allegations made against Schuyler, neither does he explain the military context from which they developed. For example, Gerlach dismisses the matter of Schuyler's military competence, his request that Congress inquire how far the miscarriages in Canada could be imputed to his direction of the army, and his subsequent court-martial in September 1778 for neglect of duty on one page (p. 288).

Bush's central concern, on the other hand, is to exonerate Schuyler of these charges, and in focussing directly (and exclusively) upon these issues, which Gerlach did not, he provides not only an illuminating narrative of Schuyler's activities during the war years, but also fascinating accounts of battlefront strategy and homefront politics. Bush believes that Congressional lack of support, sectional antagonisms between New York and New England, and the circumstances of war were the basic reasons for Schuyler's difficulties during these years.

Selected by Washington to command the Northern Department, which contained the Great Lakes and Forts George,
Ticonderoga, and Crown Point at which constituted the
outermost shield of defense against British-Indian penetration
from Canada, Schuyler found himself faced with an under-
manned army and a Congressional order to invade Canada.
The Canadian invasion seemed foredoomed from the outset,
and Schuyler, an officer during the French and Indian War,
realized it.

Nevertheless, Bush demonstrates, Schuyler in a "Herculean
effort" built and trained an army early in 1775 and personally led the initial phase of the campaign from a sickbed.
Only continued illness forced him to withdraw to Fort
Ticonderoga at the beginning of the attack. By December
1775 the Canadian expedition had failed, the Army of the
Northern Department was in disarray, and Schuyler's reputation tainted. Bush comments that even had Congress
completely supported Schuyler — which it did not — the Canadian invasion would have been a longshot, considering the
advantages of terrain and generalship possessed by the other
side.

Despite Schuyler's determined efforts, the situation did not
improve. According to Bush, "Schuyler organized Lake
Champlain's defenses and successfully blocked Sir Guy
Carleton's attempt to seize Fort Ticonderoga in October
1776. Still the military picture did not brighten." As a result,
by late 1776 Schuyler believed "America had exhausted its
resources and could no longer raise or support an army on
the pretense of fighting for independence" and then, demon-
strating this limited faith and vision, Schuyler sought "to
promote, if possible, reconciliation with Great Britain."

From this point, events moved swiftly. Under considerable
pressure, Congress replaced Schuyler as Commander of the
Northern Department with New Englander Horatio Gates,
but New Yorkers mounted a shrewd parliamentary campaign
and secured his reinstatement. Meanwhile, Schuyler was
defeated by Clinton in New York's first gubernatorial elec-

tion and Bush suggests that this was due in large measure to his besmirched reputation. Then, when General Arthur St. Clair evacuated Fort Ticonderoga rather than defend it, this, too, was blamed on Schuyler. His usefulness seemingly at an end, Congress again replaced Schuyler with General Gates. Dr. Bush then details Schuyler's almost year-long effort to secure an official statement of charges against him, and thus have an opportunity to clear himself of the "slanderous" allegations of incompetence and disloyalty which swirled about him.

Bush's judgments in these matters are always clear and sound. Though he is partisan, Bush knows he really has the best of the case and is content to let the evidence speak for Schuyler. In the process of vindicating Schuyler, Bush provides masterful descriptions and analyses of the major campaigns in the Northern Department of the Revolutionary War between 1775 and 1778. The chapters concerning the Canadian Campaign, the struggle for Lake Champlain, and the fall of Fort Ticonderoga are absorbing. Another theme which Bush handles with a sure touch is the bitter power struggle over personal interests and sectional schemes between leaders in Rhode Island, Connecticut, New Hampshire, Massachusetts, and New York "To see who would rule at home."

In summary, then, Martin H. Bush has written a lucid and absorbing account of an important, though neglected, phase of Philip Schuyler's public career and students of New York History and of the American Revolution will find it of considerable value.

Southern Connecticut State College
March, 1969

REVOLUTIONARY ENIGMA

Chapter One

A SOLDIER'S HERITAGE

The thirteen American states appeared to be on the brink of disaster in September, 1777, in what might well have been their most critical moment. Enemy troops were converging on Albany in a daring attempt to cut off New England from her southern allies, while in Pennsylvania, Washington's forces were being battered by repeated British assaults at Brandywine and Germantown. As news of defeat upon defeat spread, morale began to crumble and with it, all chances of a victory seemed to slip away.

It was a dark moment for Americans, perhaps the darkest they would face. Then, suddenly and unexpectedly, hope surged across the land. Burgoyne's invading army was overwhelmed in a spectacular victory at Saratoga, the first big American success of the war. This startling victory so shook the enemy's confidence that Sir Henry Clinton thought it advisable to recall units moving up the Hudson Valley to join Burgoyne. At Fort Ticonderoga and Crown Point, Burgoyne's rear guard abandoned their positions and hastily retreated to Canada. With the exception of New York City, New Yorkers were free of British control for the first time in months, and expectations of French support made the future look brighter. Never again would Great Britain have so good an opportunity to suppress the American rebellion.

On October 19, 1777, Burgoyne and his officers were brought into Albany amid great fanfare. Drums beat out a martial air as little boys darted in and out of the jubilant

3

crowd taunting the handsome Englishmen. From the tiny
brick houses lining the streets, housewives strained forward
to catch a glimpse of "Gentleman Johnny," the man they
had heard so much about. Six months before, this same man
had boasted that he would eat Christmas dinner in Albany.
Now he had arrived for dinner, to be sure, not as a con-
queror as planned, but as a prisoner of Major General Philip
Schuyler, the officer who had so expertly impeded his advance. Although it was not apparent to those who witnessed
the scene, Burgoyne's meeting with Schuyler symbolized the
decline of British power in America.

The Schuylers were superb hosts. Their cordiality so moved
Burgoyne that he turned to Schuyler and asked almost un-
believingly: "Is it to me, who have done you so much injury,
that you show so much kindness?" Schuyler smiled warmly
and replied: "That is the fate of war, let us say no more
about it."[1]   But much more remained to be said, for fate
had played worse tricks on Schuyler than the mere burning
of his Saratoga home by Burgoyne. Congress had stripped
him of his command in the middle of the campaign, enabling
Horatio Gates to accept Burgoyne's surrender and become
the hero of the hour, leaving Schuyler to be remembered
only as the discredited officer who had been dismissed under
questionable circumstances. This so blackened Schuyler's
reputation that later generations of Americans soon forgot
the man contemporaries admired as a courageous leader and
entrepreneur, and vaguely recall instead that he might have
been a traitor to his country.

Forty years before the Battle of Saratoga, on November
10, 1733, Johannes and Cornelia Schuyler brought Philip
John Schuyler into the world at Albany, New York. He was
a fine boy with a fine Dutch heritage. His great-grandfather,
Philip Pietersen Schuyler, settled in New York in 1650, and
his grandfather, Johannes Schuyler, became one of Albany's
most influential citizens, serving at one time or another as
mayor, militia officer, alderman and Indian commissioner.[2]

His father, John, Jr., had a promising public career cut short by an untimely death, but he provided well for his children. By marrying Cornelia Van Cortlandt, daughter of the first lord of the Cortlandt Manor, he assured young Philip of thousands of acres of land and great social status and prestige.

Life without a father was difficult for a boy whose childhood days were dominated by two women: his mother and his father's sister Margaretta. They raised Philip in a rather traditional Dutch home, characterized by discipline, openness and generosity. He was tutored by the two women at first. Then, after a brief introduction to school in Albany, they sent him to New Rochelle in 1748, to study at the Reverend Peter Stouppe's fashionable Westchester County School.[3]

These were profitable years for Schuyler. He was an eager student, anxious for success, even though illness sometimes slowed his progress. The eccentric French Protestant minister schooled him well in French and mathematics, and Schuyler learned so quickly that even the stern old man marveled at the lad's keen mind. Like many young men, however, Philip had his weak moments too, for he loved a good time now that he had gotten away from his mother. Anne Grant remembered him as a careless good-humored fellow "little what he seemed, with regard to ability, activity, ambition, art, enterprise, and perseverance, all of which he possesses in an uncommon degree...."[4]

In 1751, Schuyler came back to Albany to participate in an expedition .deep into the upper reaches of the Mohawk Valley.[5] This was a man's work, and he wanted to prove himself the equal of any man. Here he could see the frontier at first hand, meet the harsh challenges early settlers faced, talk to savage Indians, see the abundance of wildlife and timber, and survey the almost endless wilderness of land. Opportunities for riches were there for the taking, and talk of speculation was common. These tales stirred Schuyler's imagination so he learned as much as he could, for he too hoped to make money this way.

Refreshing though it was, frontier life was less to Schuyler's liking than New York City. The latter was a charming place with many attractions for a young bachelor. Schuyler loved meeting beautiful ladies there and enjoyed many useful acquaintances who were anxious to get into politics and follow that road to power. These were great days. He could argue and debate for hours with the DeLanceys, the Livingstons, William Smith, Jr., and John Morin Scott, men destined to be leaders of their time. One of New York's greatest attractions, however, was the theater, for it was still a treat in America in the eighteenth century. Schuyler recalled with delight having seen Richard Steele's "Conscious Lovers" at Hallam's Theater, and told how pleasing the performance had been.[6] Whenever possible he would attend the theater with a lady friend and he soon became known as one of New York's most popular young men. Anne Grant had changed her mind about him a little by then, and described him as a slender, well-mannered youth with "perfect command of temper, acuteness...and in the hour of social enjoyment...(always) active and companionable...."[7] It was during one of these visits to New York City that he met "sweet Kitty" Van Rensselaer and immediately fell in love with the lady who would one day become his wife.

Young Schuyler was a true aristocrat in every sense of the word. He dreamed of acquiring wealth and of serving his country to protect the heritage of aristocratic rights and privileges which he loved. Yet he had another facet to his personality that is often overlooked — sincerity and thoughtfulness. On becoming of age in 1754, he showed great magnanimity by waiving his right to primogeniture to enable his sister and two brothers to share their father's estate.

A martial atmosphere seemed to shroud America in gloom in 1754, as representatives from New England, New York, Pennsylvania, and Maryland gathered at Albany. Trouble was brewing with France and the Indians were restless. It was an exciting moment for Schuyler. Benjamin Franklin was there to propose his "Plan of Union" and reports arrived daily that other colonies had acted to strengthen their military forces. Schuyler was thrilled. All he wanted was a chance to show what he could do. His opportunity came in May, 1755, when Lieutenant Governor James DeLancey announced that eight companies of volunteers would be raised to build fortifications north of Albany under Sir William Johnson. Schuyler begged the lieutenant governor (his cousin) to commission him as a captain and DeLancey finally agreed even though Schuyler was not yet twenty-two. It proved to be a good decision because Schuyler raised a company by July 14, the first to be completed.[8]

The governor immediately ordered Schuyler's unit to join Colonel William Cockcroft's regiment at Lake George where an enemy attack was expected momentarily. But the young captain was destined to miss the fighting in spite of his energetic work. Just before Johnson's forces routed Baron Dieskau's troops at the Battle of Lake George on September 8, a hurried call from "sweet Kitty" sent Schuyler scurrying home. She was expecting his child so they were married the day before the Battle of Lake George. "In the year 1755," he wrote, "on the 7th of September did I, Philip John Schuyler (being 21 years, 9 months, and 17 days old), enter the holy state of matrimony with Catherine Van Rensselaer (being 20 years, 9 months, 27 days old). The Lord grant this marriage last long and in peace and to His honor."[9] The baby girl, named Angelica, was born in February, 1756.

A family gave the young captain a greater sense of responsibility and he asked to serve under Colonel John Bradstreet, the British Deputy Quartermaster General for New York, for he thought it was the best way to get ahead quickly. His relationship with Bradstreet could not have been better. Schuyler's natural talent for business made the handling of military supplies easy. Nothing got by him. Bradstreet took to Schuyler immediately and soon made him his secretary and deputy.[10] Although administrative duties took up most of his time, Schuyler proved he had courage too—far beyond the call of duty. As Bradstreet's troops were returning from an attempt to supply a hard-pressed British garrison at Oswego in 1756, they were ambushed by a much stronger force of French and Indians. After a short skirmish Bradstreet's men broke contact by crossing the Oswego River to comparative safety. It had been a near disaster and the British troops breathed a sigh of relief for having escaped with their lives. But when a wounded enemy soldier, who had been left behind, begged for help, Schuyler swam to the rescue, dragging the man to safety just as gunfire erupted again.[11]

The following year, Britain's campaign in North America bogged to a standstill and opportunities for advancement appeared limited. This annoyed Schuyler. He wanted to get ahead faster so he returned to civilian life where more money appeared available. But after serving in minor governmental appointive offices, most notably as commissioner of excise imposed upon foreign tea retailed in Albany (January 10, 1757), he concluded he had made a mistake and re-entered the service.[12]   Bradstreet was delighted. Poor health had plagued him in Schuyler's absence, and the young officer's return enabled Bradstreet to shift more and more responsibility into the latter's capable hands. "Your zeal, punctuality and strict honesty in his Majesty's Service, under my direction..." are, he wrote, "sufficient proofs that I can no(t) leave my public accounts and papers in a more faithful hand than in yours to be settled should any accident happen (to) me this Campaign."[13] Throughout 1759 and 1760 the now Major Philip Schuyler worked out of Albany collecting and forwarding provisions to Lord Jeffery Amherst's forces. He did well, so well that Bradstreet asked him to go to England to settle his military accounts. Going abroad appealed to Schuyler, but he declined since plans had just been completed for his new home south of Albany. When Bradstreet insisted, Schuyler agreed, on one condition: that the colonel advise Mrs. Schuyler as construction progressed.

It proved to be an unforgettable journey. Schuyler booked passage on the *General Wall* sailing for Falmouth, England, on Friday, March 3, 1761. The voyage was routine, however, until the eighteenth day at sea when Captain Lutwidge sighted the *Biscayne,* a powerful 24-gun French privateer. At first Lutwidge attempted to outrun the enemy in a desperate five-hour chase, but the French forced him to fight. It was no match. The *Biscayne*'s heavy guns quickly shattered the *General Wall*'s rigging and mortally wounded Captain Lutwidge. Faced with certain destruction, the English threw their mail overboard and struck their colors.

After disarming the *General Wall,* the French demanded, and received, a six hundred pound ransom and two hostages as their price for permitting the British to proceed. Five days later, on March 23, lookouts sighted land and the English vessel finally managed to limp into port. Fortunately for Bradstreet, Schuyler had not panicked when the enemy boarded the *General Wall.* Instead, he succeeded in outwitting them by paying fifty pounds of the ransom money while at the same time concealing Bradstreet's accounts.[14] Thus, in spite of near catastrophe at sea, he was ready to carry out his assignment upon reaching England.

Not much is known of Schuyler's visit to England even though he remained there for more than a year. In between working and settling Bradstreet's accounts he found time to purchase huge quantities of goods, most of them destined for his new home. These included items such as "Crimson Flock" wallpaper (an imitation tapestry), hinges, locks, doorknobs, glassware, chests, candlesticks, decanters, figures for the chimney pieces, and cutlery.[15] By May 29, 1762, Bradstreet's accounts had been approved "by Warrant of the Lords Commissioners of His Majesty's Treasury" so Schuyler returned home.

He first saw the now famous Schuyler Mansion, by then well on its way to completion, from the Hudson River sloop that brought him to Albany. It was a thrilling sight. The

mansion stood high on a ridge at the city's southern edge
near the communal meadow land. From its windows one
could see the Catskill's forest-clad slopes and the steep cliffs
of the Helderberg Mountains which seemed to be reaching
for the sky. For over forty years, this building became a
meeting place for the great and near-great who visited
Albany.

Discontent with British colonial policy had spread rapidly
in America after 1763, yet Schuyler chose to ignore it for
the time being to concentrate instead on developing his own
fortunes. Land, available in almost endless quantities in
western New York, naturally became the basis of his wealth
and he purchased thousands of acres whenever possible. On
occasion he even speculated on tracts as far west as Detroit.
His first sizable acquisition came, as we have seen, with the
division of family holdings after his mother's death in
1762.[16]   The Treaty of Fort Stanwix (1768) opened the way
for further land speculation; so did his associations with the
Livingstons, the Van Rensselaers, and especially Governor
Sir Henry Moore.[17]

Schuyler was an extremely successful landlord. Not only
did he acquire land, he continually sought to develop his
holdings. He built a country house in Saratoga (now Schuy-
lerville), surrounded it with a colony of workmen and slaves,
constructed saw mills, and, in 1767, his men began raising,
dressing, and spinning flax into linen.[18]   Within a short
time, his Saratoga property included "a very good dwelling
house, exceeding(ly) large storehouses, great saw mills, and
other outbuildings, to the value altogether of perhaps ten
thousand pounds."[19]

Leasing farms also proved to be among Schuyler's most
profitable ventures. In the spring of 1776, he told Charles
Carroll, a delegate to Congress from Maryland, that the
"most advantageous way of leasing lands was" to require on
every transfer "of property, from one tenant to another, a
quarter part of what the land sells for..."[20]   By exploiting

tenants in this way, as many did during that period, Schuyler accumulated a considerable fortune. This was not done easily, however, for at times these activities forced him to deal with inheritance problems, tenant riots, land claims, and boundary disputes. It was well worth the trouble to Schuyler, for the development of western lands brought Schuyler into contact with Governor Henry Moore and later Governor William Tryon, whose acquaintances proved to be of great value. Schuyler knew he could profit from their friendship and he did. They made him a colonel in the provincial militia, granted patronage authority in making public appointments, and gave him the power to keep order in the countryside.

Success in land speculation and various commercial ventures made Schuyler a comparatively wealthy man by 1768. Greater economic gains could only come through influence in colonial affairs, so he turned to politics. Two powerful New Yorkers, Sir William Johnson and Colonel Robert Livingston supported Schuyler, practically assuring his election to the Provincial Assembly. Sir William was so confident Schuyler would win that he congratulated his young friend four days before the freemen and freeholders of Albany County voted.[21]

America's dispute with Parliament over its taxing and regulatory policies had approached critical proportions as Schuyler entered the Assembly. Some radicals had already begun to consider taking extralegal actions as a means of settling their differences with English officials. Schuyler was not one of these people although he eventually cast his lot with the rebels. For the time being, he remained a rather conservative aristocrat, and fellow members of the Livingston faction referred to him as "a gentleman of great independency of spirit" and a true son of liberty, but not a radical patriot.[22]

Schuyler thought the best government was one controlled by the rich, the well-born and able; men of wealth from aristocratic families, not the common man, should dominate the colonies. Property above all must be protected and maintained. He had no intention of giving up his land or power to the masses, and supported Britain's stand on the collection of royal quit-rents because it enabled him to make sizable additions to his own holdings when the government auctioned off forfeited land. Idealism may have permeated his thinking at times, but not when it meant spreading democracy among the common people.

As a member of the agrarian group, it was only natural that he side with the Livingstons in attempting to wrest power from the DeLancey faction which was, by and large, controlled by urban and commercial interests.[23] Both parties were fundamentally conservative, aiming more at using imperial power for their own advantage in ruling New York, rather than in trying to overthrow British rule. Their ties with the Empire helped keep the Revolution from being violent or terroristic and this is why Schuyler always tried to check any great swing toward democracy.

Schuyler generally opposed the DeLancey faction and supported Governor Moore's policies. But he took a firm stand against the governor when the occasion warranted it, opposing a bill to raise the governor's salary, on one occasion, until the governor approved several measures favored by Schuyler's friends. Indeed Schuyler proved himself to be a bold and resourceful politician by successfully resisting DeLancey's attempt to weaken the Restraining Act which could suspend the legislative powers of the Assembly. The measure should not have been passed in the first place, but since it had, Schuyler believed violence might break out if it were tampered with.[24] This typified his attitude toward the controversy raging between America and Great Britain. He favored a firm, thoughtful, and responsible approach to solving New York's problems with Britain, and endeavored to avoid a complete break with the mother country at almost any cost. When debate over the Massachusetts Circular

Letter threatened to dissolve the Assembly, he fought to delay approval of the Letter until all important legislation was passed, especially legislation on appropriations.

These were not the only considerations that motivated Schuyler in public life. He always sought to keep the doors of conciliation open, hoping British officials would amend the Townsend Acts and reduce tension in the colonies. Until fighting finally broke out in America, he wanted to keep an open mind on the great issues because he cherished the hope of a peaceable settlement so America could remain within the economic framework of the British empire. Only local loyalties prompted him to support the address to King George III (December 31, 1768), protesting the unfairness of so much imperial legislation.[25] Even though it practically forced Governor Henry Moore to dissolve the Assembly, Schuyler tried never to push English officials too far if such action could be postponed.

As the acknowledged leader of the opposition in New York's Assembly "and the special favorite of the more conservative patriots," he did not want an independent America.[26] He was present at a November, 1769, meeting of the Sons of Liberty, to be sure, but he never joined that organization or approved of its activities.[27] His opposition to Britain's heavy-handed imperial legislation appears to have been directed more at the DeLanceys who supported Parliament's policies, than at England itself. When American affairs continued to worsen, Schuyler had to choose between allegiance to Congress — and perhaps rebellion and independence — or adherence to British demands, which implied submission. He chose to oppose Britain even if it meant rebellion, but he never wanted independence for America and continued to search for a solution to avoid a complete break with the mother country.

During the final session of the New York Assembly he fought the ultra-conservative DeLanceys, who, for the most part, later became Loyalists. His was a difficult course. "The controversy between the mother country and this begins to wear a dark and disagreeable aspect," he wrote on October 2, 1774, as the First Continental Congress debated American grievances. "I fear the result will be very serious. The Grand Congress Continues to Sit, but very little transpires as they have entered into Engagements of Secrecy."[28]   Throughout the session, he supported the First Continental Congress's intention to use extralegal methods to gain redress from Great Britain. Although he came to favor some changes in government, he nevertheless insisted on maintaining privileges and responsibilities which belonged to the ruling class. This is where Schuyler's aristocratic philosophy differed from that of the radical patriot. He wanted a change, but not a radical change. The DeLancey faction, on the other hand, was far more conservative than Schuyler and his friends, opposing all expressions of grievances by the colonies. For this reason, probably more than any other, Schuyler joined the fight against British rule.

Once he had aligned himself with the patriot cause, he tried to obtain Assembly approval of the First Continental Congress and make the Assembly select delegates to a second congress. He believed it important to keep New York's affairs in aristocratic hands, and asked the Assembly to list New York's grievances against the mother country and approve Congress's extralegal actions. Abraham Ten Broeck, a fellow member of the minority, spearheaded a drive to do this by proposing that the Assembly consider the proceedings of the First Continental Congress, but the DeLancey group vetoed the measure eleven to ten.[29]

The Assembly then chose a committee to formulate a list of New York's grievances against England. When the committee did not act, Schuyler once again attempted to stir up fellow members, lest they lose control of New York's affairs to the masses. On February 17, 1775, he asked the Assembly to enter in its journals, and then publish in New York's newspapers, all of its communications with Edmund Burke, the New York Committee of Correspondence, and the Connecticut Committee of Correspondence, to show that the Assembly understood how the people felt. Unfortunately, Loyalist strength had increased, and the proposal was turned down sixteen to nine. The same thing happened when John Thomas moved to have the Assembly consider naming delegates to the next Continental Congress.[30]   In spite of these frustrating defeats, Schuyler continued to urge the Assembly to defend New York against British misrule. This exasperated Cadwallader Colden and he accused Schuyler and his supporters of purposely causing trouble.[31]   Indeed this may have been true, but they did not have to invent incidents as Colden claimed. Britain gave them plenty of assistance by trying to divide the colonists and increase tension. Only a major policy shift could have improved affairs, and English officials refused to compromise. Once America learned that Britain would rather risk civil war than yield to colonial demands, the colonies moved to convene a Second Continental Congress.

Since New York's Provincial Assembly would neither approve the actions of the First Continental Congress nor select delegates to a second one, those opposed to British policy were forced to call an extralegal convention for that purpose.[32]   Philip Schuyler was among those present when this body met on April 21, 1775, at New York City's Exchange.[33]   Most of the delegates who had represented New York in the first congress were reappointed, and five new members were added to the delegation, the most important being Philip Schuyler, George Clinton, and Robert R. Livingston.[34]   They represented the minority dedicated to opposing royalist policies. After the convention adjourned, Schuyler left for Saratoga to put his personal affairs in order before proceeding to Philadelphia.

While he relaxed on his voyage home, word of a fight near Boston reached New York City. But news traveled slowly in 1775, and Schuyler did not learn of the clash at

Lexington and Concord for several days. The report did not surprise him, however, for he was convinced as early as 1774, that "civil war" would occur in America unless Britain softened her colonial policy. Upon hearing the news, he said Americans would be unworthy of themselves if they meekly submitted to the Ministry's demands and he preferred to see the colonies desolated for a time, rather than have them retreat one step from their stand. Like most patriots, he considered colonial actions to be defensive measures aimed at reconciliation, not as an attempt to gain independence from Great Britain.

Chapter Two

WITH FIRMNESS AND DETERMINATION

When Philip Schuyler arrived in Philadelphia to attend the Second Continental Congress on May 15, 1775, its proceedings were rather friendly and without the suspicions or sectional rivalries that soon developed. Personal ambitions had temporarily been pushed aside after fighting broke out at Lexington and Concord on April 19, and the American colonies were united as never before.[1] According to Richard Henry Lee of Virginia: "There never appeared more perfect unanimity among any set of men than among the Delegates, and indeed all the old Provinces, not one excepted . . . were directed with firmness and determination."[2]

Although the delegates easily organized, their wonderful spirit of cooperation did not last, as precedents were established in a most haphazard manner. Glaring weaknesses soon became apparent, especially the decision to keep secret congressional deliberations. Secrecy not only gave the delegates a false sense of security, it led outsiders to believe that Congress possessed more authority than it actually had, or could possibly exert in colonial affairs. Whenever Congress failed to act with vigor and directness in an emergency, many Americans lost faith in it, thinking its members acted more on selfish motives than for the good of their country. Yet Congress could do little more than it actually did, for it had practically no money or the authority to collect taxes, and very little power.

Danger signs appeared everywhere as legislation bogged

17

down under the weight of uncertainty. More often than not, committee meetings proved to be futile and congressional debates were frequently marred by suspicions, anger, and recriminations. Unfortunately, the delegates did nothing to remedy the situation and let bureaucratic inefficiency go unchallenged. Their failure to govern better almost proved disastrous for America, and the United States probably won the Revolution in spite of Congress, not because of it.

Congress did manage to act with vigor on occasion, however. In the spring of 1775, when British troopships dropped anchor off Sandy Hook, a wave of apprehension swept through New York City. Upon hearing the news, Congress issued recommendations to prevent enemy landings and advised New Yorkers to avoid provocations unless the British made aggressive moves.[3] If the enemy seized property, started fortifications, or attempted to isolate the city, Congress told New York to stop them with armed force if necessary.[4] These instructions indicate that Congress still considered its role to be a defensive one since it had been the British who provoked the fight at Lexington and Concord. Their position was weakened, however, when Ethan Allen and Benedict Arnold seized Fort Ticonderoga on May 10, 1775.[5] Not content with modest success, Allen and Arnold captured Crown Point and then went after bigger things and actually invaded Canada to temporarily occupy Fort St. Johns.[6] These were not defensive moves by any stretch of the imagination and they embarrassed those delegates who wished to avoid an open conflict.

Congress initially recoiled in anger upon hearing the news from Canada, although a few delegates approved of what Allen and Arnold had done, arguing that their actions were justified. They maintained that the English had massed troops and supplies in the area, provoked Indian raids, and were making plans to invade northern New York.[7] If Allen and Arnold had not taken the initiative to disrupt the enemy's preparations, they believed New York's northern frontier would be vulnerable to an enemy attack. Philip Schuyler and Silas Deane took this stand. What is more, they appear to have helped Allen and Arnold plot the assault, because Deane's enemies quickly nicknamed him "Ticonderoga."[8]

Congress refused to condone the act in spite of Schuyler's stand. Instead, it ordered New York to abandon Fort Ticonderoga and Crown Point, and withdraw all troops, cannon, and stores to the southern end of Lake George in what appears to have been a strategic blunder.[9] By removing troops from the lakes, the Americans relinquished control without a shot being fired, leaving New York and New England open to an invasion. The enemy could build a fleet, concentrate troops, and stockpile supplies within sixty miles of Albany, and launch an attack that would be almost impossible to stop.

Why then did Congress act so irresponsibly? More than anything else, the order to withdraw from Ticonderoga appears to have been a concession to Great Britain in an all-out effort to settle differences amicably. Many delegates still were anxiously seeking to placate the King and insisted on the withdrawal. This theory takes on added weight when one considers that Congress also asked for an exact inventory of everything at the fort to insure its safe return when peaceful relations were resumed with the mother country. Most Americans wanted to settle their differences with Great Britain at this point, yet in their desire to do so, they foolishly left unprotected five hundred frontier families friendly to the American cause. Although Philip Schuyler and several other delegates made this clear, Congress refused to change its orders as hopes for reconciliation ruled the day. It did, however, in a small concession to Schuyler, tell New York to prepare its defenses in case conciliatory measures failed.[10]

Schuyler devoted most of his early days in Congress to the Ammunition and Military Stores Committee. These meetings did not produce any tangible results, but they did help to establish a rapport between men of widely different backgrounds who would soon fight side by side on the field of battle. Schuyler and Washington worked together on the Ammunition Committee, trying to raise ammunition and military stores for the colonies.[11]   Even though they failed to find solutions for their most perplexing problems, being able only to suggest that each colony collect supplies or manufacture gunpowder to strengthen America's bargaining position with Parliament, they became lifelong friends.

From the negative point of view congressional committee reports also served a useful purpose. They made America realize that a war with Great Britain would be a long and bitter experience. After all, colonial resources were limited to men, timber, and food, while Britain possessed tremendous material wealth and the finest military forces in the world. Once the delegates were faced with the hard truth, much of their enthusiasm began to flag and many were more insistent than ever on finding a peaceful settlement to the crisis.

Before long, signs of discontent appeared in Congress as the larger and more prosperous colonies accused several of the smaller colonies of not meeting their ammunition and military stores quotas. At the same time New Englanders provoked New Yorkers by intimating the latter would withdraw from the struggle once the going got rough, rupturing the already strained relations between the two sections. Bickering became so commonplace that factions began to form and members appeared to be spending most of their time arguing with one another, rather than trying to solve the urgent problems facing the colonies.[12]

Fortunately for America, Massachusetts helped Congress overcome one of its most difficult hurdles when American militia troops surrounding Boston badly needed reinforcements. Since neither Congress nor the other colonies made any move to assist them, Massachusetts called on its own people to put 13,600 men in the field. They responded remarkably well, and this prompted Massachusetts to urge New Hampshire, Rhode Island, and Connecticut to furnish troops in the same proportion.[13]   It was a bold move. No colony had acted with such vigor in the past, but Yankee leaders had apparently become convinced that a powerful army could stop Britain's tyrannical actions and put an end to civil strife. Only with a force far greater than any England could place in the field, could America expect to escape suppression at the hands of George III. Joseph Warren described the plan as "the means to an immediate end ... to the human ravages of mercenary troops in America ... "[14]

By crystallizing thinking in America, Massachusetts paved the way for the creation of a Continental army capable of resisting England, a defensive force at best, but nevertheless an army. When the militia around Boston showed signs of collapsing, despite the great enthusiasm it had generated, Congress finally decided to show Massachusetts its people were fighting for all of the colonies, and the Yankees, in turn, could expect support from all of them. On June 14, 1775, Congress ordered ten rifle companies to be raised in Pennsylvania, Maryland, and Virginia to aid the militia troops surrounding Boston.[15]   Actually it was not much more than a token reinforcement, yet it was significant in that it marked the beginning of the American Continental army.

Finding the funds to enlist, supply, and transport Continental troops would prove to be a tremendous task, for no one knew how much money might be needed, or where to get it. Guesses as to the probable length of the struggle varied from months to years, with most people agreeing on only one thing: a long hard fight was ahead if the colonies did not reconcile their differences with Britain.

Congress kept Schuyler busy, drawing upon his experience whenever possible, and appointing him to a committee to suggest ways of financing the army.[16]   While Schuyler, Washington, Silas Deane, Thomas Cushing, and Joseph Hewes attempted to see what solutions they could come up with, Congress planned enlistments, established pay scales, and set troop quotas; but when its members could not agree on rules or regulations for the army, they again turned to Schuyler and Washington for assistance.[17] Even though the New Yorker and the Virginian were terribly overworked at the time, both were flattered, perhaps from the knowledge that Congress would soon choose officers to command the army and that they appeared to be in line for important appointments if they wanted them.

Sides soon formed over the choice of a commander-in-chief. New England wished to have a Bostonian at the head of the army, with John Hancock figuring prominently in their plans, while a southern bloc opposed Hancock since his selection would give New England too much power in the new Government. A third group, those still seeking reconciliation, wanted to postpone any move toward independent action until another petition could be sent to the King. As one might expect, there were also differences of opinion within these groups to further complicate the already complex situation.[18]

Fortunately for the colonies, George Washington emerged as the choice for Commander-in-chief, but the command controversy had just begun. Selecting other high-ranking officers promised to be far more difficult for delegates who usually sought or were given advice by their respective Provincial Congresses before voting. Concessions had to be made, often on a political or geographic basis, and these deals often led to poor appointments when a small hard-core of good officers was desperately needed.[19] David Wooster of Connecticut and Thomas Mifflin of Pennsylvania were two officers who were clearly not up to the duties given them. Worst of all, such bargaining created ill feelings no matter how popular or how deserving a choice may have been.

In keeping with the characteristic practice of the hour, the New York Provincial Congress instructed its delegates to support Schuyler for Major General and Richard Montgomery for Brigadier General.[20] No record remains of the debate over Schuyler's appointment although the fight must have been bitter. The most violent protests came from Yankees who claimed New York had been given too much power, at their expense, in the person of General Schuyler, their bitter enemy in a recent New Hampshire Grants boundary dispute. Since Schuyler would command large numbers of their troops, Massachusetts, Connecticut, New Hampshire, and Rhode Island showed their resentment by attacking New York for dragging its feet in the controversy with Great Britain.[21] This sectional jealousy had a bad influence on Schuyler, and his political and military reputation declined in a steady pattern from that day on. In such an atmosphere he would find it almost impossible to get support from the New England colonies. According to Eliphalet Dyer, a delegate from Connecticut, Schuyler received approval merely "to sweeten and keep up the spirit of..." New York and nothing more.[22]

Few men in the colonies could match Schuyler's knowledge or qualifications even though the Yankees considered them inadequate. As a rich landowner, he had considerable experience in business affairs and his interest in land speculation had given him a good understanding of New York's frontier and its people. Service in the Seven Years War provided battle experience, along with a superb understanding of military supply problems, and seven years in the New York Assembly had sharpened his political acumen.

Schuyler was delighted that Washington had selected him to command in northern New York even though the task ahead would be one of the most difficult in the land. Enlisting, supplying, and financing a new army, and then getting it into fighting trim, promised to be an almost insurmountable problem. Yet in the enthusiasm of the moment he eagerly accepted the challenge until America could rejoin the mother country.

After leaving Philadelphia, Schuyler and Washington, and their party, rode toward New York City until they encount-

ered a messenger with news of a battle at Boston. From him
they learned that British regulars had clashed with American
militia at Bunker Hill and had succeeded in dislodging the
Americans after repeated assaults and heavy losses. According to the messenger, the militia fought with a tenacity
befitting the finest soldiers in the world and gave in to the
British regulars only after running out of ammunition. This
was good news indeed. The Americans could fight and
would fight British regulars. A few more such battles might
convince George III he would lose a war with America and
prompt him to stop the rebellion. If the King did not end
the fighting, the American officers thought they could force
Britain to agree to American demands.

Occasionally Schuyler and Washington were able to forget
the war and the dusty roads, and enjoy the crowds who
turned out to greet them. At New Brunswick, however, news
reached them that Governor William Tryon planned on
returning to New York City on the same day they expected
to arrive.[23]   An accidental meeting between the two parties
might cause trouble. And if trouble broke out, it threatened
to take the form of mob violence at its worst, and mob
violence might turn public opinion against the patriot cause.
Governor Tryon could then call in British troops to restore
order. If he did, they would cut communications between the
northern and the southern colonies. Trade would suffer, the
interior would be isolated from the sea, and recruits and
supplies from New York City would be lost to Continental
forces. Worst of all, an English base in the heart of the
colonies, on top of the threat of an invasion from Canada,
would make the situation critical.[24]   To prevent anything
like this from happening, General Schuyler asked the New
York Provincial Congress to have one company greet the
governor while another met Washington's party when it
arrived.[25]

New York City stirred with excitement as the Commander-
in-chief and his staff crossed the Hudson River at 4 p.m. on

Sunday, June 25, 1775, to land amid cheering throngs of well-wishers near Colonel Leonard Lispenard's house about two miles north of the city.[26]   Bells were ringing, drums were beating, and nine militia companies stood rigidly at attention. After being entertained at Lispenard's, they toured the city. Four hours later, Governor Tryon arrived at a place called Long Island Bridge. Excitement had still not subsided and shouting and cheering crowds continued to mill around the streets. "Is this all for me?" he asked two of his aides. They told him it was not and hurried him to safety in a home near the City Hotel.[27]   Later, according to Mrs. Richard Montgomery, he nearly fainted when he saw Washington's party pass, surrounded by scores of admirers. From her window next to the City Hotel, she (and perhaps Governor Tryon also) witnessed a ceremony in which General Schuyler and her husband were formally given commissions and instructions by General Washington.[28]   Although Tryon and Schuyler were long-time friends, neither made an attempt to see the other while they were in the city.[29]

Before continuing on to Boston, General Washington helped Schuyler lay plans for the Northern army. The tall Virginian liked the New Yorker and gave him all the assistance he could, for Schuyler would have to overcome many material shortages and fight with little more on his side than hope, luck, and a will to survive.[30]   The following day Schuyler accompanied Washington to New Rochelle, New York, where they parted. Then Schuyler put his plan into operation. He ordered Brigadier General David Wooster's units to New York City to oppose the British if they attempted to land troops from the eight transports anchored off Sandy Hook.[31]   The British made no threats although rumors were heard everywhere. Some said the fleet would go to Boston, others said troops were preparing to land in New York. If this were so, Schuyler believed a show of force might discourage, or at least delay, an invasion.

Once Wooster's regiments moved into position, Schuyler

turned his attention to the northern frontier. Strengthening this area and building an army in the wilderness appeared to be a formidable task. No ammunition could be procured; finances were low; flour was in short supply; commissions for officers had not yet arrived; and the army Schuyler expected to inherit proved almost non-existent.[32]   To find out where he stood at the moment, he ordered all officers to make troop and supply returns immediately, and to obtain, if possible, information about Governor Guy Carleton's plans.[33]   He also tried to get more support from the Continental Congress and neighboring colonies.[34]

Before leaving for Albany, Schuyler received an unexpected and rather discomforting order. Congress directed him to make preparations to invade Canada as soon as practical.[35] This came as a shock. The day before, defending New York's frontier appeared difficult, and invading Canada almost impossible. Now Schuyler was asked to accomplish what had seemed impossible: an invasion through a vast and hostile wilderness.

Chapter Three

"IF JOB HAD BEEN A GENERAL..."

General Schuyler took over the Northern Department in June, 1775, with only 1,352 poorly trained troops under his command.[1] This was far below the estimated four thousand needed to invade Canada, and almost nine weeks would be lost before he could attack St. Johns. They were weeks filled with confusion and frustrations, for conditions at strategic Fort Ticonderoga were deplorable. The walls were crumbling and most of the garrison was unruly and without shelter or adequate clothing. The few reinforcements who reported there brought with them practically no equipment or provisions. Even when supplies were obtained, they moved north slowly due to poor transportation and bad roads; at one 45-mile stretch between Fort Ticonderoga and Fort Edward there was no road at all. Faced with such a task, it is no wonder that Schuyler was not optimistic about chances of successfully launching the expedition as preparations got underway.

The situation was further complicated when Ethan Allen seized British posts on Lake Champlain in May, 1775. Allen's precipitate action had jolted Canadian Governor Sir Guy Carleton into making plans of his own. Carleton reacted so swiftly that Schuyler heard Sir Guy was building a fleet and stockpiling supplies at St. Johns for an attack against New York. This disturbed the General, but he could not find out how far Sir Guy's preparations had progressed, and thought of himself as being in a race with Carleton without knowing where he stood.[2] Schuyler did realize, however, that an invasion of Canada would be impossible if the enemy naval force moved out onto Lake Champlain first. Such a fleet might even threaten New York itself since American vessels on the lake were not nearly strong enough to defeat it. This was not the only bad news for Schuyler. His paper army had little organization and practically no discipline or training. Yet it had several good qualities; the hardy frontiersmen were accustomed to the hardships of frontier life and most officers thought they would give a good account of themselves in a fight.[3]

From the beginning, Schuyler appears to have questioned Congress's decision to invade Canada. An assault with the small force under his command might, he warned, result in the loss of the lakes as well as Crown Point, Ticonderoga, and Fort George. He told Congress this on July 3, 1775, so delegates would know what could happen in an invasion he was "not at liberty to desist from making, without orders to the contrary."[4] But Congress ignored these remarks even when Schuyler persisted in pointing out how poorly prepared he was to launch an attack. At the same time, he told George Washington of the confusion among Fort Ticonderoga's officers: "Some have taken the liberty to disband troops; others refused to serve unless this or that particular person commanded; the sloop is left without either captain or pilot, both of which are dismissed or come away; much provision wasted or embezzled, and..." there is only one barrel of flour.[5] Since General Washington faced similar problems, Schuyler found little comfort in his friend's replies.

The complex task of building an army and navy moved slowly at first. There was no set plan; there could not be one. The grand design had to evolve as orders were issued because little thought could be given to any decision. Shortages and emergencies called for immediate substitutions and improvisations. Yet on the whole it was an orderly, if hastily conceived, enterprise.

While General Schuyler attempted to put an army into the field, other problems required attention. Tories and Indians were an ever-lurking menace and to combat them Schuyler developed a complex intelligence network to obtain information of enemy movements.[6] Travelers were questioned, scouts patrolled the frontier, and Indian commissioners went into the forests to keep the Iroquois tribes at bay. But there were other dangers besides those on the frontier. Schuyler also kept close watch on Governor William Tryon in New York City and Sir John Johnson and Guy Johnson in Tryon County.[7] The latter proved to be most troublesome for he incited the Indians and actually raised a force to threaten the Mohawk Valley settlements.[8]

Because of Guy Johnson's activities, Schuyler believed western New York, northern Pennsylvania, and northern New Jersey might be the targets of Indian raids. To prevent surprise attacks, he asked Congress to send troops into Indian country to keep them neutral.[9] This was particularly true of Tryon County in western New York where inhabitants found themselves in an almost defenseless position. Few soldiers and practically no ammunition were available to them even though they momentarily expected an Indian uprising. "In this defenseless condition, should eight hundred Indians, or half the number, come down, and be joined by the Highlanders and others that are disaffected in Tryon County," warned Schuyler, "they may with impunity not only march where they please through that or this County, but so effectively cut off all supplies from the Troops to the northward, that they must disperse or starve."[10] Thus, in many respects, the fate of Schuyler's invasion force depended on the situation in Tryon County.

On advice from Schuyler and the Committee on Indian Affairs, Congress established three Indian departments on July 12, 1775, the northernmost of which included the powerful Six Nations and all tribes north of them. Philip Schuyler, Major Joseph Hawley, Turbot Francis, Oliver Wolcott, and

Volkert P. Douw were appointed commissioners of the Northern Indian Department, empowered to deal with the Iroquois in any way necessary to preserve peace and friendship and keep them from siding with Great Britain.[11]   With this in mind, Schuyler called for a conference with the tribal chieftains to persuade them to agree to a treaty of peace. But the council could not meet until mid-August.

Sir John Johnson remained at Johnstown to wait for a more favorable opportunity to act. As for Governor Tryon, he made no hostile moves even though rumors hinted that he had been given military rank to command troops scheduled to arrive in New York City. These stories appear to have been fomented by New Englanders who wished to take the governor prisoner, but Schuyler blocked the plan because he believed it might provoke a general uprising among heretofore peaceful Tories. Nevertheless, the intriguers refused to yield until Schuyler told them General Washington had left written orders not to molest Tryon unless he became troublesome.[12]

One can trace Schuyler's progress in organizing an army through orders issued by his aides, John Lansing and Richard Varick, to subordinate commanders, and through his correspondence with congressional delegates and leaders of the separate colonies. He and General Richard Montgomery worked hard to mold their troops into a disciplined, orderly, and obedient military machine. By demanding that their soldiers live up to regulations and perform their duties in strict military fashion, they hoped to develop a unified spirit. Drunkenness and disorderly behavior were frowned upon and strict orders were given to prevent destruction of private property.[13]

Although Schuyler pressed colonial legislatures and Congress unceasingly for help in obtaining proper clothing, tents, flour, fresh meat, rum, medical supplies, and money to pay the troops, most of these items continued in short supply. Yet Schuyler never relaxed his efforts. He frequently used rumors of impending disaster to stir the colonies into sending him aid. At first this approach received a good response, but as time went on colonial leaders looked upon him as a perpetual complainer. Hence it became increasingly difficult for him to obtain assistance after sending urgent pleas so often in the past. Be that as it may, Congress did its best to aid him during the summer of 1775. It authorized $200,000 in hard money to put an army into action.[14]　Then, several tons of ammunition were shipped to Albany from Philadelphia, and more was promised.[15]　In an effort to ease the ammunition shortage, two powder mills were put into operation in New York and three in Pennsylvania.[16]　When the British fleet standing off Sandy Hook weighed anchor, Congress ordered the Connecticut troops stationed in New York City to march to Ticonderoga.[17]　By this time dozens of recruiting parties were working throughout the colony raising troops to serve against the King. "Is it not astonishing," remarked Nathaniel Hazard, "that the loyal, highly distinguished Province of New York should be the first . . . except the 4 rebellious Colonies to raise Troops to fight the King's Troops?"[18]

Transporting troops, provisions, and supplies continued to be one of Schuyler's major headaches. Goods had to be shipped from Albany to Half Moon by batteau. From there they were transferred by wagon to Stillwater on the Hudson, then they were placed in another batteau for a trip to Saratoga Falls. There they were taken across a small portage and on to Fort Miller Falls. At this point they were moved overland and then again by water to Fort Edward. From Fort Edward they could either be shipped on to Ticonderoga via Fort George or by way of Fort Anne. In the former case they were taken overland to Fort George at the southern tip of Lake George, then by water to the north end of the lake, where they were shipped overland to a place on Lake Champlain called the Saw Mills, and finally across the lake to Fort Ticonderoga. The route from Fort Anne appears to have been more manageable. Provisions were moved overland to Fort Anne and then down Wood Creek by batteau to Skene's Falls. There the batteaux were rolled across a small portage to the south end of Lake Champlain where they sailed over to Fort Ticonderoga.[19]

Few colonists could imagine the time and effort involved in transporting military necessities through a pathless wilderness to the expedition gathering on Lake Champlain. Delays at any of the transfer points sometimes forced other workmen along the line to sit and wait for days at a time. Furthermore, the constant loading and reloading of provisions gave thieves ample time to take their share. For Schuyler, this problem always remained difficult to manage at best; but to colonists in far off cities and villages the task appeared easy.

Although Schuyler continued in his reluctance to launch an invasion force against Canada, he took steps to construct fighting ships and a fleet of transports capable of moving four thousand men. Keels were laid at Skenesborough, and carpenters were offered as much as five dollars a day in hard money to lure them to the shipyards. Good pay in hard money brought workmen to the area from all directions. Soon the sawmills were repaired and the whole village came alive with activity. Although shortages of boards, oakum, nails, and other material still caused delays, Schuyler attempted to keep the workmen supplied by constantly prodding Congress and the various colonial governments to obtain assistance. "I have neither boats sufficient nor any materials prepared for building them," he wrote on July 21, and "the stores...from New York are not yet arrived. I have therefore not a nail, no pitch, and no oakum..."[20]

General Schuyler did not get around to inspecting Colonel Benjamin Hinman's defenses at Fort Ticonderoga until July 17. At 10 p.m. that night, the General and his staff landed near the fort. One hundred men were stationed at this debarkation point, but only one sentry halted the party even though the guard could not tell whether they were friendly or hostile in the darkness. Schuyler's aides persuaded the man to leave his post, to awaken his comrades, and while the soldier tried unsuccessfully to rouse them, the General approached a second sentry. This sentinel challenged him, but permitted him to get too close. "With a penknife," wrote Schuyler, "I could have cut off both guards, and then have set fire to the block-house, destroyed the stores, and starved the people..."[21]

The new Commander-in-chief of the Northern Department took immediate steps to prevent a repetition of this incident. He issued orders to tighten security and reprimanded the guards for their foolish conduct. Because these troops had not been accustomed to discipline they naturally resented their new commander. Discontent increased, especially among the Connecticut militia, when Schuyler ordered a cutback in their daily rations. After all, the Connecticut government had promised them a food allotment in excess of what other troops would receive, and when Schuyler ordered standard rations for everyone the Connecticut enlisted men bitterly protested. Had he not done so, however, greater discontent undoubtedly would have occurred in the army.[22]

Other incidents marred Schuyler's relations with the New England soldiery. On one occasion, he stopped cattle shipments to Ticonderoga after hearing that oxen already there were starving due to a prolonged drought. As might be expected, Yankee troops screamed that they were being deprived of fresh beef by the haughty New York aristocrat. On another occasion, a Connecticut blacksmith tried to speak to the General, but Schuyler dismissed the man because he had not gone through proper military channels, a procedure the General was trying to teach his troops. Even though he later consented to talk to the blacksmith, critics said he did so only after learning the soldier had once owned an estate in England.[23]

Such incidents provoked malicious rumors which were

spread about the General with more and more frequency as
the months passed. Some even alleged that Schuyler was
secretly a Tory. As these stories drifted back to the New
England colonies, many Yankees began to suspect Schuyler
of treasonable intentions. The rumors became so persistent
that the Reverend Cotton Mather's wife wrote to her husband to ask if Schuyler really was a Tory. Although Mather
had been the Chaplain at Ticonderoga for only a few weeks,
he knew the gossips had been unfair. "General Schuyler,"
he replied, "is as earnest a patriot as any in our land and
he has few superiors in any respect."[24]

Logistic problems continued to plague the Northern Department, possibly because of the inability of Congress to
understand the probable length of the struggle with Britain.
Since most delegates believed provisions and ammunition
would be needed for only six months, they were unwilling
to commit themselves to large expenditures. This so irritated
Schuyler that he told General Washington, "If Job had been
a general, in my situation, his memory had not been so
famous for patience."[25]

Pressure to invade Canada began to mount in Congress
and throughout America as July drew to a close and several
Canadian messengers arrived seeking help against the Ministry's forces. One claimed that Canadians would "subdue the
Regular Troops themselves..." if their fellow colonists
would "send only three Commissioned officers to take command..."[26] Another said his countrymen were "praying
for...the Americans to arrive, or they must for their own
safety be obliged to join the King's troops."[27]

In spite of such statements, there were discouraging reports
from Canada too. The English fleet at St. Johns appeared to
be nearing completion and Schuyler saw little chance of de-
stroying its warships before they sailed out onto Lake Champlain; nevertheless, he was determined to make an attempt if
at all possible to put it out of action.[28] If the enemy fleet
reached the lake, American chances of a successful invasion

of Canada would be considerably lessened. This was not all. Some Canadians were so eager to stay out of the controversy that they were attempting to keep the Indians neutral as well.[29]

More disturbing rumors arrived from Boston, where British officers were evacuating their army by sea and moving it, or so these reports stated, to Canada. If this were true, Schuyler knew all chances of success in Canada had come to an end; so work on the invasion force slowed to a standstill.[30] Fortunately, it soon became apparent that there was no basis to such gossip, yet for some strange reason battle preparations continued to lag. Ammunition stores could not supply more than one pound of gunpowder per man, and sickness reduced the army at Ticonderoga to a mere five hundred effective militia.[31] There were, it is true, another thousand militia at Albany, but they could not be ordered to Ticonderoga until more provisions were available to support them.[32]

The commander of the Northern Department was not alone in his reluctance to prematurely invade Canada. Brigadier General Richard Montgomery also harbored doubts, because a successful attack on Canada would considerably enlarge the American sphere of operations. This, in turn, would necessitate a great defensive force to prevent Great Britain from recapturing the provinces. But Montgomery, like Schuyler, thought it was worth the risk, for an invasion would show the world what strength the rebellious colonies could muster against Britain if they were forced to fight. The Iroquois, too, would realize that New Yorkers would keep them from ravaging the frontier, and cut them off from English agents such as Guy Johnson if they took the warpath.[33] Thus it appears that both Schuyler and Montgomery wanted to attack Canada, although they were both reluctant to proceed until adequate preparations were made.

They may have differed significantly on only one fundamental point, however. Schuyler appears to have dreaded the possibility of defeat in his first campaign as a general, whereas Montgomery took a much more realistic stand. "Perhaps the inconvenience of a failure may not be so great as you apprehend," he informed Robert R. Livingston. "We must be exceedingly unfortunate indeed not to be able to act on the defensive at this end of Lake Champlain and to keep the command of that lake tho' we were obliged to retire from Canada we still have the enemy at arm's length..."[34] Montgomery also reminded his friend that New York itself really had little to fear from the few ships and troops under Governor Carleton's command.

Gradually the American army and navy began to take shape. It was a small force, nowhere near the four thousand he had hoped to raise, and hardly enough, or so Schuyler reasoned, to strike a crippling blow at Canada. While he may have been a bit gloomy about this, others felt the picture had begun to brighten. Benjamin Trumbull reported that rapid progress had been made after Schuyler took command, and he went on to tell what an outstanding job the General had done. His men "repaired the Mills, sawed Boards, procured Carpenters, Nails, provisions, Teams... and forwarded Matters with so much Dispatch, that it was thought proper to have the Troops on their Way to..." Ticonderoga by August 1.[35]

Soon Schuyler himself spoke with some optimism about launching the expedition, but apparently he still hoped Congress or General Washington might rescind his orders until he could build a more powerful army. "I am prepared," he told Washington, "...to obey my orders, and move against the enemy, unless your Excellency or Congress should direct otherwise." Then he added: "In a few days I expect to receive the ultimate determination."[36] From whom the "ultimate determination" would come no one can say. Neither Congress nor the Commander-in-chief ever gave Schuyler the slightest idea that they wished him to delay the attack or await further orders although Schuyler obviously hoped they would grant him a delay. Samuel Chase of Maryland emphasized this point for Congress on August 10, and General Washington did the same thing a few weeks later.[37]

When Schuyler next heard from Washington, he learned that his Commander-in-chief had ordered an expedition against Quebec over the Kennebec River route. With this small force, led by the gallant Benedict Arnold, he hoped to draw Governor Carleton's attention away from Lake Champlain long enough to keep opposition to Schuyler at a minimum as he pushed toward Quebec. Washington believed two attacks might be decisive since the Canadians would not hesitate to resist the British. Unfortunately, this proved to be wishful thinking.

Historians, as a rule, have questioned Schuyler's intention to move against Canada, but Washington never doubted it. He simply asked for definite word as to when Schuyler planned to embark.[38] All available evidence indicates that Washington had judged Schuyler correctly, for the latter resolved early in August to move his tiny army against St. Johns without further delay. Naturally, he continued to complain and demand more assistance where help was needed, but such grumbling was part of his nature.[39]

Even before General Schuyler received the encouraging news from Washington, he wrote freely of his own intention to start moving forward soon. The 1,300 troops, with provisions for only 20 days of fighting, were far below his original estimate of 4,000 militia, supplied with provisions for three months; so were his artillery and ammunition supplies.[40] Yet Schuyler realized the British fleet had to be contained before it hit the waves or he must give up all thought of advancing into Canada. Knowledge of the sympathetic attitude of many Canadians, coupled with the obvious weakness of Carleton's forces, inspired him to act.

With an Indian attack on New York's frontier still a possibility, Schuyler had to be certain that the Six Iroquois

Nations would remain neutral before attacking St. Johns. When a large Iroquois delegation arrived at Albany on Tuesday, August 22, Schuyler could ill afford to miss such a good opportunity to confer with them and he hurried there to obtain a treaty if possible. The Indians, for their part, wished to avoid taking sides in what they considered a family quarrel, and promised to remain neutral.

Shortly after Schuyler arrived at Albany, General Montgomery received alarming news from one of his best scouts, Major John Brown, which he relayed to his chief by special courier on August 25, the day it arrived.[41] Brown said two large enemy vessels under construction at St. Johns were almost finished. At that very moment their hulls were being covered with pitch to the gunwales and the masts were nearing completion. According to Brown, they would be ready to sail within a week because workmen labored until after dark each night to get them ready.[42] James Livingston of Albany sent a similar report to Schuyler, but Livingston claimed there were three vessels of fifty tons each, capable of sailing within a week.[43]

General Schuyler had expected something like this to happen so he had taken steps to move quickly. Once he learned there would be no Indian trouble he told General Montgomery "to get everything in the best readiness he could..." because he wanted to "move immediately, weak and ill appointed...as they were."[44] When a third report arrived from Peter Griffin, there was no doubt that any further delays might prove fatal to the American cause and Montgomery prepared to attack.[45] When Schuyler heard Montgomery had carried out his standing orders to embark, he reported the event to General Washington with a great deal of satisfaction.[46]

This decision has usually been interpreted adversely for General Schuyler. Readers often have been led to believe that Montgomery anxiously waited for Schuyler to leave so he could launch an attack. Most authors also claim Schuyler used the Indian negotiations as another excuse to postpone action; and then there are those who claim Montgomery had become so completely frustrated and disgusted with Schuyler's continued delays that he took matters into his own hands once Schuyler departed. This does not appear to be so. General Schuyler clearly used every means in his power to begin the invasion although he worked under the most trying circumstances. He even expressed regret that Washington had not thought of the Kennebec expedition sooner. Once operations began, Schuyler boldly predicted a victory and said defeat could come only if large numbers of Canadians opposed them.[47]

Schuyler's order to move and Montgomery's report that he would try to prevent the launching of the British vessels undoubtedly crossed in the mail. But Schuyler probably told Montgomery before he left that he would order him to prepare to embark once he learned of the disposition of the Indians. Many critical problems of transportation, supplies, equipment, money, men and Indians had improved to a point where an attack became feasible. It is clear, therefore, that General Schuyler had decided to act as Congress had instructed, and that he was in favor of the decision to embark because he encouraged it.

Chapter Four

THE CANADIAN CAMPAIGN

Sir Guy Carleton, an experienced veteran of the French and Indian War and governor of Canada since 1772, proved to be a skillful opponent. Like Schuyler, Sir Guy was also handicapped by poor communications, supply shortages, and the lack of trained personnel. The few regular troops available to him in Canada could not possibly defend the province so he called on the militia for help.[1] This proved disappointing. He soon learned that most Canadians preferred to remain neutral and supply provisions to those who could pay in hard money, rather than fight the Americans with whom they had no quarrel. They had become embittered with the Government in 1774 when dry weather and poor crops brought on inflation and the threat of famine. Politically the situation was just as unsettled. Many English inhabitants of Canada resented the Quebec Act of 1774 and demanded a return to English common law.[2] Feelings were so strong that three hundred people were said to have been imprisoned by the Government in an attempt to crush opposition to the Act.[3] Because of Carleton's heavy-handed treatment, those still agitating appeared anxious to join Schuyler's forces if the threatened American invasion materialized.

On July 17, 1775, this threat to Canada became a reality. Colonel Guy Johnson, the British Superintendent of Indian Affairs in New York, brought Carleton definite information about Schuyler's invasion plans.[4] Johnson had tried to gain time for the governor before leaving New York by attempting to turn the savages against the colonies. He told Iroquois leaders of a secret congressional plan to take away their land, to prevent them from hunting on the lakes, and to force them to become Christians, while also characterizing the Americans as poor, starving beggars with no money for anyone.[5] His strategy worked surprisingly well. After talking to Johnson, the Six Nations promised to protect and keep water communication between New York and Canada open, and, at the same time, menace Schuyler's line of communications. When Johnson fled to Canada several days later, two hundred Indians accompanied him. More would have gone along with Johnson, or so he claimed, had transportation been available.

Because of Johnson, the Indians might easily have played an even more decisive role in the Canadian invasion of 1775 had Governor Carleton not given orders to restrain them. The Indians were forbidden to go beyond the 45° parallel, or, in other words, beyond the southern boundary of the province.[6] Naturally this displeased the blood-hungry savages. When one of Schuyler's patrols clashed with them at Point au Fer on August 5, Colonel Johnson urged General William Prescott to let the Indians take the warpath, but the General refused. Prescott's answer discouraged the savages who by now had become restless. To prevent the Indians from leaving, Johnson tried to keep them busy with scouting missions.[7] A small party of Schuyler's troops encountered some of these Indian scouts on August 22, whereupon the savages killed Captain Remember Baker, whose bloody head they placed on a pole at Fort St. Johns. The taste of blood made them impatient and Johnson began to fear they would all leave him unless they were given more freedom. To prevent this, he once again urged Governor Carleton to let them harass Schuyler's communications in New York. Still, Sir Guy continued to reject his requests.[8]

It is difficult to tell why Carleton refused to let the In-

dians cross the Canadian border to attack Schuyler's forces.
When one considers that General Thomas Gage had directed
him to enlist a corps of Canadians and Indians to menace
the New England frontier, it is even more confusing.[9] Despite these directions, Sir Guy did not choose to let the
savages ravage the colonies. The governor apparently pinned
all of his hopes on one possibility — that of prevailing on the
Canadians to defend themselves. He undoubtedly expected
them to fight; yet he appears to have erred in his judgment
because most Canadians refused to arm themselves. Carleton
may also have feared an Indian attack would turn inhabitants
of Canada against him, especially if they got out of hand.
To avoid being branded as the aggressor, he chose to restrain
the savages almost completely; so, as the campaign opened,
most of Canada remained neutral.

Although there were only a few Indian raids in New York,
they created a great deal of apprehension among Schuyler's
troops at Fort Ticonderoga, who remained unaware of the
General's negotiations. Had they known why he had left
them, they probably would have been less critical of Schuyler
and more relaxed in their frontier posts. Instead, they cursed
the damned Dutchman for enjoying the comforts of home
while they momentarily faced an Indian attack.[10] But
Schuyler had been effective, more effective than his critics
realized. By the time the American army sailed toward
St. Johns, most of the savages were proclaiming their
neutrality.[11]

While the main body of American troops pushed slowly
down Lake Champlain, General Schuyler hurried to join
them. But long hours of work and travel, the rugged conditions of a military encampment, and tedious Indian negotiations had taken their toll. His fragile body appeared thin,
his face pale, and indeed the General looked more like a
feeble invalid than a fighting officer. Just after arriving at
Ticonderoga he began to run a fever. The symptoms were
nothing new. He had been troubled with fever and gout

before. Generally these attacks passed, and Schuyler expected this one would too; therefore, he prepared to join Montgomery in Canada.[12] Before leaving Ticonderoga, he issued orders to forward artillery, ammunition, provisions, and troops to his advancing army. Although a heavy rain and strong winds temporarily delayed him, Schuyler resumed command of the army at Isle La Motte on September 4, 1775. Immediately he ordered an advance to Isle aux Noix where he planned to launch the attack against St. Johns.

On September 5, Schuyler sent messengers into Canada with a "Declaration to the Inhabitants" in which he told them the Americans had come to rid their province of British tyranny.[13] This proclamation made a bid for active Canadian support; but on the whole it failed, since the Canadians appeared to lean toward those in power, whether British or American, and as of the moment the Americans had not proved they would win.

Early on September 6, one thousand troops left Isle aux Noix to assault St. Johns twelve miles down the lake. St. Johns was a square fortification with bastions at each corner, protected by a dry ditch at the base of stiff clay walls. From a redoubt to the northwest, a battery covered the fort's approaches on three sides. The fourth side was an open area facing the water, where shipyards, ships, and naval storehouses were located.[14] At 2 p.m., the Americans approached within two miles of the enemy post. From this point, General Montgomery led an advance party a little closer until a surpisingly heavy British cannonade drove him back.[15] After this first setback, he decided to regroup at a beachhead out of range of enemy guns to try again. The second assault fared no better than the first. His troops were forced to form for battle in a deep, almost impenetrable, swamp because their officers considered the underbrush an excellent cover. As they moved forward, carefully picking their way through a dense thicket, an enemy patrol hit their left flank with a deadly volley. The Americans did not lose

their poise in spite of the surprise, returned the fire, and
pursued their attackers in a spirited charge. Within half an
hour, the skirmish ended with the enemy fleeing headlong
back to the fort. Short though it was, the fight halted Montgomery's advance. Nightfall was not far off, so he decided
to make an encampment back at the water's edge. Unfor-
tuantely for the Americans, enemy gunners had pinpointed
their location. As dusk fell, the guns of St. Johns opened
up on the invaders forcing a hurried retreat to a point three
quarters of a mile away.[16]

That evening, an informant entered the American lines to
see General Schuyler. A quick interrogation brought to light
some startling information about Sir Guy Carleton's military
capabilities. He apparently had gambled on stopping the
Americans right where they were. All except fifty of the
British regulars in Canada were concentrated at St. Johns
and Chambly, where they were supported by one hundred
Indians. The remaining regulars were posted at Montreal with
Colonel Guy Johnson's Indians. In spite of St. Johns'
strength, Schuyler's informant insisted that an attack would
be successful if the Americans struck at once. If it were
postponed too long, however, a recently launched 16-gun
vessel could, if it were allowed to break out onto Lake
Champlain, threaten the position of an American army in
Canada. On the other hand, information about the Canadians themselves was not altogether encouraging. Most of
them would not oppose the Americans provided their property and crops were left unharmed, but few Canadians would
take up arms against the King. They preferred instead to
sell provisions to both sides for gold and silver.[17]

Upon hearing this news, General Schuyler called his officers for a conference. They decided it probably would be
best to go back to Isle aux Noix since they had neither
cannon nor shells to begin a siege of the fort, inviting as
the chances for success appeared. Furthermore, they could
scarcely hope to sink the 16-gun warship while it stayed

within the fort's protective cover. The Americans knew, moreover, that they had to prevent the vessel from slipping out of Lake Champlain. If it did, communications with Fort Ticonderoga might be cut, and the Canadian invasion could not continue. Its escape might be prevented, they thought, by a boom across the channel at Isle aux Noix where a mud bank six feet below the lake's surface made navigation difficult. The situation changed quickly and the boom became unnecessary when seven hundred American troops with three cannons and two mortars unexpectedly arrived on the scene.[18] They strengthened Schuyler's army enough to permit an immediate attack on St. Johns.

Although a high fever had forced Schuyler to bed by this time, he still managed to complete plans for the assault. Operations began on September 10 with the landing of eleven hundred troops at the old beachhead.[19] As eight hundred of them advanced toward the fortress, the whole force suddenly panicked and scattered even though not a shot had been fired. Apparently one company had accidently strayed in the thick woods, and, in trying to rejoin the advance, fell in between two other units. Since the heavy underbrush concealed their movements, they so frightened the others that the whole force fled in disorder. Twice more Montgomery tried to rally his troops for another attack, but without success. On one of these occasions the men had to be restrained "from pushing off without their officers." In disgust, therefore, Montgomery ordered the expedition to return to Isle aux Noix the following day.[20]

With the exception of Schuyler and Montgomery, most American officers were completely disillusioned. "The behaviour of our Troops on the discharge of a few Booms of the Enemy is such that I should not name it...," wrote Philip Van Renssalaer, an officer from Albany.[21] But Schuyler and Montgomery were determined to shame their men into redeeming themselves. They stung the pride of their troops with caustic statements about cowardly conduct. These tongue lashings, coupled with several barbarous acts by the savages, put the Americans in a fighting mood. The Indians, it seems, had not been content with scalping captives; they dug up the American dead and "mangled them in the most shocking manner."[22] If anything more were needed to further raise spirits, it came in the form of an enemy attack. A hostile ship boldly approached the American camp and opened fire with a barrage of grapeshot, but Schuyler's artillerymen met the challenge with a direct hit which sank the enemy vessel. After this incident optimism surged through American ranks.[23]

Before ordering an advance, Schuyler and Montgomery decided to set a trap for the 16-gun schooner in a daring maneuver to take it out of action. They realized the warship might attempt to scatter their landing craft, or sneak out onto Lake Champlain in the confusion of an attack. Therefore, Schuyler armed two row galleys with twelve-pound cannons, and supported them with a sloop, a schooner, and ten batteaux. This little squadron would wait in hiding for the enemy warship to strike; once it exposed itself, the men would board her and overpower the crew.[24] In case the plan miscarried, two hundred troops were positioned to cover a retreat. Meanwhile the main army would begin its siege of St. Johns.[25]

As the Americans prepared to strike, sickness caused by insufficient food, inadequate shelter, and unsanitary conditions swept through camp. Six hundred of the seventeen hundred American troops became too ill to move, and General Schuyler's condition also grew worse.[26] It was well known that Schuyler had been directing operations from his bed for more than a week, yet even this now became impossible.[27] Bad weather had finally ended all hopes for the General's quick recovery, so he turned over command of the army to Montgomery and returned to Ticonderoga for treatment. For a while, he appeared to have a chance of returning to Canada to resume command in the field and he expressed his optimism in a letter to General Washington. "The fever has left me," he wrote, "and I hope soon to return where I ought and wish to be. Unless a barbarous Relapse should Dash this Cup of Hope from my Lips."[28] His recovery was only momentary, however, for the fever soon returned.

Being at Ticonderoga had unexpected advantages. Schuyler could coordinate affairs with Congress and the various colonial governments with more effectiveness. More important, he was able to deal directly with the deteriorating situation at the fort itself. Not more than one hundred soldiers remained there because Colonel Benjamin Hinman had permitted many troops to leave for home, even though they were desperately needed. Some of the men had no weapons, while others refused to be mustered or to obey the Rules and Articles of War because they had not been paid. Worst of all, shipments of men and materials destined for General Montgomery had slowed to a standstill. "If I had not arrived here," said Schuyler, "even on the very day I did, as sure as God lives, the army would have starved."[29] Montgomery counted heavily on Schuyler because supplies and ammunition were running low. Port rations were cut in half; Canadian flour was too expensive to purchase; and shortages of ammunition and cannon threatened to end the siege.[30] Although Montgomery had been shelling the fort with his twelve pounders, he told Schuyler the siege could not continue without immediate support.[31] Since disaster threatened the army, Schuyler was determined to stay at Ticonderoga, in spite of his illness, to get materials moving north at once.

Boats were plentiful; so were sailors to man them. Yet huge quantities of provisions and supplies had accumulated at Fort George. Schuyler soon found out why. Sailors and teamsters idled away much of their time drinking and gambling, and made only one trip a week. Even when they did work, their boats and wagons were often half filled with

sutlers' goods.[32]   Schuyler put a stop to this immediately.
He prohibited boats from spending more than three hours at
either end of Lake George except at night or in bad weather.
All boats had to be unloaded at once and manned by fresh
hands at each end of the trip.[33]   Sutlers' stores were to be
seized and destroyed, while officers and workmen were
threatened with severe punishment if they disobeyed orders.[34]

Soon General Schuyler's aggressive measures began to take
effect. Within a week, two hundred troops arrived at Fort
Ticonderoga, along with four hundred barrels of provisions
and three batteaux of artillery stores.[35]   Sick and ailing
though he was, Schuyler's exceptional organizing ability
helped to save the American army in Canada. Had it not
been for him, all chances of conquering the province would
have ended early in the autumn of 1775. But Canada alone
did not occupy Schuyler's thoughts. That winter he also
assisted Colonel Henry Knox by providing cattle, men, and
equipment to help him transport Fort Ticonderoga's cannon
to Boston so General Washington could drive British troops
from the city.

In spite of this progress, all was not well at Fort Ticonderoga. Violent winds and heavy gales on Lake Champlain
prevented troops from embarking. Some New Englanders
told Schuyler they did not choose to move until General
David Wooster arrived. "Do not choose to move!" ex-
claimed Schuyler. "Strange language in an Army..." [36]
Strange language indeed, but necessity forced him to overlook such behavior. Even after Wooster arrived, most of the
men were reluctant to proceed. They feared being stranded
in Canada all winter or perishing because of the cold and
disease.[37]   These quarrels again pointed up the underlying
animosities between individualists fighting for a common
cause. "The New England troops were universally disaffected
with General Schuyler," wrote James Lockwood, and "the
disaffection is by no means confined to the New England
troops, there being none who return from across the Lake,

a few of his particular friends excepted, that speak well of him."[38]

With their supply lifeline open once more, the colonial forces pushed on with the invasion of Canada. Fort Chambly capitulated on October 18, 1775, and two weeks later four hundred British regulars and one hundred Canadians surrendered St. Johns to General Montgomery. The gallant Irishman was not one to rest on his laurels. He quickly pressed on to Montreal where a committee of citizens acknowledged defeat on November 12.[39] The Americans struck so swiftly that they trapped Governor Carleton himself for a time, without knowing it, but Sir Guy succeeded in escaping to Quebec in a small boat. If Montgomery's troops had siezed the Canadian Governor, resistance in the province probably would have disintegrated.

In the meantime, Benedict Arnold's half-naked troops had emerged from the wilderness after one of the most astonishing journeys in history. Arnold immediately sent word of his arrival to General Schuyler whom he believed to be in Canada, but his Indian messenger delivered the news to Governor Carleton instead. Thus forewarned, Carleton fortified Quebec with nineteen hundred men and brought in many heavy guns from outlying districts.[40] By the time Arnold reached the city to demand its surrender, all hope of an easy victory had vanished. This forced him to fall back to Point aux Trembles to await Montgomery's arrival. Once more fate had stepped in to keep victory from the Americans. Had the Indian messenger not deserted, or if Arnold had arrived ten days earlier, Quebec might have fallen. As it was, the two ragged armies united on December 3, 1775, with little chance of defeating Carleton.

While American forces were penetrating deeper and deeper into Canada, Schuyler struggled to keep them supplied with food and clothing, an almost impossible task since the army was three hundred miles from its base of supply. Buying these much-needed goods in Canada appeared to be the best way to handle the dilemma, but the Canadians refused to accept American currency as payment for their products. Accordingly, Schuyler sought to find gold and silver for this purpose even though it could not easily be obtained. "I tremble for the consequence," he wrote, "should we not get a speedy supply of gold and silver."[41]

Once most of the St. Lawrence Valley had fallen under American control, steps had to be taken to govern occupied territory, so General Schuyler asked Congress to send a committee into the province to help establish American policy. Robert Treat Paine, John Langdon, and Robert R. Livingston were designated to look over the situation. Although these men did confer with Schuyler, bad weather prevented them from going into Canada for a first-hand look. The committee learned, however, that General Montgomery had been forced to make numerous concessions to his soldiers to prevent them from returning home. He had given them an issue of clothing at government expense, plus a one dollar bounty. Still the men showed little enthusiasm; some, including Seth Warner and his Green Mountain Boys, returned home anyway even before their enlistments expired.[42]

Schuyler and Montgomery were thoroughly disgusted with the troops. "Nothing can surpass the impatience of the troops from the New England Colonies to get to their firesides," complained Schuyler. "Habituated to order, I cannot, without the most extreme pain, see that disregard of discipline, confusion, and inattention, which reign so generally in this quarter, and I am, therefore, determined to retire. Of this I have advised Congress."[43] Fortunately, General Washington convinced him to continue in the service. Had he not done so, the Northern Department would have fallen into a chaotic state.

Although the Canadians were, for the most part, friendly, General Montgomery told Schuyler they could not be counted upon. "They will be our friends as long as we are able to maintain our ground, but they must not be depended upon especially for defensive purposes."[44] Still, the Americans did everything in their power to secure the cooperation of inhabitants. Otherwise the hoped-for alliance between Canada and the American colonies would not come to fruition even if the invaders were victorious. Had the Canadians been friendlier to the Americans, General Montgomery probably would have been content to blockade Quebec until Schuyler could send enough reinforcements to overpower the citadel. Montgomery thought a four-month siege would create a good deal of distress in the city, perhaps weakening it to a point where it would easily be overrun.[45] But food was beginning to run low in the American camp and "an unhappy homesickness..." prevailed among the men; therefore Montgomery decided to attack the city.[46]

Having made a decision to attack, Montgomery begged Schuyler for reinforcements even though they could not possibly arrive before his first assault. They would be needed to hold the city if the attack should prove successful. Schuyler urged Congress to send him three thousand men, guaranteeing that he would get them to Canada by mid-January to assist Montgomery. Again and again he appealed for assistance, yet few troops arrived. Montgomery realized Schuyler was making every effort to help him; still he had to decide whether it would be best to wait for more troops, or to risk a surprise attack with what men he had before too many of their enlistments expired. Faced with no really good alternative, Montgomery decided on an attack. "I shall be very sorry to be reduced to this...," he informed Schuyler, "because I know the melancholy consequences, but the approaching severe season and the weakness of the garrison, together with the nature of the works, point it out too strong to be passed by."[47] Unhappily for the Americans, Montgomery had underestimated Carleton's strength.

As heavy snow began to fall, Montgomery readied his forces for an assault. On December 31, 1775, the Americans struck Quebec in the midst of a driving snowstorm, only to find that Carleton had been waiting for them. A deserter had betrayed the Americans. Shortly after attacking, Montgomery lay dead from grapeshot and Arnold was badly wounded. Their troops were hopelessly lost in Quebec's maze of crooked streets, all the while under heavy sniper fire. The battle ended in disaster for the Americans and almost all hope of conquering Canada was shattered against the walls of Quebec that night.

Courageously the wretched, freezing, half starved band of men hung on, keeping up the pretense of a siege for the benefit of their Canadian friends as Edward Antill dashed to Albany with the sad news. General Schuyler immediately sent him on to Philadelphia with new appeals for help (January 13, 1776), while similar messages were dispatched to Washington and neighboring colonies. Congress responded at once to Schuyler's plea. New Jersey and Pennsylvania were asked to send troops; blankets were gathered from Philadelphia's citizens; and Colonels John Bull of Pennsylvania and William Maxwell of New Jersey were ordered to report to Schuyler with their units without delay. Congress also asked Washington for a battalion, while New Hampshire, Connecticut, New York, and Pennsylvania were urged to raise battalions for Canadian service. To encourage assistance, enlistment bounties of six and two-thirds dollars were offered.[48]

Schuyler himself could not send any troops to Canada because Tory uprisings along the Mohawk River threatened to throw Tryon County into chaos. This new menace to New York was caused by Sir John Johnson who had fortified Johnson Hall and gathered three hundred Indians and six to seven hundred Scotch Highlanders around him, apparently with the idea of stirring up the frontier. No one can be certain why Sir John chose this moment to take action against the colonies. Perhaps word of Montgomery's death and the crushing American defeat at Quebec prompted him to act, since news of the battle probably reached Johnstown on January 10, three days before Edward Antill reported the disaster to Schuyler in Albany.[49]   Sir John at once took steps to harass the Whigs in Tryon County. His move may either have been designed to completely cut off supplies from the American army in Canada, or simply to disrupt communications and discourage those who might otherwise support the rebel cause.

Isaac Paris, chairman of the Tryon County Committee, told Schuyler of Johnson's plans.[50]   Paris said three hundred Indians were laying an ambush near Johnson Hall with orders to destroy anyone who might seek to oppose Sir John.[51]   Upon learning this, Schuyler acted quickly. Urgent requests for assistance went out to the countryside, and men whose homes and families were threatened soon began to converge on Albany despite the cold weather. When Schuyler gave orders to march on Monday, January 16, 1776, almost three thousand troops were with him.

By Tuesday evening, the expedition had reached Schenectady, where Schuyler encountered several Mohawk Indians who told him they came as mediators. Little Abraham, their spokesman, asked General Schuyler to delay his advance, but the General refused. He insisted on bringing Sir John into line before his rash acts inflamed the frontier. Schuyler did take this opportunity, however, to assure Little Abraham that no American units would march into Iroquois territory unless the Indians joined Sir John. The savages appeared to like this and quickly promised not to take sides in the quarrel.[52]

That night, General Schuyler sent word to Johnson in an attempt to set up a meeting the following day. When they met to discuss their differences, Schuyler demanded that Sir John end at once all hostile activity in the Mohawk Valley, surrender his arms and ammunition, and help to relieve tension in Tryon County. Sir John refused. He claimed the Indians were poised to aid him if fighting broke out. But Schuyler could not be bluffed. He told Johnson force would be met with force and suggested that he think it over. Shortly after the meeting ended, Little Abraham visited Schuyler again to seek some kind of a compromise. This time Schuyler was more blunt with him, for it was obvious that Sir John was using the threat of an Indian attack in his war of nerves with the Americans. Schuyler warned Little Abraham not to meddle because he would destroy Mohawk villages if the Indians continued to let Johnson use them as a threat against western settlers.[53]

On Thursday, January 18, Schuyler advanced to within four miles of Johnstown when a counter-proposal from Johnson arrived. Schuyler considered Sir John's terms unsatisfactory, so he prepared to take Johnson Hall by force. "I give you until twelve o'clock this night," he said, "after which I shall receive no proposals... This condescension I make from no other motive than to prevent the effusion of blood..."[54] The Indians soon returned, begging Schuyler to wait until 4 a.m. By then they hoped to bring Sir John to his senses. They also insisted again that they intended not to fight and General Schuyler now realized he might be able to humiliate Johnson in the eyes of the Iroquois. With this in mind, he told the Indians he would agree to their request because of his love and esteem for them. At the same time, he wanted to prove to the Iroquois they could get what they wanted by cooperating with the Americans, but not by using threats of force. Hence, he told the savages to make Johnson see his error and alter his conduct or he would be crushed by American arms.

The four-hour extension proved to be unnecessary because Sir John came to terms at exactly midnight. The next day, Schuyler's troops triumphantly marched into Johnstown where they took possession of Johnson's weapons and military stores. On Saturday, the Americans formed in Johnstown's main street to formally accept arms from Johnson's previously recalcitrant Highlanders. Schuyler's troops soon rounded up other troublemakers in the area, disarming be-

tween six and seven hundred Tories before they had finished.[55]   With the Tryon County situation well in hand, Schuyler returned to Albany to oversee preparations to send troops and supplies to Canada. His aggressive measures had ended Sir John Johnson's activities, while forcing the Indians to look upon the colonists' power with considerably more respect. No battle had been fought, yet Schuyler had won a bloodless victory of great significance. This had not been done without a great personal sacrifice by Schuyler himself, however. Although he had recovered enough to lead the expedition in spite of his weak and unsteady condition, exposure to the severe cold weather, excessive activity, and poor food brought on a relapse which forced him to bed for the rest of the month. "I have been Confined to my room for 8 days by my Ancient Enemy who has attacked In the Foot, Supported by an auxiliary more formidable who has made a lodgement in my lungs and threatened destruction..."[56]
In spite of his physical condition, his recent successes in the field and the flood of supplies pouring into Albany made him more optimistic than usual. He knew that if troops and supplies could be rushed to the army in Canada before help for Carleton arrived from Britain, success might still possibly come to the American troops in front of Quebec.

Chapter Five

THE STRUGGLE FOR LAKE CHAMPLAIN

The weeks following Montgomery's ill-fated assault on Quebec were filled with suffering and sadness for those who survived the attack. Temperatures often dropped to 20° below zero as icy winds pounded the ragged little army huddled outside the town. Benedict Arnold, in spite of being bedridden with severe wounds, tried to maintain the appearance of a cordon around Quebec. It was an empty gesture, however, since General Schuyler's chances of getting help to him were slim. Arnold realized an enemy relief force would probably arrive to break the siege before Schuyler could help, yet he never stopped trying to keep alive America's fading hopes for a Canadian conquest. Unfortunately, not many of his troops showed as much determination. Morale began to crumble, discipline collapsed, desertions increased, and the once-friendly Canadians turned their backs on the Americans, cutting off what little support they had given the invaders in the past. Most of them wanted nothing to do with an army which could offer neither protection for them nor hard money for their goods. Since Arnold's troops had only depreciated Continental currency, they further alienated the Canadians by looting wood and foodstuffs to avoid freezing and starving.

Everything appeared to go wrong. Some of the troops complained of a high fever and violent headaches. When red spots on their bodies turned into thickly set pimples, there was no doubt about what they had — smallpox. By mid-

February, the dread disease swept through camp in epidemic proportions.[1] The furious itching was almost more than men could bear. Had he wanted to, Carleton probably could have wiped out the Americans. Instead he chose to wait for relief to arrive from England rather than expose his own people to smallpox, for experience had taught him that the rigors of winter, starvation, and disease would eventually reduce Arnold's army to a disorganized mob anyway. Why not wait within the relative comfort of Quebec's walls and watch the elements do their job? This is what he decided to do.

At Fort Ticonderoga, meanwhile, General Schuyler hurried with arrangements to personally lead a relief expedition to aid Arnold.[2] Even though sickness stopped him once again before he could depart, he managed to get troops, supplies, money, and ammunition rolling toward Canada. When they reached Quebec on April 1, 1776, General David Wooster replaced the wounded Arnold.[3] Wooster, a Connecticut militia officer, was popular with his troops but he lacked the ability necessary to rally them in a difficult spot. That was not all. He and Schuyler had clashed several weeks before when he overstepped his authority at Fort George.[4] Although Wooster grudgingly accepted a reprimand, he felt Schuyler had persecuted him. Once Wooster crossed into Canada, however, he told Schuyler he no longer considered himself subordinate to the commander of the Northern Department. This display of arrogance so enraged Schuyler he sent a letter to Congress, written almost as an ultimatum. In it, he emphasized the difficulties involved in serving with an officer who showed contempt for his orders and made "insults of the grossest kind."[5] One of them had to go. This proved unwise for Schuyler because many New Englanders wished to see him replaced.[6] They countered by pointing out that a general belonged with his troops and Schuyler had not been with the army for almost five months. They claimed this was the reason why New Englanders responded slowly to calls for reinforcements. No one wanted to serve under a general who disappeared just before an attack. The Yankee delegates concluded their arguments by demanding to know why he remained at Ticonderoga when the army needed him at Quebec.[7]

When Congress learned Schuyler's health would prevent him from going to Canada for many weeks, it used the opportunity to get rid of him. In reorganizing the army on February 17, 1776, Congress directed Major General Charles Lee to take command in Canada.[8] Lee was an adventurous officer who had seen service in Europe and with James Braddock and Sir William Johnson in America. His experience and fighting background might have improved operations in Canada, but before he could take over his orders were changed. Intelligence reports indicated Britain planned an intensification of operations in the middle and southern colonies. Hence Congress preferred to give Lee command of the Southern Department and send General John Thomas, fresh from outstanding service at Dorchester Heights and Boston, to Canada. In this reorganization, Schuyler was told to take over forces in New York as soon as his health permitted, to maintain his headquarters at Albany, and to do everything possible to strengthen Thomas's forces in Canada.[9]

While Congress attempted to inject some new life in the Northern army, Governor Guy Carleton called for assistance from Britain. His request reached London on Christmas Day, 1775, and English leaders made arrangements at once to send a small fleet of troop transports to the mouth of the St. Lawrence River to be on hand to aid Carleton when the spring ice jams broke up.[10] Severe cold hampered preparations in Britain, but three ships managed to leave for Quebec by February 22, and others got underway several weeks later. Steps were also taken to follow the first relief expedition with a much larger military force of eight British regiments, five artillery companies, and five thousand German mercenaries. These troops were to be supported by workmen and supplied with batteaux, clothing, and trinkets for the Indians. Carleton had to contribute six thousand Canadians so the army could, if necessary, drive American troops out of the province.[11] British leaders also had a secondary objective. They talked in March, 1776, of severing New York and establishing contact with British units on the Atlantic seaboard. Once the King's forces succeeded in cutting New England off from the other colonies, British leaders intended to let the Indians menace the frontier farmers and force them to flee to safety. This would cause a food shortage and perhaps encourage some Americans to stop fighting.[12]

Many members of Congress still did not understand the desperate situation in Canada even though Schuyler warned of an impending disaster. Troops and provisions had been sent, to be sure; so had some hard money, but this was not enough to reverse the trend. Congress betrayed its ignorance by ordering Benjamin Franklin, Samuel Chase, and Charles Carroll to Canada with authorization to officially bring that province into the Colonies.[13] There was no chance of this. Schuyler knew it; so did many others. Yet Congress continued to entertain the idea. When the congressional commissioners arrived in Canada after a short conference with General Schuyler in Albany, they realized how ill-conceived their mission was. Many Canadians had been exploited and humiliated at the point of a bayonet that winter by the desperate, half-starved, half-frozen American troops. Because of such treatment, the Canadians were hostile to American aims and little enthusiasm could be generated among them. Only one slim chance appeared to remain. The commissioners thought eight or ten thousand troops might still conquer Canada if they arrived before Britain reinforced Carleton. Troops alone would not do it, however; faith had to be restored in American credit.[14] This meant an initial outlay of at least twenty thousand pounds in specie. These were bold measures, indeed, yet Congress did not hesitate to carry out the commissioners' advice in its gamble to hold Canada.[15]

When General John Thomas superseded old David Wooster on May 1, 1776, he realized the ragged little army could not possibly force Quebec to surrender, so he gave orders to raise the siege.[16]   Unfortunately, his troops could not withdraw before three British men-of-war broke through the ice on May 6 to reinforce Carleton. Quebec went wild with joy. Carleton siezed the opportunity to deal Thomas's troops a devastating blow. He quickly struck the muddy, half-starved, and discouraged Americans who scattered in headlong flight, leaving their cannon, food, clothing, ammunition, and hospital cases behind them.[17]   Forty miles west of Quebec, Thomas tried to rally his fearstricken troops, but it was useless. He described them as: "A retreating army, disheartened by unavoidable misfortunes, destitute of almost every necessity to render their lives comfortable or even tolerable, sick and (as they think) wholly neglected and (with) no prospect of speedy relief."[18]   Their flight came to an end at Sorel on May 17, when two thousand advancing musketmen reached them. The relief column was commanded by Brigadier General William Thompson who had recently served under Washington as colonel of a Pennsylvania rifle regiment. Meanwhile Thomas's sadly battered, almost helpless, troops continued to Chambly where Thomas himself died of smallpox on June 2.[19]

The day before Thomas died, prospects for a counter-offensive momentarily improved. Thirty-three hundred additional reinforcements arrived with Brigadier General John Sullivan, who had come to take command of the army. Sullivan marched two thousand fresh troops halfway back to Quebec in an attempt to retake Three Rivers. Unluckily for them, six thousand British regulars had concentrated there while awaiting two thousand reinforcements, but the Americans had no idea that the enemy had assembled there with such force. Indeed they were advancing into a veritable trap.

When the unwary Americans attacked, they were thrown back with terrific losses and almost half of them never re-

turned to Sorel. Despite this costly defeat, Sullivan was still determined to block the advancing British regulars at Sorel. At the last moment, however, he decided against it. "I found myself at the head of a dispirited Army, filled with horror at the thought of seeing their enemy... Smallpox, famine and disorder had rendered them almost lifeless... I found a great panick... among both officers and soldiers... no less than 40 officers begged leave to resign... However strongly I might fortify Sorel, my men would in general leave me."[20]
The game in Canada was up. As Sullivan headed for New York, Arnold told Schuyler he also intended to abandon Canada rather than risk complete annihilation. Several days later Sullivan and Arnold joined forces at St. Johns. But Schuyler had seen their defeat coming and provided numerous boats for a retreat to a low flat swampy brush-covered island called Isle aux Noix. Unfortunately, it proved to be a poor choice for the battered American troops because thunderstorms turned the island into a steaming sea of mud. Tents were scarce; some hospital cases had no shelter or heat; and there was not enough food to go around. The rain soon brought out swarms of tiny black flies and mosquitoes which tormented the critically ill and healthy alike. Within 48 hours a quarter of the Americans had malaria, smallpox, or dysentery, with but little medical aid available to relieve their suffering. The pitiful cries of sick and dying soldiers pierced every corner of the encampment. Men died so fast that common graves were filled with bodies day after day. To continue at Isle aux Noix meant certain destruction for those who still were healthy, so General Sullivan evacuated his army to Crown Point.

The realization that five thousand Americans had lost their lives in ten months of campaigning in Canada spread gloom throughout the eastern colonies. Each reversal brought new demands for generals with fighting backgrounds. When Congress learned how Sullivan's troops had walked into a virtual trap at Three Rivers, it directed General Washington to make Major General Horatio Gates commander of all forces in Canada.[21]   Gates was looked upon as an ideal choice because of his service under Prince Ferdinand of Europe, and with General Braddock in America, and it was felt that he could restore the army to fighting efficiency. Once he arrived in Albany, however, Gates learned his army had left Canada. This came as a disappointment, but he was not discouraged. He apparently thought Congress had also given him Schuyler's command in New York, and indeed this may well have been what a strong New England faction intended to do, so a showdown became inevitable.

Trouble between Schuyler and Gates was not long in coming. Gates introduced David Avery to Schuyler and said Avery needed money to carry out his duties as Deputy Commissary General. Schuyler was astonished. But Avery insisted that Commissary General Joseph Trumball had commissioned him to supersede Walter Livingston before he left New York City. While Schuyler sent for Livingston, he told Gates and Avery that Trumbull had no authority to make such an appointment. When Livingston reported, he brought a letter from Trumbull which contradicted Avery's claim. This forced Avery to back down and Schuyler considered the matter closed until he learned that Gates still was not satisfied. A few minutes after leaving Schuyler, Gates promised Avery he would hire him anyway, but one of Schuyler's aides overheard the comment and told Schuyler about it. The latter angrily confronted Gates and pointed out that he (Gates) had replaced Sullivan as his second in command in the Northern Department, and he had no authority to contradict the order. Gates disagreed. After a heated argument both officers decided to ask Congress to clarify Gates's orders, and on July 8, Congress supported Schuyler.[22]   It explained that it had intended to give General Gates a superior command to General Schuyler only while Gates headed an army in Canada. When the army left Canada, it then became Schuyler's responsibility.[23]   Gates, as a result, had no choice other than to work with General Schuyler. It is good to note that he probably would not have made an issue of the matter in the first place if several New England delegates had not encouraged him to do so. Elbridge Gerry made this clear when he wrote: "We want very much to see you with the sole command in the Northern Department, but hope you will not relinquish your exertions, until a favorable opportunity shall effect it." [24] Obviously Gates planned to try again.

Even before the issue had been settled, Schuyler and Gates set out for Crown Point to assess the Northern army's military capabilities. At a council of war there on July 7, Schuyler, Gates, Sullivan, Arnold, and Prussian General Baron de Woedtke unanimously decided it would be foolhardy to defend Crown Point.[25] Its defenses were crumbling; contagious diseases infected the fort; supplies were a long way off; and it could easily be by-passed and cut off by an enemy fleet. Faced with such a situation the council thought it best to make a stand at the more defensible Fort Ticonderoga and move the two thousand sick, wounded, and dying soldiers to Fort George. By isolating smallpox cases there, the council believed militia troops would be more willing to go to Ticonderoga. Since control of Lake Champlain was important, the council also recommended the construction of "a naval armament of gondolas, row-galleys" and armed batteaux to oppose an expected enemy invasion.[26]

Surprisingly enough, discontent with the council's orders erupted among the field officers at Crown Point. Twenty-one of them termed the intended withdrawal uncalled-for and unwise.[27] Although General Washington disapproved of such mutinous action, he, too, questioned the council's decision to abandon Crown Point, until Schuyler and Gates explained their reasoning. Schuyler pointed out that time and careless construction had left the post useless. Gates agreed: "The Ramparts are Tumbled down," he said, "the casements are Fallen in, the Barracks Burnt, and the whole so perfect a Ruin that it would take Five times the Number of our Army for several Summers to put Those Works in Defensable (sic) Repair."[28]

The arrival of troops from Crown Point swelled Ticonderoga's garrison to twenty-five hundred by July 15, but trouble came with them. Intense provincial jealousies made the separation of Pennsylvania and New England troops a necessity. Brigades composed of troops from Massachusetts, New Hampshire, Connecticut, New Jersey, and New York were positioned on Mount Independence on the east side of Lake Champlain, and the Pennsylvania units were encamped on the Ticonderoga side. Worst of all, the survivors of the Canadian campaign were like a mob without discipline. Most of them were not New Yorkers, and they made no secret of their intention to make General Schuyler the target of their discontent. Mismanaged shipments of supplies were attributed to him; so were food and ammunition shortages. Some of the more bitter individuals even said he would sell his wife and plunder his country to·make a few dollars.[29] This started other Americans thinking about Schuyler. "Is it possible that he can be sacrificing the Interest of that Country to his Ambition or Avarice?" asked Robert Morris.[30] Those close to Schuyler knew charges of dishonesty had no basis; however, they were unable to stop them. For the time being Schuyler ignored these attacks; he chose instead to concentrate on other problems which plagued the Northern Department, yet there can be no doubt that he was deeply hurt.

Ordnance and ordnance stores were inadequate at Fort Ticonderoga. Although 120 guns varying from three-pounders to a 32-pounder were on hand, only forty-three gun carriages could be located to mount them. Powder, lead, flints, sponges, rammers, and cartridge paper were also in short supply.[31] The fleet intended for Lake Champlain continued to be a problem. It consisted of three schooners: the *Royal Savage,* captured at St. Johns by Montgomery the previous year; the *Liberty,* taken from the British at Skenesborough; the *Revenge,* a vessel recently constructed at Ticonderoga; and a sloop called the *Enterprise,* which Arnold took when Ticonderoga fell into American hands in 1775. It was a fleet in name only, since its vessels were more like floating logs than warships. Nevertheless, Schuyler still hoped to win the shipbuilding duel then in progress with Sir Guy Carleton.[32] Reports from St. Johns indicated British workmen had transported partially constructed ships to St. Johns where they were being fitted out to move an army against Ticonderoga by late summer. This meant no time could be lost if Schuyler expected to block Carleton's advances.

Finding a capable officer to command the American fleet became the first order of business, but Benedict Arnold solved this quickly by volunteering to oversee construction of the fleet and take command of it when it was ready to sail.[33] Schuyler and Gates were pleased with Arnold's offer because he possessed great spirit and courage in addition to some knowledge of naval affairs. Schuyler also realized that construction of schooners and sloops might take too long, so he decided to concentrate instead on building the less complex row galleys and gondolas. The row galleys were sixty to eighty feet in length with an 18-foot beam, and a round bottom and keel. They were generally manned by eighty men and armed with six to ten guns. At best they had one 12-pound gun and one 18-pounder in the stern, two masts, lateen sails, and thirty-six oars which made them easy to handle. The gondolas, on the other hand, were slower, smaller, and so difficult to handle they could sail only before a fair wind. They were flat-bottomed craft, forty feet in length, one mast, two square sails, oars, and a forty-man crew. Their fire power was supplied by one 12-pound and two 9-pound guns.

The Americans soon began constructing these vessels in a dockyard at Skenesborough under the supervision of Brigadier General James Waterbury, Jr., of Connecticut.[34] Construction went slowly at first. Supplies, equipment, and workmen were practically non-existent, although a search of the Northern army produced a few experienced carpenters and mechanics. Schuyler had thirty more sent from Albany, but these craftsmen were not nearly enough for the job at hand.[35] Therefore, hurried calls went out to New England coastal towns with the promise of wages as high as five dollars a day in hard money to those who would come to northern New York. Gradually several hundred blacksmiths, oar makers, riggers, sailmakers, and shipwrights from Massachusetts, Connecticut, and Rhode Island seaports arrived at Skenesborough. A few even came from far off Philadelphia.[36] While this was going on, shipments of naval stores, nails, and paint from the seacoast towns moved slowly over wilderness trails and roads to the shipyard. Too frequently there were delays and at one time or another workmen were idled by nail, rope, and canvas shortages before these hard-to-get supplies became plentiful.

Although the slopes surrounding Lake Champlain were covered with fine stands of virgin timber, lumber was difficult to obtain. Felling axes, broadaxes, and crosscut saws were so scarce that two hundred soldiers worked with tomahawks until General Schuyler obtained fifteen hundred axes in Albany. When Governor Jonathan Trumbull of Connecticut added a thousand more, the welcome sound of hundreds of axes rang through the forest.[37] The long-inactive sawmills at Skenesborough, Ticonderoga, and Crown Point soon buzzed with activity, while at the dockyards a small armada began to take shape under General Waterbury's watchful eyes.

Conditions in general improved in the Northern Department. Bread was plentiful; cattle driven to Ticonderoga provided the garrison with fresh beef; and settlers cheered the troops by bringing them vegetables, sugar, butter, cheese, chocolate, rum, and wine. When militia units arrived from New England in substantial numbers on July 3, 1776, and again in early August, the picture brightened considerably. Troop returns for August 24, listed 10,657 rank and file, although only 6,399 were said to be fit for duty.[38]   In general, the improved defenses, more plentiful supplies, and Arnold's rapidly growing fleet, greatly helped to improve morale.

With the situation well in hand at Ticonderoga, General Schuyler turned his attention toward western New York where rumors indicated trouble was brewing. British agents who had long tried to get the Iroquois Indians to destroy villages in the Mohawk Valley were apparently making some headway. This was partially substantiated by an unconfirmed report that Indian warriors had assisted British forces in a landing at Fort Oswego.[39]   A two-front battle appeared to be in the making, so Schuyler rushed to German Flats to confer with Iroquois leaders. He felt they had to be kept out of the fight at any cost. After a lengthy conference which lasted until August 13, the Indians promised to honor their earlier pledge of neutrality. To prove their sincerity, they even agreed to let Schuyler refurbish Fort Schuyler (old Fort Stanwix) as a means of strengthening New York's western frontier.[40]   This meeting was of great strategic importance since it enabled Schuyler to forget about a possible Indian uprising and turn his attention toward Sir Guy Carleton's threatened invasion. Yet most Americans did not understand what Schuyler had accomplished, and they condemned him for being away from the army when it badly needed him.

Frustrations at every turn, charges of misconduct and disloyalty, and endless hours of work pushed Schuyler's patience to the breaking point. He finally exploded in anger when an unofficial council of army officers in New York City took it upon themselves to practically censure him for his decision to evacuate Crown Point. Instead of ignoring the incident as he should have done, Schuyler sent a sharply worded letter to General Washington and to Congress in which he defended the move.[41] Bristling with anger, Schuyler urged Congress to investigate charges of disloyalty being made against him; to find out why reverses in Canada were blamed on him; and to check his accounts to see if shortages were caused by his greed and negligence, as many claimed. Then, in a defiant mood, he formally submitted his resignation to John Hancock, President of the Continental Congress.[42] Hancock tried to calm Schuyler by promising to look into these charges, while the General's friends rallied to his support. In addition, Congress refused to consider Schuyler's resignation, assuring him that it had complete faith and confidence in him in spite of aspersions cast upon his character.[43] This pleased Schuyler until he realized Congress had appointed a committee to confer, not with him, but with General Gates, on conditions in the Northern Department.[44] Even though he still resented the implications of its most recent resolution, he decided to push aside personal considerations until Sir Guy Carleton made his move against Ticonderoga.

By August 20, a fleet of eleven American vessels was ready for action. It was an awkward looking armada, rather slow and over-gunned and so short of powder none could be spared even for target practice. In general, the crews who manned these ships had never before served on one, but Benedict Arnold's daring and resourceful nature gave them considerable confidence. Arnold hastened northward rather than wait until five other boats were completed. He hoped to bottle up Carleton's fleet in Champlain's narrow Canadian waters where its superior fire power would be minimized in battle. When this position proved untenable, however, Arnold retired to a concealed anchorage between Valcour Island and Champlain's western shore. There, late in September, the five remaining vessels joined him to await Carleton's advance.

But Carleton moved slowly. Although British forces had pursued Sullivan's army to St. Johns in June, they were unable to strike at New York until October. A quick thrust proved impractical because of Schuyler's decision to build warships on Lake Champlain. The new American fleet caused the overcautious Carleton to make extraordinary preparations before he dared venture out to battle Arnold. Finally, on October 4, Sir Guy took up the chase with twenty-nine vessels carrying ninety-three guns. Fifty-three of them could be swung into action at one time. The odds were high against Arnold since his armada could counter with no more than thirty-two of its fifty-three guns at one time. Furthermore, members of the Royal Navy were handling Carleton's ships and they could fire 500 pounds of metal in a single cannonade compared to Arnold's 265.[45] On October 11, the British, a bit overconfident under the circumstances, sailed past Arnold and lost the windward position. This slight advantage proved insufficient in combat, however, and Carleton's superior fire power severely punished the Americans in a desperate seven-hour battle.[46]

Arnold's losses were heavy. A schooner and gondola were sunk; sixty men had been killed or wounded; three-quarters of the ammunition was gone; and the fleet's sails hung in shreds among a mass of tangled rigging and twisted wreckage. As darkness fell, defeat appeared certain for Arnold, so Carleton decided to wait until morning before finishing him off. But Arnold refused to give up. Using darkness and fog for cover, he made a daring escape through the midst of Carleton's fleet. At sunrise British officers were shocked to learn that the Americans had slipped away. They quickly pursued Arnold and struck him again at Split Rock and Buttonmould Bay on October 13. When most of the American vessels could no longer continue, Arnold ran them ashore and burned them as their crews fled into the woods in complete defeat.[47] Afterward the British units proceeded to Crown Point to await orders to attack Fort Ticonderoga.

News of Arnold's defeat soon reached American headquarters. Although eleven boats had been lost, Schuyler realized Arnold's men might have successfully delayed Carleton long enough to keep him from assaulting Fort Ticonderoga because winter was rapidly approaching. Since only Sir Guy could provide the key to his theory, Schuyler waited for him to act. One day passed, then another, and still no enemy units appeared in front of Ticonderoga. Although rumors of a British withdrawal began to spread through the army, Schuyler and his generals remained skeptical. Arnold hoped it was not just a feint to throw the Americans off guard and encourage short-term militia troops to return home.[48]   Gates, on the other hand, told Schuyler his scouts could not make contact with enemy troops even though they probed forty miles below Crown Point.[49]   Soon inhabitants of the area where the British were supposed to be, told his scouts that Sir Guy had returned to winter headquarters in Canada; and these reports turned out to be true.

Although the lateness of the season undoubtedly played an important part in Carleton's decision to pull back, it was by no means the only reason for his withdrawal. More significant, perhaps, was the presence of 13,500 entrenched troops at Ticonderoga. They could not be easily or quickly driven back without a long and bitter struggle which might have stretched well into the winter months when Lake Champlain usually froze over. This would have been risky for Carleton, since his army's ability to sustain such an attack rested precariously on an extended lifeline across Lake Champlain. Any disruption in communication, no matter how slight, would have left his forces open to destruction. Thus, Carleton returned to Canada to await a more favorable opportunity to bring New York back under British control, while Schuyler looked ahead to the next campaign.

Chapter Six

"TO THE DEPTHS OF DESPAIR"

By late November, 1776, most Americans thought the possibility of an invasion from Canada could be forgotten until spring; not General Schuyler. He told two congressional commissioners, Richard Stockton and George Clymer, to expect an attack that winter because Carleton could get enough sleds to transport artillery and provisions for ten thousand men.[1] By then the American militia would be gone and the Northern Department would be considerably weaker. Therefore he appealed to Congress and the New England states for help. None came, so he repeated his requests. Still no one answered except Governor Jonathan Trumbull of Connecticut. Trumbull assured Schuyler that he would do everything possible to help but he was handicapped by the threat of an invasion by an English fleet standing off the coast.[2] Upon hearing this Schuyler realized he could not expect much support from New England so he carefully worked out strategy to defend New York's frontier with the troops that were available. Twenty-five hundred were stationed at Fort Ticonderoga, 400 at Fort George, 100 at Skenesborough, 100 at Fort Anne, 400 at Fort Edward, 1,000 at Saratoga, 100 at Schenectady, 200 at Johnstown, 200 at Fort Dayton, 400 at Fort Schuyler, and about 400 at Albany.[3] By cantoning the army in this manner, Schuyler hoped to contain any surprise attacks until other units could be thrown into battle. The presence of troops at strategic points might also help to discourage Carleton from attacking until spring.

As Schuyler completed these arrangements, the mighty force which had gathered at Ticonderoga began to disperse. On November 9, Colonel Caleb Hide's Berks County men were released;[4] a few days later 1,107 troops from Winds', Maxwell's, and deHaas's New Jersey regiments (their enlistments had already expired) left with General Arthur St. Clair,[5] while Brigadier General James Bricket's ten militia regiments — 5,106 men in all — were slated to move out late in November.[6] Therefore Schuyler advised General Gates to send as many troops as possible into winter positions.[7] Gates complied by moving eight Continental regiments toward Albany, leaving 2,500 Pennsylvania and New Jersey troops at Fort Ticonderoga under Colonel Anthony Wayne.[8] This deployment was temporary because Wayne's troops were scheduled to leave the army on January 5, 1777, and the New Jersey regiments under Colonels Elias Dayton and Charles Burrell would complete their enlistments a fortnight later.[9] Consequently, positive steps had to be taken to enlist replacements for them, but this promised to be difficult, since recruiting lagged in the colonies.

Schuyler, Gates, Arnold and Bricket analyzed the situation at a council of war in Saratoga on November 21, 1776, and, after considerable discussion, they concluded that few of the troops then in New York would re-enlist unless they were first allowed to return home. Since the enlistments of eight New England regiments would be up on December 31, 1776, the council decided to let them go early to recruit their own replacements.[10] Unfortunately, the plan was foredoomed to failure. To begin with, most New Englanders who had served in New York were loath to enlist for duty there again. Those who had participated in the Canadian invasion and retreat the previous winter had bitterly complained of suffering from sickness and shortages of medicine, provisions, and clothing. Some said they had been forced to pay exorbitant prices for necessities sold by sutlers. Sometimes they spent their entire wages to prevent starvation.[11]   Statements such as these prompted New Hampshire's affable physician delegate to Congress, Josiah Bartlett, to suggest an inquiry to find out why sick soldiers had been deprived of medicine when large quantities had been sent to New York. Until this state of affairs was corrected, Bartlett feared Schuyler would be unable to raise any troops at all.[12]

In view of the rout suffered by the army in 1776, and the almost intolerable conditions then prevailing at most frontier posts, the situation could not be improved as easily as Bartlett and others appeared to think. Ticonderoga had no barracks or permanent hospital; some men slept on the ground in "poor thin tents," while others had no tents at all. As a result many soldiers suffered from pleurisy and colds. According to Colonel Wayne, the fort's temporary hospital contained invalids of all descriptions. There were no medicines or regimen, no beds, not even straw to lie on, and no covering to keep the suffering warm.[13] When Joseph Wood entered this so-called temporary hospital, the sight of ill and dying men sprawled on the damp floor horrified him. The poor wretch nearest the door was dead, the next two alive, and on the other side of them lay two more lifeless comrades. The dead had been allowed to remain among the living for twenty-four hours. "If you was (sic) here," said Wood, "your heart would melt."[14]

Men died so fast their comrades grew weary of digging graves in the frozen ground. On one occasion the New Jersey troops dug two graves. While they were busy bringing corpses to the place, some Pennsylvanians buried two of their dead there. Just as the Pennsylvania men were covering the bodies the Jersey men appeared, and a fight ensued. When the Jersey soldiers proved stronger, they dug up the dead Pennsylvanians and buried the Jersey bodies where they belonged. This forced the Pennsylvanians to cover their dead in gullies with logs and stones. It was "too hard to labor so much for those for whom they might never expect any return as to cover them with frozen earth."[15]

The more fortunate had no great appetite for war, especially those whose enlistments would soon expire. The Revolutionary patriot, like most soldiers, disliked making defensive preparations for an enemy he would not have to fight; he preferred instead to drink, play cards, and think about getting an early release from duty.[16] Cornelius Wynkoop, commanding at Skenesborough, complained that the militia would not do a thing for him, nor could he make them.[17] Two of Wayne's officers, Colonel Francis Johnson and Major Persifor Frazer, actually went to Congress to seek an early release for their men, under the pretense that all of them would "probably" re-enlist if permitted to return home.[18] When the Pennsylvania Committee of Safety learned about the plight of its troops at Ticonderoga, David Rittenhouse, acting as the committee's spokesman, called the situation "the most important matter which can at this time attract the attention of Congress..." Until a thorough reform is made, he wrote, opposition to Carleton's forces would be in vain because "a few naked, sickly, and illtrained troops must fall prey to their own distress, if not to the enemy." [19]

No one could deny the gravity of the situation, and Schuyler realized it might become worse if Washington's forces continued to be stampeded. Fort Washington's surrender (November 16, 1776), with the accompanying loss of 2,500 men and enormous quantities of equipment, came as a severe blow to him.[20] He ordered Gates to detain all regiments scheduled for an early release until more information arrived from the Commander-in-chief.[21] The implications of this disaster were clear. It might be necessary to transfer these units to New Jersey.

When General Howe began to push toward Philadelphia, Congress directed General Washington to recall the Pennsylvania and New Jersey troops serving with Schuyler.[22] Since Gates had deployed the Pennsylvania and New Jersey units at remote areas on the frontier, they could not possibly report to Washington for several weeks or perhaps even a month, and even then it might not be done safely.[23] Therefore Schuyler had to send the eight recruiting regiments waiting to be released, even though this undermined his plans to enlist a new army.[24]

This greatly displeased Schuyler. He felt Congress had acted too quickly because it did not know how critical affairs were in the Northern Department. Therefore he viciously lashed out at the delegates, telling them he was astonished by New Jersey's and Pennsylvania's lack of support for Washington. "It appears," he wrote, "as if they intended to give up the cause." Then he needled Congress for its decision to move to Baltimore before it was forced to do so, because such a step would cause alarm throughout the colonies.[25] Finally, he accused Congress of ignoring letters asking for help on New York's frontier.[26] Although these complaints may have been justified to some extent, on the whole they were unfair to Congress. Had Schuyler known that Stockton and Clymer had not yet reported, he might have reacted differently. It can be seen, therefore, that poor communications and lack of trust and faith on both sides probably contributed most to the deterioration of Schuyler's relations with Congress, but he also failed to realize the seriousness of General Washington's position when Congress requested reinforcements from the Northern Department. Congress, on the other hand, did not know what Schuyler faced on the frontier. When Stockton and Clymer reported on November 27, 1776, its members learned that New York faced an invasion threat over the ice that winter and their attitude changed considerably.[27]

The following day Congress took strong steps to aid Schuyler. It asked Governor Trumbull to send twenty cannon to New York; experts were sent to the Salisbury and Livingston foundries to see whether cannon could be forged at those places; and the Commissary General was ordered to supply provisions. A day later, it ordered the Medical Committee "to provide sufficient quantities of antiscorbutics for the use of hospitals in the northern army," and authorized construction of one hundred batteaux.[28] On December 7, Congress ordered its President to "write to the four New England Governments, and request them to use their utmost influence in raising their respective quotas of Troops, and to hasten their march, with all possible diligence, to the places appointed for their rendezvous by General Schuyler."[29]

By this time, however, Schuyler was disgusted with Congress because of his clash with Gates and the knowledge that he had long been the point of bitter attacks by many delegates. Thus he wanted a showdown more than ever, but it was impossible for him to leave Albany until General Chevelier de Fermoy arrived.[30] General Gates, on the other hand, insisted on leaving at once. At first Schuyler demurred, but when Gates became insistent he agreed to let him accompany the regiments destined for Washington's army.

Certainly Schuyler must have realized that Gates would go directly to Congress and attempt to have Schuyler removed. Why then, did he allow Gates to leave when no other general remained in the Northern Department? In the first place, it had become increasingly difficult for them to work together since neither trusted the other. Inasmuch as a break between the two was inevitable, Schuyler probably did not care to prolong their disagreeable relationship. Furthermore, Schuyler thought Congress did not appreciate his service even after Carleton withdrew British troops from New York. Perhaps a touch of cynicism also shaped his thinking by this time, for late in November he appears to have become disillusioned by the war. He told his Loyalist friend William Smith that hardships and suffering were driving many patriots over to the British side. Then, according to Smith, he spoke "in Despair of the Abilities of the Colonies and with Disgust at the Conduct of their leaders."[31]

In spite of his discontent, General Schuyler did everything

possible to defend New York's frontier. Couriers were sent to New England with new calls for help, but again practically no one replied and the situation looked more critical than ever. Only five hundred reinforcements were on their way to Albany, and no further aid could be expected from the Hampshire Grants or Berkshire County.[32] Meanwhile, Schuyler had fortifications at Ticonderoga redesigned and a fort begun across the lake on Mount Independence. He also tried to replace the cannon that were lost in Canada and at Valcour Island and stockpiled eight months of provisions for five thousand men at Albany and Fort Anne. While these defensive measures were being pushed, Schuyler told Congress it would be wise to renew work on the shattered navy; but too little time and practically no supplies remained, so no vessels were begun.[33]

All the while, death, desertion, and sickness weakened Ticonderoga. The garrison there dwindled to seventeen hundred troops and fewer than one hundred men remained at each of the other posts. Worst of all, not many would stay after the first of the year.[34] This faced Schuyler with the possibility of being left with a skeleton force to meet the probable enemy attack.

Late in December, a chill went through the American camp when large numbers of enemy troops were sighted at the northern end of Lake Champlain. Two regiments were at St. Johns, three at Isle aux Noix, and a small advance party at Isle la Motte. This meant the enemy would probably strike as soon as the ice froze on Lake Champlain.[35] When Congress received these reports, it asked the New Hampshire, Massachusetts, and Connecticut assemblies to send Schuyler 4,500 troops.[36] Sam Adams, in a personal appeal, told his friends that the British governor would seize Ticonderoga unless he is "prevented by an immediate Exertion from New England..."[37]

Nonetheless, as the new year began, the situation continued to worsen. On January 7, 1777, Colonel Edmund

Phinney's troops left Fort George and they were followed by their officers several days later when the latter's firewood ran out.[38]   At the same time, Nathaniel Buel asked Schuyler for permission to withdraw his forces from Mount Independence to prevent their "leaving the Ground in a Dishonourable way."[39]   Similar requests came from other posts, all of them at a time when it was extremely difficult to send replacements. Even the arrival of seven hundred Massachusetts troops at Fort Ticonderoga did not help.[40]   Their appearance merely triggered demands for an early release from the disgruntled garrison. Rather than risk a mutiny or mass desertion, Anthony Wayne decided to let eight infantry companies (about six hundred troops) go home.[41]   Schuyler was practically distraught. He told Congress Fort Ticonderoga could not be saved once the ice froze over on Lake Champlain. He suggested that this in turn might lead to the loss of New York and possibly New England and "bring on the Subversion of American Liberty."[42]

In an effort to obtain more support from New York, Schuyler rushed to Fishkill for a hurried conference with his friends in the New York Convention. At several informal meetings he told them that his army was so short of troops, cannon, provisions, and money that the British could advance almost unopposed to Albany within five weeks after launching an attack.[43]   Although they assured him the Convention would give him all the support he needed, he had little hope of raising an army under the pretense of fighting for independence. He believed America had reached the point of exhaustion and only direct French intervention might save them. France had to declare war on Great Britain at once and assist the colonies with a fleet, arms, ammunition, cannon, clothing, and money, or the American war effort would collapse.[44]

Before meeting with the Convention officially, Schuyler told James Duane what he planned to say. He came, he said, to promote "some Application in the Continental

Congress for a Treaty of Reconciliation" with Great Britain because he was against disunion of the empire and hoped negotiations for peace would soon be opened. Duane replied that if New York meddled, "it would be destroyed by the other Provinces," but Schuyler interrupted and told Duane he missed the point of his statement. This colony "should speak its mind to the Cont(inental) Congress..." he said, for "all Overtures must be made by them..." After all, New York might "as safely submit to the British Power at once as treat separately—but as a colony she might suggest her advice" to Congress. Duane admitted that he, too, was also against independence, but he believed Congress had probably gone too far in its negotiations with France to stop. Therefore he thought the Convention would not consider Schuyler's suggestion and told him to forget it. In spite of Duane's advice, the General still pressed his views on the Convention until he realized most of its members "were more afraid of the other colonies than of British arms." Then, in what may have been a gesture of contempt, he attempted to resign his commission. But the Convention told him it would not back him if he persisted. Faced with this possibility, he decided to drop the matter for a while because he suspected that the Convention might even have arrested him if he had pushed its members too far.[45]

Before Schuyler left for Albany, the Convention tried to reaffirm its confidence in him by offering him what amounted to dictatorial powers, including the authority to call out militia units whenever he wished. Since Schuyler felt no good would come of it if the resolution became generally known, he decided not to publish the act or use the power unless it was absolutely necessary.[46]

There were many reasons for Schuyler's failure to draw an army together in the Northern Department. Public enthusiasm had turned to disillusionment after the series of defeats in 1776. Almost eight thousand Americans had been lost in battle during the abortive Canadian campaign, and this

greatly discouraged recruiting, particularly in villages which
had been hard hit.[47]   Once the colonists learned a quick and
easy victory was impossible, they exhibited an almost universal reluctance to serve at Ticonderoga.[48]   For example,
Colonel Pierce Long enlisted a regiment of Continental troops
in New Hampshire by telling them they would remain there.
When his regiment received orders to leave for Ticonderoga
the men did everything they could to avoid marching. Some
deserted, others boarded privateers, a few enlisted for service
on the *Raleigh,* a man-of-war lying in Piscatagua Harbor,
and several joined a regiment being raised for the duration
of the war.[49]   Prejudices and jealousies also slowed enlistments whenever New Englanders were asked to serve with
New Yorkers. They were reluctant to consider themselves
as one people struggling for a common cause. But these were
not the only things which hindered Schuyler in his attempt
to put a strong army into the field.

Empty state treasuries left many governments without
bounty money to encourage enlistments and clothe recruits
as Congress had recommended.[50]   This became especially
irritating in New York where interior villages were cut off
from the ocean by the British occupation of New York City.
Recruits from this area complained of being deceived when
no clothing was issued and many became recalcitrant about
taking orders.[51]   This discouraged others from enlisting.
Similarly the generous bounties given by Massachusetts often
retarded recruiting in adjoining colonies. Some feared the
Bay State's excessive inducements would "stop any further
Inlistments till the Soldiers can Extort from their Townsmen
50 dollars a piece in Addition to the Bounty already..."
promised.[52]

The New York Convention gave additional reasons for its
inability to fill quotas. Many of its best young men had been
sent to raise drooping spirits in New Jersey, while another
force was kept busy attempting to rid Westchester of enemy
troops. A number of them would undoubtedly have joined

Continental units had they not been sent elsewhere. Colonel Moses Hazen's unscrupulous recruiting tactics also came under fire from the New York Convention. It claimed Hazen had been given permission to recruit men in New York for a unit called "Congress's own Regiment." He became very successful, at the state's expense, by pretending to raise men to be stationed near Congress for its immediate defense. To add to New York's troubles, one general insisted on discharging soldiers who enlisted in his units because they were inhabitants of neighboring states, or, in the case of foreigners, because they previously had served in a regiment of another colony.[53]

A large British fleet hovering off the Connecticut coast also added to Schuyler's woes. In December, 1776, this naval squadron landed more than five thousand troops at Newport, Rhode Island, and threatened all of New England. As a result, many towns hesitated to send militia units to New York because it might encourage the English to make destructive raids into the interior of New England. Their troops were either sent to Rhode Island to oppose the British or kept near home to await an attack.[54] In view of this, it is easy to see why troop shortages plagued Schuyler although an attack appeared imminent.

On January 25, 1777, Samuel Kirkland sent a report which confirmed Schuyler's suspicions about Sir Guy Carleton's intentions. A climax to the crisis appeared likely just as Schuyler had predicted. Meanwhile, the garrison at Ticonderoga grew steadily weaker as some of the newly-arrived recruits deserted or died.[55] In a frantic last effort to save the frontier, Schuyler renewed his appeals to the New England governments and the Continental Congress. To Meshech Weare, President of the New Hampshire Council, he wrote: "I...most earnestly entreat you to forward at least one compleat Regiment...without the least Delay for I have a Variety of Reasons to apprehend, that Ticonderoga will soon be attacked..." and taken if it is not reinforced.[56]

General Washington tried to help by ordering new units being raised in New England to report to the Northern army.[57]   He also offered to send General James Clinton, but Schuyler declined. "I wish Brigadier General Clinton to remain where he is. I am personally acquainted with him and have a high Respect for him as a Friend and a Citizen and, altho' I believe him to be a brave Officer, yet he is amazingly slow and I believe no Disciplinarian."[58]

Ironically, Schuyler's luck began to change. On February 4, 1777, Colonel Wayne told him Lake Champlain still had not frozen. Otherwise, Wayne thought the enemy would have attacked since he had learned that all the sleighs in Canada had been collected for that purpose.[59]   When two Frenchmen were taken prisoner nine days later, they said Indians and enemy regulars had begun to advance down the west side of Lake Champlain.[60]   But winter slowly drew to a close with parts of Lake Champlain still unfrozen. This ended all chance of a British invasion over the ice and New York was temporarily spared from the ravages of war.

Chapter Seven

THE SCHUYLER-GATES CONTROVERSY

By March, 1777, Schuyler realized his long-delayed trip to Congress could not be postponed much longer if he hoped to keep British forces from overrunning New York. His failure to obtain badly-needed reinforcements and supplies had convinced him that drastic measures had to be taken, especially after the chaos of the previous winter.[1] Since cooperation with New England appeared almost impossible, Schuyler wanted to make a defensive stand until some kind of reconciliation with Great Britain could be arranged. He was certain this was inevitable. Until reconciliation took place, he would defend New York's frontier and protect himself from those who wanted Horatio Gates to command the Northern army. He knew leaders in Rhode Island, Connecticut, New Hampshire, and Massachusetts would leave no stone unturned in their effort to get rid of him because they had already resorted to a vicious whispering campaign in an attempt to shroud his reputation with charges of disloyalty, incompetence, and greed.[2]

The Schuyler-Gates controversy went much deeper, however, for it was a manifestation of a "power struggle" being waged between New Yorkers and New Englanders.[3] Both sections were fighting for more than independence: they were squabbling among themselves to see who would rule at home. Therefore a local success meant as much to them as a victory over Great Britain. New York's Hudson Valley landlords, for example, were defending their trade, their property,

and their aristocratic privileges against the leveling influence
of America's new congressional government which appeared
at times to be dominated by New England.[4] New Yorkers
particularly resented a newly-implemented embargo on trade
initiated by the eastern states.[5] Prices in New York had
risen rapidly as a result and the situation threatened to get
worse because British troops in New York City cut the
Hudson Valley off from the sea. Until the trade embargo
ended, or the British were driven from New York City, New
Yorkers were almost at the mercy of their eastern neighbors.[6] The two sections had also clashed over the so-called
New Hampshire Grants issue. This problem had arisen when
inhabitants of an area that later became Vermont wanted to
break away from New York, a move vigorously opposed by
most New Yorkers including General Schuyler. Since New
Englanders had encouraged the inhabitants of the Grants to
revolt against New York, they increased the bitterness
between New York and New England.[7] Now the Yankees
and New Yorkers were at each other's throats once more so
they placed a great deal of significance on the Schuyler-Gates
controversy.

The first disagreement involving Schuyler and Gates (June,
1776) had apparently been settled satisfactorily, or so thought
Schuyler. It proved to be short-lived, however, for several
months later a greater falling-out took place after Schuyler's
appeals to Congress for aid went unanswered.[8] He bluntly
told its members they spent more time on personal interests
and sectional schemes than they did on the war effort.[9] This
so incensed his enemies that they lashed back by placing the
blame for America's military inadequacies on Schuyler and
the other commanding generals. "Many persons are extremely dissatisfied with numbers of general officers of the highest
rank," wrote John Adams. "I don't mean the Commander-
in-Chief, his character is justly very high, but Schuyler,
Putnam of Connecticut, Spencer, and Heath, are thought by
very few to be capable of the great commands they hold.

We hear of none of their heroic deeds of arms. I wish they would all resign...."[10] Although there may have been some truth in this statement, Adams failed to appreciate the difficulties under which these officers labored. In Schuyler's case, for instance, New York's remote frontier, Congress's poor administration, and despondency among the people had generated considerable turmoil. Hence he found himself being swept onward by a current of events over which he had no control.

Schuyler carefully worked out plans for his impending visit to Congress. Before leaving headquarters, he asked the Albany Committee of Correspondence to nominate him as a prospective delegate to Congress.[11] Cloaked with this authority he could go to Philadelphia on an equal footing with his enemies, not just as a discredited officer attempting to obtain retribution. Once he had established himself in Congress, Schuyler hoped to challenge the misconduct charges lodged against him by requesting official inquiry into his affairs that would provide the showdown he had looked forward to for almost two years. Once his record had been cleared, he hoped to formulate military strategy with congressional cooperation and advice, and save New York from an enemy invasion.[12] This was important to him because congressional participation in the planning stages of the campaign might insure stronger support from Congress in the future.[13]

Since no brigadier general had arrived by March 8 to take command while he went to Congress, Schuyler decided to go anyway. This was indeed a desperate and foolish move for him because he deliberately left himself open to justifiable criticism for leaving the Northern army without a commanding general. "I wish to see one before I go down to Philadelphia," he wrote, "but if none comes in a Fortnight I shall then begin the journey and immediately on my arrival shall request an Enquiry into my Conduct."[14] Under the circumstances, he appears on this occasion to have placed his personal interests before his duty to his country.

Meanwhile in Philadelphia, Horatio Gates moved swiftly to win command of the Northern army. He cultivated friendships with newer members of Congress to gain their backing in trying to remove the New York aristocrat. The popular Englishman was in an excellent position because many influential delegates were eager to have the unpopular Schuyler replaced. But finding a sufficient reason to dismiss him had heretofore upset their schemes. Insults had not worked; neither had investigations, nor hardships and frustrations.[15] The catalytic agent so necessary for their plan's execution still escaped them. "Gates is here," wrote Sam Adams. "How shall we make him the head of that army?"[16]

The Gates clique decided to act before General Schuyler appeared on the scene. Using slanderous charges against the General appeared too dangerous, so his enemies seized upon the idea of discrediting Schuyler with his own words. The instrument of destruction would be a long and somewhat cantankerous three-page letter he had written to Congress on February 4, 1777. "Dr. Stringer," observed Schuyler, "had my Recommendation to the Office he has sustained, perhaps it was a compliment due to me that I should have been advised of the Reasons for his Dismission." He said no more about his friend Stringer and continued on to the Trumbull incident. "I was in Hopes some Notice would have been taken of the odious Suspicion contained in Mr. Commissary Trumbull's intercepted Letter to..." William Williams. "I really feel myself deeply chagrined on the Occasion. I am incapable of the Meanness he suspects me of and I confidently expected that Congress would have done me that Justice, which it was in their power to give and which, I humbly conceive, they ought to have done."[17]

These were the offensive words Congress took exception to in its trumped-up charge to discredit Schuyler and strip him of his command. Although historians have generally led their readers to believe that the letter in question was disrespectful to Congress, it·was typical of Schuyler's correspondence and nothing more. In fact, most of it dealt with administrative and logistic problems, and not the irritating incidents referred to by Congress. With this as their weapon, the Gates faction urged Congress to give Schuyler a sharp reprimand for being offensive and disrespectful to the dignity of "a representative body of free and independent States... and to his own character as their officer."[18] Having gained a slight advantage, Gates's friends then attempted to turn neutral delegates against Schuyler and force the issue to a showdown.[19] Their strategy worked well. On March 25, 1777, Congress passed a resolution ordering Gates to take command of the army at Fort Ticonderoga.[20]

General Schuyler still retained his title as Commander-in-chief of the Northern Department in the technical sense, but the General's enemies expected him to resign once he learned of their latest insult. After all, he had been reduced to being a commander without an army in his own state. When John Hancock sent Schuyler the congressional reprimand, he must have done so with some misgivings, for Hancock, not Schuyler, had secretly blocked Trumbull's appointment.[21]

As the New England delegation executed its parliamentary maneuvers with ruthless precision, General Schuyler, entirely unaware of what had happened, hurried over snow-covered roads toward Kingston where he soon heard rumors about the appointment of General Gates.[22] Evidently, Schuyler thought there was some credence in these stories for he asked Richard Varick to confirm them, if possible, since he "would not by any means Chuse to be in the least obliged to..." his successor.[23]

Much to Schuyler's embarrassment, matters did not go well at Kingston. Francis Lewis used his influence to block the General's attempt to obtain a seat in the Continental Congress by a vote of 21 to 14.[24] Lewis's unexpected activity caught Schuyler's aristocratic friends by surprise, but they moved aggressively and swiftly to reverse the vote. By applying great pressure on several members they were more successful in a new vote.[25]   Although Schuyler won, this incident had dark portents for him. An acute contemporary observer believed the Dutch landlords had overstepped the bounds of propriety in demanding a second vote and thereby caused "great Discontent."[26]   One reason for discontent, aside from the manner in which the vote had been handled, was the disillusioned outburst Schuyler had made before the New York Convention in January. Apparently some New Yorkers believed this statement was the cause of Schuyler's conduct being questioned by the Continental Congress. Since it is probable that the New England delegates had heard of the January rumblings in New York, Schuyler's own words may have helped pave the way for his reprimand. Schuyler saw it in a different light. "The convention have a proper sense of the ill treatment I have sustained," he said, "and are resolved that justice shall be done me."[27]   For a man who had just had trouble getting elected by his fellow New Yorkers, this appears to have been wishful thinking.

In the meantime, Gates had taken over the Northern Department. It was in a deplorable state. Only fourteen hundred troops were stationed there and nearly half of the people living in the area favored a return to British rule.[28]   At first he thought Schuyler had been negligent in permitting military stores and cannon badly needed at Ticonderoga to remain at Albany.[29]   Yet he too soon fell victim to the same circumstances. Bad roads and unreliable waggoners quickly proved to him that Schuyler had done his best. Try as he might, Gates could do nothing about the situation either. A "general apathy seems (to) have pervaded . . . " the whole system, he said, which "nothing but the cannon of the Enemy will awaken."[30]   He sent requests for men, supplies, and stores everywhere in the tireless effort to improve the situation, but they failed to bring results.[31]   Governor Jonathan Trumbull could dispatch nothing more than sympathetic letters. "The Hardships, Severities and Losses in the last Campaign . . . " he said, "have made deep Impressions on the Minds of the

Soldiering," therefore the Connecticut men would not fight, not even for Gates.[32] To expect a man to "Voluntarily exchange a peaceful Employment, and Domestic Happiness for the Labours, Sufferings and Dangers of a Soldier's Life for less Wages than he can have at Home...." wrote Trumbull, "is a strain of Virtue and Public Spirit we do not expect to find...."[33]

Colonel Anthony Wayne tried to repair Ticonderoga's defenses, but shortages of workmen, equipment, and material made it hopeless. He also failed to stockpile food and stores. Gaunt and disgruntled, Wayne called the fortress the last place in "the world that God made...finished in the dark ...the ancient Golgotha or place of skulls."[34] When conditions in the Northern Department failed to improve, Gates grew apprehensive because he could not understand why his Yankees were so reluctant to serve on New York's frontier.[35] Still, General Gates believed Fort Ticonderoga would not have to be abandoned if only more troops, artillery, stores, and provisions could be brought there by mid-June.

Meanwhile Schuyler learned, after arriving at the State House in Philadelphia, that the rumors about Horatio Gates's appointment were true.[36] Even so, old friends and new greeted him with warmth and respect, and his enemies appeared anxious to avoid an open rupture in their relations with New York. Others, less concerned with what had happened, assured Schuyler they never believed the malicious reports propagated about him, and said they had no complaints about affairs in the Northern Department.[37] In spite of these statements, Schuyler believed Congress "had gone too far." Unless every injurious entry in the journals was expunged, he threatened to quit the services. New York's other delegates — William Duer, James Duane and Philip Livingston — urged him to be patient because New York's position, as well as his own reputation, would be at stake in the ensuing dispute. They reminded him that many old supporters, such as Benjamin Harrison, Joseph Hewes, William

Hooper, George Read, Edward Rutledge and Thomas Stone, had been succeeded in Congress by newcomers, whose friendships had to be cultivated while New York's primary objective remained a secret.[38] James Duane urged a cautious and deliberate approach to the problem of unseating Gates, and advised his friends to suppress their personal feelings until they became better acquainted with the new members. In addition, the New York delegation made it a rule never to push its complaints upon Congress in the early sessions since this might irritate and disgust the new legislators. The four New Yorkers also limited their attention to a single point until it could be settled.[39] On the whole, therefore, they conducted themselves with propriety and grace. While they were laying the groundwork for their plan, several members told Duer and Duane they could not expect any reversal of Schuyler's case because Congress had already gone too far in the matter.[40] Nevertheless, the New Yorkers did not give up hope.

Shortly after Schuyler's arrival in Philadelphia, Thomas Wharton, President of the State of Pennsylvania, asked him to take command of Pennsylvania's military forces.[41] Although at first reluctant to become involved in that state's troubled affairs, he finally agreed to take on the added duties.[42] More likely than not, he based his decision on practical rather than altruistic motives, with the hopes of gaining Pennsylvania's support in the command controversy. From his new post, General Schuyler set to work shoring up the province's defenses. He established a military camp on the west side of the Schuylkill River and completed defensive fortifications at Red Bank and Fort Island. In addition, he managed to send some reinforcements and supplies to General Washington's army.[43] Despite these military duties, Schuyler also found time to help the Continental Congress reorganize the Commissary Department. In fact, Congress benefited considerably from his experience and frequently adopted the General's suggestions while formulating new rules to govern the department.[44]

It was not until April 18, 1777, that the New York delegates made their bid to unseat Gates. By that time they
believed the apparent abeyance of the command controversy
had given New Englanders a false sense of security. Yet when
New York moved to have an investigation committee look
into Schuyler's past conduct, the New England delegation
rose in opposition.[45]   There is "no Accuser, no Complaint..." and no charge against the General, they pointed
out. Nothing had ever been said to his "Disadvantage or
Dishonor..." in the halls of Congress. They then asked
why New York demanded a hearing. To approve such a
motion, they insisted, would be "an implied Censure, or at
least an Indication of Suspicion..." of Congress.[46]   Therefore, the New England states asked to have the matter
dropped without further consideration. Schuyler's colleagues
refused to be swayed by such arguments, however, and
asked why the General's authority had been reduced to practically nothing at the very time he was most needed in
northern New York. "Why is he thus disgraced?"[47]   Such
a plea could not be ignored by the other delegates. Even
many of those who had voted to send Gates to New York
now began to wonder what really was going on in the Northern Department, so they supported New York's motion.[48]
    A week elapsed before this committee could convene. Once
its members began sifting through the evidence, they were
favorably impressed with the General's record. "Such a
change has taken place in the sentiments of the members
who were unacquainted with me, that it is thought that they
will expunge the resolutions of March 15th..." observed
Schuyler.[49]   Still there were difficult hurdles to pass before
he could again become sole commander of the Northern
army. "They wish me to remain in command," he said,
"but having already appointed (or, at least implicatively so)
General Gates to command...they do not know how to
manage the matter; they wish to make Ticonderoga a separate command...but they know I will not serve at Albany on

those conditions...therefore, I shall return Mr. Schuyler only to Albany."[50]

The committee showed little sign of progress toward an early conclusion. After a short time had passed, General Schuyler tried to speed the decision with a different approach. He asked the treasury commissioners to examine his accounts because he was certain they would show how honestly and unselfishly he had handled public funds.[51] Nevertheless, the delays continued until Schuyler's patience reached the breaking point and he again began to talk of resigning.[52] At last on May 4, 1777, New York's tactics began paying off. The Committee of the Treasury reported that in 1775, General Schuyler had sent more than $3,250 in specie to his troops before he ever received any money from the government. More sums, raised on Schuyler's private credit, had been dispatched from time to time, and by spring, 1776, ten thousand dollars of his own money had been furnished to the army. Furthermore Congress still had not reimbursed him for $3,250 in specie.[53] When this news broke, the tide began to turn. Even the worst gossips knew the infamous stories about Schuyler's embezzlements were false. James Lovell, the youthful Massachusetts delegate who kept Gates informed, became pessimistic. He was not certain how the matter would be resolved, but he guessed it would not be favorable to General Gates.[54] According to Schuyler's friends, the report had a "powerful Effect on many of the Members, who heard it with the utmost Pleasure, and Frankly acknowledged that they had been deceived."[55]

If New York's delegation could only expunge from record the resolutions of March 15, 1777, its mission would be accomplished. With this goal in mind, Duane, Livingston, Duer, Schuyler, and John Lansing, Jr. prepared a statement to bring the whole controversy out into the open.[56] This memorial pictured Schuyler's actions as being consistent with the public good at all times. It also showed the case against him to be unfounded and unwarranted. The General told Congress he had delivered the letter dismissing Dr. Stringer within thirty minutes after it arrived. After carrying out this order, he subsequently tried to persuade the doctor to continue caring for the sick until another physician arrived. "If this part of your memorialist's conduct, which was dictated by common humanity and regard to public economy, be deemed as disobedience," he said, "I must plead guilty."[57]

Next he discussed the derogatory remarks for which he had been censured. He insisted they were by no means as impolite as his opponents had maintained. The first merely expressed a wish to be informed as to why Stringer had been dismissed, "not as a right, but merely as a matter of compliment, and not from impatience and curiosity, but with a view to obviate that gentleman's complaints..." of ill treatment.[58] While Schuyler did not question the power of Congress to dismiss public servants without a formal enquiry, he did suggest that the continuance of such a high-handed policy might discourage good men from serving their country.[59] This point was well taken, for many delegates realized they too might someday find themselves in a similar situation.

The second remark referred to the letter printed in *The New-York Mercury* alleging that Schuyler had detained a commission for John Trumbull. This charge had come as a surprise to the General. Once his honor and integrity had been publicly questioned, the matter could not be ignored. He therefore asked Congress for an explanation.[60] Such a request should not have been offensive to Congress, according to Schuyler, "because their honorable President must have known...that the commission had not...been transmitted..." at the time the letter was written. "Without this evidence," he asked, "how could it have been possible to convince the world that the suspicion was ill-founded, Or to have brought Colonel Trumbull to a Court-Martial for slandering a superior officer...."[61]

By drawing an analogy the General sought to prove his point. He reminded Congress what the consequences might have been if he had arrested General Gates when the latter disputed his command after retreating from Canada.[62]

Would the service not have suffered if he had done so? Was it not more desirable for an officer to refer the Gates and Trumbull incidents to Congress rather than deal peremptorily with them himself as he had every right to do?[63] Upon hearing Schuyler's point of view, his fellow delegates decided to expunge their earlier resolution from the record in the interest of justice. Congress unanimously resolved: "That the explanation given in Major General Schuyler's memorial, of the expressions used in his letter of the 4th of February last, to Congress, is satisfactory; and that Congress entertain now the same favorable sentiments concerning him which they entertained before that letter was received."[64] Time, truth, Schuyler's own merit, and a shrewdly managed parliamentary campaign had carried the day for New York; but the drama had not yet finished because Horatio Gates still remained in command of Fort Ticonderoga.

Congressional meetings during the next few weeks were filled with weary hours of wrangling over Ticonderoga. Past misconceptions about the northern military jurisdiction had to be clarified. The delegates had to decide whether it would be more desirable to keep the Northern Department as a single military district under one commander, or whether it would be preferable to establish Fort Ticonderoga as a separate district. Outsiders believed this to be the only point at issue. Those who knew better realized much more was at stake. New Yorkers felt they had to make Schuyler the commanding officer in the Northern Department or sacrifice much of their influence in Congress. On the other hand, delegates from New England and New Jersey sought to forestall New York's bid for power.

Some delegates believed Fort Ticonderoga's commanding officer should not be forced to act under absolute orders from a superior officer a hundred miles away. This was particularly true because Schuyler was frequently involved in Indian negotiations or with obtaining provisions for the army. "A commander-in-chief and Commanders of the separate armies," said James Lovell, "is the only distinction which should be known."[65]   But this was contrary to the system Congress had established, and he knew it.[66]   The more detached delegates probably began to swing away from Gates when they heard about the unrest near Albany.[67] Under the circumstances, Schuyler appeared better qualified to handle such a situation near his own home.[68]   Opponents of Gates hammered away at his presumptuous claim to command in the Northern Department.[69]   This was good strategy because members of Congress knew they had sent him north simply to take command of Ticonderoga. In an effort to settle the dispute once and for all, Congress asked the Board of War to make a ruling.[70]

On May 15, the Board reached a decision. It recommended that Schuyler should be given command of the Northern Department, and that Gates should serve under him or join General Washington.[71]   This favorable report and the absence of several unfriendly delegates momentarily gave New York the upper hand. Consequently, the New York delegation asked for an immediate vote on the Board's recommendations.[72]   Maryland, New York, North Carolina, Pennsylvania, South Carolina, and Virginia cast ballots in favor of Schuyler's reinstatement, but Connecticut, Massachusetts, and New Hampshire voted against him. Two states, Georgia and New Jersey, were divided, and two others (Delaware and Rhode Island) were not represented.[73]   Thus by a vote of six to three, the delegates resolved "That Albany, Ticonderoga, Fort Stanwix, and their dependencies, be henceforward considered as forming the Northern Department." They also repealed a resolution (March 6, 1776) requiring the General to establish his headquarters at Albany, and ordered Schuyler to resume command immediately.[74]

The contest was closer than the vote indicates. Virginia's ballot for Schuyler was described as "rather a phenomenon," and the tie in New Jersey's delegation came as a result of the absence of Abraham Clark and Jonathan Dickenson Sergeant, both of whom were Schuyler's enemies.[75]   If one of them had been present, and Rhode Island had been represented when the balloting took place, Gates would not have been replaced.[76]

New Yorkers were pleased with the outcome of this affair because General Schuyler had been fully reinstated and every point at issue had been decided in the state's favor.[77] Yet no one could guess how costly their success would be. Had Schuyler lost his parliamentary contest, Gates would have been in command of the Northern Department when General St. Clair abandoned Ticonderoga. Schuyler might then have been called upon to replace Gates and thus he, and not the latter, might have tasted the fruits of victory at Saratoga. The real losers in this affair, however, were the American states.[78] Congress's failure to work out a solution because of sectional rivalries and interests again betrayed its inability to act effectively in a crisis and use profitably the abilities of two officers such as Schuyler and Gates. The episode is revealing in still another respect. General Gates had created a magnificent public image for himself as a great military leader. Consequently, many New Englanders thought he could best defend Ticonderoga because militia units would flock to aid him although they would not fight for Schuyler. Even though this did not happen when Gates took over, the idea has gained almost universal acceptance.

Chapter Eight

POLITICAL EXPECTATIONS

When Schuyler returned to New York to reassume command of the Northern Department in June, 1777, his name was among those frequently brought up as a possible candidate for governor. The General's close friends knew he liked the idea of being the state's first chief-executive even though he had stated that he would not run for public office. Besides, he seemed rather confident of winning and boasted to his friend William Smith that: "They may chuse (sic) who they will I will command them all."[1] John Jay, Chief Justice of New York, was another popular figure mentioned as a gubernatorial aspirant, but Jay tried to discourage such talk in an effort to close Conservative ranks behind Schuyler. "For my own part," said Jay, "I know of no person at present whom I would prefer to General Schuyler."[2]

Even though high-pressured political campaigning, as America grew to know it, had not yet been born, a great deal of political bargaining did take place on the eve of New York's first election. For months, candidates for office were discussed, but there were no formal nominations, nor were there organized parties as they exist today. Each faction or combination of men endorsed its particular choice and sought to gain support for him through personal contacts and a letter-writing campaign. Besides Schuyler, the other candidates for governor included George Clinton, John Morin Scott, and Philip Livingston.

Ulster County's George Clinton appeared to be the only

97

real threat to Schuyler's political expectations. Between 1768 and 1776, Clinton had gained quite a reputation as a fiery though somewhat radical Whig in New York politics, and, as such, he had become the idol of the common man.

John Morin Scott, the third leading candidate, was an easy-going, sensible, and forthright individual, but, unfortunately, one whose drinking habits and democratic inclinations made him unacceptable to the Conservatives. Like Clinton, Scott looked to the radical Whigs for most of his support. But in actuality, Scott stood only an outside chance of getting elected.

Philip Livingston, whose brother William Livingston had little opposition for the same office in New Jersey, did not have much of a chance because of objections to "having two brother Governors."

The Livingston family, as a result, were supposed to have swung their support to Schuyler rather than see the "government drowned in a bowl of grog" — an obvious slap at Scott.[3] Schuyler had some doubts about the Livingstons' sincerity, however, and he may well have been correct. Mrs. Janet Livingston Montgomery, undoubtedly echoing her family's sentiments, said Schuyler should not be both governor and general at the same time and hoped that he would resign the latter post at once. The extremely ambitious Livingstons appear to have considered Schuyler's military and civil position in state affairs as undeserved and unwarranted, and it is probable that they may have refrained from voting, or even turned to Clinton once Philip Livingston's candidacy collapsed. This conclusion appears plausible for there is a Livingston family tradition which credits Mrs. Margaret Beekman Livingston with having called a meeting at Clermont, the Livingston Manor, to discuss potential candidates for public office. When those present could not agree on a choice for governor, she is supposed to have suggested George Clinton's name in a compromise move to unite the group.[4] If this is true, and it might well be, it could be one of the reasons why Clinton won such a surprisingly easy victory at the polls.

As the election drew near, Conservative circles seethed with suspicions, due in large part to John Morin Scott's activities. He attacked those aristocratic leaders who had formed the new government, particularly the Livingstons, whom he characterized as being "rapacious after Office." Discontent grew to such a degree among Conservatives that indiscriminate accusations appeared to be aimed at everyone. William Duer and other leading aristocrats were appalled by such attacks, and these men urged their fellow Conservatives to exhibit some common sense and consider the possible consequences that political feuding might cause once the election was over.[5] Despite the bitterness of the campaign, the general public appeared rather apathetic about the election, being more concerned with the exigencies of war and the possibility of an imminent enemy invasion by Burgoyne.

The popular choices for governor soon narrowed to Schuyler and Clinton, although neither man actively attempted to do much on his own behalf because of the pressure of military duties. Their friends and supporters, on the other hand, worked vigorously and diligently in an effort to secure votes. Typical of electioneering letters they sent was one mailed to Egbert Benson on behalf of the Schuyler-Clinton ticket. "These gentlemen are respectable at home and abroad," it states, "their attachment to the cause is confessed, and abilities unquestionable. Let us endeavor to be unanimous as possible. Interest is making for others, but we hope that care will be taken to frustrate the ambitious views of those who have neither stability, uniformity or sobriety to recommend them."[6]

Most informed observers believed Schuyler's election had been reduced to a certainty, but political machinations and dissatisfaction among the Conservatives were destined to undermine his strength. This became apparent when five respected members of the New York Committee of Safety recommended Schuyler for governor and George Clinton for lieutenant governor. They failed to realize, however, that the supporters of each candidate were reluctant to accept the other as a running mate.[7] Yet such an attitude was understandable, since Clinton carried upon his shoulders the aspirations of small farmers, artisans, and village tradesmen, while Schuyler represented the patrician class. The former were undoubtedly repelled by Schuyler's overbearing attitude and his quickness to resent a slight familiarity by the common man; while the latter probably accepted Clinton only as a vote-getting expedient to aid their cause. Then there were a few landlords, especially those around Albany, who refused to condone this so-called practical compromise and proposed instead General Abraham Ten Broeck as their choice for lieutenant governor to run with Schuyler.[8]

On June 9, two more tickets appeared in Albany, one naming Schuyler and James Duane, the other Philip Livingston and Abraham Ten Broeck.[9]   These Conservative nominations must have brought delight to George Clinton who shared, only with Scott, radical support for governor. When residents of Esopus heard the northern counties were backing Ten Broeck instead of Clinton for lieutenant governor, considerable ill-will developed and many voters turned away from Schuyler in disgust. Although aware of the danger inherent in this situation, John Jay still believed such resentment could not seriously hurt Schuyler because it did not have time to spread throughout the state.

The overconfident Conservatives appeared to believe that Clinton's candidacy would falter because he permitted his supporters to push his name for both the offices of governor and lieutenant governor. They also thought Scott's play for radical support would take enough votes away from Clinton to assure his defeat and make Schuyler the winner.[10]   In theory their reasoning was sound, but in reality the Conservatives had underestimated the resourcefulness of their opponents.

Major Christopher Tappen, Clinton's brother-in-law, had a notion that the vote of small farmers, artisans, and village tradesmen would not be large enough to carry Clinton into office because too many were away on militia duty, and, therefore, unable to vote. Why not, he wondered, make arrangements to bring the soldier vote into the election. If the support of a large segment of militia friendly to Clinton could be cornered, he believed the voting scales would record a victory for Clinton. Thus he hatched a plan to grab the gubernatorial prize.

Several officers from Clinton's brigade were advised to petition the Committee of Safety for the right to vote.[11] John Morin Scott pushed this petition in hopes of aiding his own chances, while Tappan argued that it should be approved because the militia were "by Express command of the Convention drawn from their Domestic Business and should notwithstanding be entitled to their privileges as freemen...."[12] John Jay saw through the plan and sought to defeat it by demanding strict adherence to the manner and places for the election as adopted by the Convention. This would exclude the petitioners. But Jay was unsuccessful, and Scott's motion passed by a five to four vote.[13] The Conservatives would not drop the matter, however, because the proposal threatened to ruin their cause, and they were determined to defeat it.

Six days later (June 6, 1777), John Sloss Hobart sucessfully moved to reconsider Scott's resolution.[14] This opening gave John Jay and Gilbert Livingston a chance to bring forth a new three-point plan to replace Scott's proposal. In urging acceptance of their plan, they emphasized the unfairness of permitting General Clinton's troops to vote while excluding troops at Fort Constitution, Peekskill, Fort Stanwix, Ticonderoga, and other areas of the state. To send commissioners to all posts to take votes would be equally impractical. Why not, they asked, permit militia troops who had a right to vote to go to the nearest polling place to cast their ballots, provided their absence did not endanger their posts?[15]   This plan appealed to the delegates, but the Conservative politicians had not, as they had hoped, won the battle. They had indeed blocked the attempt to permit only members of Clinton's brigade to vote, but they had unwittingly thrown open the vote to many more Clinton supporters than they realized. In view of General Schuyler's unpopularity and declining influence among the common people, a law enabling more of them to vote could only hurt his chances of success.

Early returns, though scattered and incomplete, appeared to justify aristocratic expectations. "The elections in the middle district have taken such a turn...," Jay reported to Schuyler, "that if a tolerable degree of unanimity should prevail in the upper counties, there will be little doubt of having erelong, the honor of addressing a letter to your Excellency."[16]

Unexpected opposition to Schuyler first came from the lower Rensselaer Manor at Claverack where less than one hundred freemen voted. Of those who did, most cast ballots for the George Clinton-Alexander McDougall ticket.[17]   Disquieting rumors also came from the Livingston Manor and claimed that none of the Livingstons had bothered to vote.[18] As might be expected in a bitterly-fought contest, confusion also appeared to reign at many other places in the state. At Little Nine Partners, for example, Morris Graham reported that agitators there had induced the inhabitants to vote contrary to their true wishes.[19]

Dutchess, Ulster, and Orange counties were being counted upon to give Clinton a large vote, while the northern counties were expected by Schuyler's supporters to carry their man to victory. But in Albany no more than half of the freemen bothered to vote and news of this stunned the Schuyler camp. Returns arriving at Kingston soon confirmed their worst suspicions as a definite swing from Schuyler to Clinton began to develop. This news, on top of the small

Albany vote, caused consternation in aristocratic circles and they began to fear their candidate might be beaten.[20]   When this early trend continued, Christopher Tappen predicted that George Clinton would be elected governor as well as lieutenant governor, and indeed, he was correct. Although the outcome was a foregone conclusion, the Committee of Safety waited to make an announcement until the official returns arrived from Orange County. When Schuyler heard the unwelcome news, he said, "General Clinton I am informed has the majority of votes for the Chair. If so, he played his cards better than expected."[21]   Clinton had played his cards well indeed and Schuyler knew it.

The Orange County returns turned what appeared to be a close race into a crushing defeat for the Conservatives. These ballots gave Clinton 963 votes to only 187 for Schuyler. Although complete results for New York's first gubernatorial election are no longer available, fragmentary records shed some light on the contest, showing that a total of 1,828 votes were cast for Clinton to 1,199 for Schuyler. Of the six counties for which returns exist, only Albany gave General Schuyler a majority vote.[22]

Before turning away from politics, the Commander-in-chief of the Northern Department tried to heal wounds in order to close the split in patriot ranks. He urged his fellow-men as good citizens to strenuously exert themselves "to counteract the wicked, the weak, and the disappointed, and . . . support the friends of the country in office against their malignant opponents."[23]   Like many fellow-aristocrats, he believed Clinton's background did not entitle him to so distinguished an office. Yet he knew Clinton to be a virtuous man who loved his country. "The Governor-elect has ability and he is brave," remarked the General, and I "hope he will experience from every patriot what I am resolved he shall have from me, support, countenance and comfort."[24] Thus, even as his world began to collapse around him in the dark days of July and August of 1777, Schuyler congratulated Clinton and promised to him all the support the times would permit.

Schuyler must have been upset by Clinton's smashing victory, for shortly after hearing of it he admitted to being "deeply chagrined at the intemperance of some people... who having wished for offices which it would be improper they should hold, and since they are not likely to obtain them become noisy and troublesome."[25]   Although this pointed reference to Scott should be kept in mind, other causes of his defeat were probably more important. The most obvious reason, of course, was Schuyler's own personal unpopularity with the masses. In addition, great numbers of northern freemen apparently failed to vote because they disliked the new form of government. This was especially true of the manorial landlords. Many of them decided, therefore, to oppose or remain indifferent to separation from the British Empire, and the best way to do this, or so they believed, was to refuse to vote.

At the same time, confused patrician military and political leadership caused increased economic hardships and suffering in the state. While New York faced an invading army in the north with almost no hope of opposition, five counties were under enemy control (Tories and malcontents threatened uprisings in three others), and good government had almost ceased to exist in the remaining six counties. Finally, the most significant reason for the crushing defeat may have been the broadening of the franchise. This enabled numerous freemen to vote for a gubernatorial candidate of their choice, the idol of the common man — General George Clinton. For the first time in New York's history, the old ruling aristocracy had been forced to share an important office with a representative of the lower classes. Yet their power had by no means been broken and the rich landlords and merchants would still exert a powerful influence in New York State for a half-century to come.

Chapter Nine

THE FALL OF FORT TICONDEROGA

While Schuyler and Gates maneuvered to keep control of the Northern Department, Lord North's Ministry concentrated on putting an end to the war by military victory. The basic responsibility for British operations in America belonged to Lord George Germain, Secretary of State for the colonies. Germain, to be sure, had disgraced himself at the Battle of Minden in the French and Indian War, and, as a result, he had been court-martialed for cowardice and forbidden to hold further military office. Yet, because of his close friendship with George III, he was now formulating British military strategy for the colonies.

Germain thought success would have crowned his plan to end the war in 1776, if only Sir Guy Carleton had continued to attack instead of withdrawing to Canada in October. After all, he reasoned, Howe had been victorious and Carleton had routed the American flotilla on Lake Champlain. Apparently all that was needed were more troops, a more daring and imaginative officer to replace the overly conservative Carleton, and an early start in the next campaign. With this in mind, Germain was determined to try again to completely suppress the American colonies.

In 1777, Germain planned to split New York by using three separate invasion forces. The main British army would push down Lake Champlain toward Albany, while a smaller diversionary force landed at Oswego for a quick thrust at Albany down the Mohawk Valley. As these troops applied pressure on General Schuyler's northern line of defense, a third British army would then advance up the Hudson Valley to Albany.[1] Before the enemy converged on that city, however, Sir William Howe was supposed to throw New England into confusion by invading Rhode Island.[2] If resistance collapsed, Howe planned to push into Massachusetts and seize Boston; meanwhile eight thousand British regulars would keep New Jersey and Pennsylvania off balance by threatening Philadelphia. British leaders believed these widely scattered operations would prevent Continental and militia units in threatened areas from marching to General Schuyler's assistance until the trap at Albany was ready to close. Then, in mid-August, Howe would suddenly cut short his coastal operations and converge on Albany to join British troops invading from Canada.

Rumors of these enemy plans circulated freely throughout the states, yet most Americans did not really take them seriously because large numbers of troops were needed to conduct operations on two distant fronts — perhaps as many as 35,000.[3] Since Germain had never been able to place an army that size in the field at one time, the reasoning of skeptics appeared to be sound. But British leaders were more optimistic in 1777. They had signed a treaty with the German states guaranteeing them large numbers of Hessian troops for the ensuing campaign. Had the English gone ahead with their scheme, New England and New York might well have been taken out of the war. As it was, Howe made several disastrous changes which completely undermined the original plan. He did this with good reason, however, because information from Philadelphia indicated that Pennsylvanians were eager to desert the American camp and rejoin the mother country.[4] Therefore, Sir William abandoned his designs on Boston to concentrate his forces on what he expected to be an easy conquest.

George III approved of Howe's changes on March 3, 1777, but asked him to make threats against New Hampshire and Massachusetts to discourage rebels who might otherwise join Schuyler's army.[5] A month later the King again allowed Howe to alter his plan. This time, operations in Rhode Island and New Jersey were canceled to enable Howe to cooperate with British troops advancing toward Albany. George III asked him to be certain to leave himself enough time to make a move in that direction. Sir William did not reply. Instead, he proposed the use of Loyalist troops in New York to invade Connecticut or advance up the Hudson River to keep pressure on Schuyler's Northern army while he crushed resistance in Pennsylvania.[6] Fortunately for the Americans, these changes remained unknown to General John Burgoyne, the newly-appointed commander of the British expeditionary force in Canada, until it was too late for him to alter his strategy.

There remains to this day a singular fascination about Burgoyne. Although he was already in his mid-fifties in 1777, he retained that youthful touch of bravura which set him apart from fellow officers and prompted his troopers to call him "Gentleman Johnny." The colorful Englishman had attracted considerable attention in the Seven Years War for his courage at Cherbourg, St. Malo, and Belle Isle. But in the American Revolution he played only a minor role until he returned to America in 1777 after a brief visit to England.

The situation at Schuyler's headquarters was not promising. The Northern Department had long suffered from a divided command and America's failure to present a united front in view of reported troop buildups in Canada caused growing alarm among its leaders. "What infatuation has seized my Yankees?" complained Gates just before Schuyler replaced him. "They take the Field as Tardily as if they were going to be Hanged."[7] When Schuyler took over from Gates on June 3, 1777, little had been done to strengthen Fort Ticonderoga. If anything, the army and its defenses in northern New York had degenerated considerably under Gates.[8] Fewer troops were then in the Northern army than were on hand when Gates took command two months earlier. Supplies were depleted, defenses were crumbling, and a general apathy appeared to grip the countryside.[9]

The reasons for the unresponsiveness on the part of many Americans are not as complex as they appear. In the first place, few New Englanders were willing to volunteer for duty in the wilderness at Ticonderoga even under a popular leader like Gates. Hardships and suffering the previous year had caused many young men to regret hasty enlistments. They were not about to repeat this mistake in 1777. Low wages, supply shortages, bad roads, fear of smallpox inoculations, and reports of an invasion fleet off the New England coast also kept troops away.[10] Yet these were only manifestations of what may have been the underlying cause for the prolonged delays. No one, not even Schuyler, Gates, or St. Clair, appears to have really believed Britain would launch a major attack from Canada in the summer of 1777. According to Schuyler, enemy troops would not attempt a "Real Attack ... soon, if at all .... " since they were unable to strike Fort Ticonderoga itself the previous autumn and again that winter. They would merely approach Fort Ticonderoga to alarm New York and draw attention from their true objectives in other parts of the colonies.[11] Although he was quite certain of this, he still planned to take every precaution against a surprise, and he asked General Gates to take command of Fort Ticonderoga. But Gates refused, claiming that he wished to report to Congress without delay.

Before heading for Philadelphia, however, Gates revealed to his friends the real reason for his decision: he told them he refused to serve under a General who kept headquarters at Albany. This was ironic indeed since Gates himself never left Albany while he commanded troops in the Northern Department during April and May. In fact, Gates did not even make an attempt to inspect the lake outposts. One must assume, therefore, that Gates's statement was probably nothing more than the opening move in a new maneuver to remove Schuyler. To fill the gap left by Gates's departure, Schuyler gave Major General Arthur St. Clair command of Fort Ticonderoga. St. Clair was a seasoned veteran well suited for the difficult task ahead. As a British lieutenant in the French and Indian War, he won respect while serving at Louisburg and Quebec.

When St. Clair arrived at Fort Ticonderoga on June 12, he was shocked to learn that his garrison of 2,200 troops could only form one thin line of defense with no reserves to back them up.[12] This resulted from questionable improvements made on advice from Polish engineering expert Colonel Thaddeus Kosciusko who had extended Ticonderoga's defense line across Lake Champlain to Mount Independence. As a result, ten thousand troops were necessary to adequately defend positions nearly two thousand yards in length. To maintain communications and prevent enemy vessels from slipping past the fort, the Americans constructed a four-hundred-yard boom, chain, and bridge across the lake to connect both posts. Although this network of defense would have given St. Clair greater mobility if he had more troops, his little army appeared incapable of successfully repulsing an enemy attack. The men were miserably clad and inadequately armed, and desertions became so frequent that several public executions were ordered to put a stop to them. General Schuyler was well aware of these conditions, yet he continued to express confidence in St. Clair's ability to meet a British attack if one came![13] Obviously, Schuyler still did not believe the British would launch a major attack on Ticonderoga.

Yet at that very moment, a deafening roll of drums followed by a blast of bugles unsettled the wilderness near Lake Champlain's northern shore. They heralded the start of an invasion destined to go down in history as the Burgoyne Campaign. "Gentleman Johnny" had assembled an army of 7,250 British and German troops supported by 156 pieces of artillery. They would be strengthened by some 250 Canadians and 400 savages before they reached Fort Ticonderoga on

June 30. At Oswego in western New York, Colonel Barry St. Leger, another veteran of Wolfe's campaign in America, pressed toward the Mohawk Valley with an army of 968 regulars, Loyalists, and Hannau Chasseurs supported by almost 1,000 braves under Mohawk Chieftain Joseph Brant.[14]

When rumors of this enemy activity reached Schuyler, he realized he might have been mistaken in thinking no attack would be made over the lakes that summer and promptly renewed his pleas for assistance. Couriers dashed off to colonial governments in New Hampshire, Massachusetts, and Pennsylvania with requests for aid, while a special messenger hastened to Washington's headquarters in an effort to get the Commander-in-chief to detach Continental troops for service at Ticonderoga. After placing New York's militia units on a stand-by basis, Schuyler himself hurried to Fort Ticonderoga for a first-hand look at the fort.

When he reached Lake Champlain on June 17, he found St. Clair making battle preparations. Although Schuyler had been optimistic about Ticonderoga's strength earlier that month, the sight of it now made him realize his error.[15] The boom across Champlain had not yet been completed; the garrison had practically no stores other than pork and flour; and only a few hundred bayonets were available. The situation was critical indeed, so Schuyler called a council of war to see what, if anything, could be done to improve America's chances of holding out against a strong enemy offensive. Other generals present were the Frenchman Matthias Alexis Roche de Fermoy, Enoch Poor of New Hampshire, and John Patterson of Massachusetts. Each agreed that Ticonderoga could not survive a British attack unless numerous reinforcements were thrown into the post at once. Since this was unlikely, they decided to defend Fort Ticonderoga and Mount Independence only until stores, cannon, and troops were safely withdrawn.[16] Schuyler returned to Albany immediately after this conference in an effort to speed supplies and troops to the threatened outpost.

No one really knew what Burgoyne was doing at the northern end of Lake Champlain because British ships controlled the lake. Even when substantial evidence of troop concentrations in Canada fell into American hands, Congress and the Board of War still refused to believe Burgoyne was preparing to attack. Washington did not think Burgoyne had strength enough to overcome Fort Ticonderoga and advised Schuyler not to send troops to the fort since they would unnecessarily consume much-needed rations. Like so many others, the Commander-in-chief thought Ticonderoga could only be overrun by a frontal assault, and Burgoyne would need more than five thousand troops to do this.[17]   Schuyler did little to change his opinion. For some strange reason, he told Washington, as late as June 25, that enemy movements on Lake Champlain were probably intended to cover plans for an invasion of New Hampshire or down the Mohawk Valley.[18]   Indian agent James Deane appeared to confirm this theory when he learned Sir John Johnson was about to move against New York's western frontier.[19]

Events began to move rapidly as June drew to a close. Lake Champlain suddenly came alive with British galleys and frigates carrying troops to battle. By June 30, advance units of Burgoyne's army approached to within three miles of American fortifications at Ticonderoga.[20]   That night, bonfires blazed in red splendor as masses of flame darted into the darkness, revealing to American scouts the outline of a huge British encampment. As they watched this spectacle to the north, they could also see a much less impressive display at their own positions to the south.

Troops and supplies arrived at Ticonderoga from Albany in increasing numbers, yet they were hardly enough to maintain the post for long. "I cannot help repeating to you the Situation we are in," wrote St. Clair, "nor can I see the least prospect of ... being able to defend the post unless the Militia come in ...." If we are attacked, he wrote, and "the Enemy protract their Operations, or invest us ... with a simple Blocade (sic) we are infallibly ruined."[21] Because of the increased tension, Washington ordered Continental units stationed at Peekskill to move toward Albany. Schuyler anxiously awaited their arrival so he could lead them to Fort Ticonderoga; but they did not appear.

Meanwhile, enemy infantrymen advanced up both sides of Lake Champlain, supported by a fleet of nine heavily armed warships, twenty-eight gunboats, and numerous batteaux in an attempt to envelop American positions. On the Vermont side, Major General Baron von Riedesel, a twenty-year veteran in Hessian and Brunswick armies, approached Mount Independence, while Brigadier General Simon Fraser, a veteran of Wolfe's campaigns in Canada, advanced up the west side. To conceal their true objective, British regulars and Indians maintained pressure on the American lines as Fraser's men worked their way through the woods toward Mount Hope.[22]

Although St. Clair realized the enemy would sever Ticonderoga's communications with Lake George, he refused to risk a fight over Mount Hope, thus permitting himself to be cut off from Lake George. At nine o'clock on the morning of June 2, Americans set fire to the blockhouse and sawmills and headed for Ticonderoga. British officers saw the smoke and set a trap for them. Luckily for the Americans, several drunken braves exposed the ambush by firing too soon. A few minutes after this clash, several Indians and regulars blundered again by rushing at an American picket of sixty men. St. Clair ordered his troops to hold their fire, but one enemy soldier approached too closely. This prompted the inexperienced Americans to unleash a heavy fire. The enemy soldiers fell back momentarily, steadied themselves, and came forward again. Once again they were repulsed. When the firing ceased, two savages were dead and one lay wounded. The British soldier who caused the skirmish was also there, but the man was not mortally wounded — he was dead drunk.[23]

Painted by J. Trumbull.   Engraved by T. Kelly.

MAJOR GENERAL PHILIP SCHUYLER.

Ph: Schuyler

Geo. Clinton

After being taken prisoner he refused to talk, so an American officer dressed in rags was thrown into a cell with him. The Englishman thought his new cell mate was a Tory spy, and, with the aid of a bottle of rum, he soon confirmed Schuyler's worst fears. The Americans learned Burgoyne had an army of 5,600 British regulars, Hessians and Canadians, supported by a band of Indians and that they intended to surround Ticonderoga and begin a seige.[24]

By this time, General Riedesel's Hessians had reached East Creek in front of Mount Independence, where they were stopped by heavy firing. British units on the west shore, however, were more successful. Despite an artillery barrage from Ticonderoga, they were able to occupy Mount Hope, which controlled the portage between Lake George and Lake Champlain.[25]   Since this position was on high ground fourteen hundred yards from Ticonderoga, it also permitted British artillery to shell the fort's outlying trenches. The next morning, both sides engaged in a savage artillery duel. Neither could gain an advantage until an explosion rocked Ticonderoga. Apparently its magazine had been hit. As a gigantic cloud of smoke rose above the fort, British officers ordered an assault, thinking the blast had made it vulnerable. But this decision proved to be a costly one. The English troops were driven back by a surprising American counterattack.[26]   When fighting subsided, the British decided that they had better reshape their thinking about an assault.

The lull in activity gave enemy officers on Mount Hope a chance to study Sugar Loaf Mountain's southern slope which rose gently from Lake George. Since Sugar Loaf's steep face overlooked both Ticonderoga and Mount Independence, they realized artillery on its summit could cut off American forces from outside aid, and perhaps even prevent St. Clair from escaping encirclement. Yet this news may not have been a surprise to Burgoyne. He knew of Sugar Loaf's strategic importance long before the Revolutionary War because an English officer had scouted it in 1759, during the French and Indian War.[27]

His chief engineer, Lieutenant William Twiss, had also reported that a wagon trail up Sugar Loaf could be constructed within twenty-four hours, so Burgoyne ordered Major General William Phillips to begin work at once. This gave Phillips the type of challenge he liked best. Years before, he had helped route French forces at the Battle of Minden with a similar move. "Where a goat can go a man can go," Phillips is supposed to have said, "And where a man can go he can drag a gun." Day and night, four hundred of Phillips's best men cleared trees and leveled ground in great secrecy. Finally, at one o'clock in the morning of July 6, two medium 12-pounders were placed into position on top of Sugar Loaf and the British renamed it Mount Defiance.[28]

At daybreak the next morning, Colonel James Wilkinson studied this mountain ridge from Fort Ticonderoga to see why fires had been reported there the night before. Much to his surprise, the glint of metal caught his eye. There in the distance, high atop the supposedly unoccupied hill, he spotted a gun battery and the unmistakable scarlet of British uniforms.[29] He could hardly believe his eyes. Until that moment, Ticonderoga's defenders had looked forward with courage and hope to the impending British attack. The frequent alarms had made them more alert. And on July 1, American spirits had been given a lift by news that Burgoyne's workmen were building a boom across Lake Champlain and digging extensive intrenchments just beyond it.[30]

This apparently meant that enemy forces were not large enough to carry out a siege and were protecting themselves against a counterattack. Indeed, as late as July 2, St. Clair boasted to Schuyler that the enemy would "go back faster than they came."[31] The following day Colonel Samuel Brewer echoed these same sentiments because his troopers seemed "determined to Conquer or die...."[32] But General Schuyler had become far less optimistic because few reinforcements had arrived at Albany. He even began to talk of losing Ticonderoga. Still, he sent St. Clair assurances of militia support within a few days, and the backing of Continental troops several days thereafter.

With the discovery of British guns on Sugar Loaf Mountain, St. Clair's troops became greatly disturbed. To many of the officers and men the situation looked hopeless. Orders were given to drive the enemy troops from the hill before they could open fire, but the American shells fell short. The guns were raised, ammunition charges were doubled, and still most shots "could not reach the Height." [33] Meanwhile, British gunners were ordered to withhold their fire except for a few shots aimed at a vessel anchored in Lake Champlain. [34] Since the American cannonade had proved unsuccessful, St. Clair began to consider his position untenable. To make matters worse, enemy troops were now reported to be nearly ten thousand in number, and they had almost completely surrounded Fort Ticonderoga and Mount Independence. Only one avenue of escape still lay open to St. Clair's forces, the narrow strip of land between Lake Champlain and East Creek, and even this was being threatened by General Riedesel's Hessians.

With the hour for an all-out British attack rapidly approaching, St. Clair called his senior officers together for another council of war. He told them British troops probably would make simultaneous assaults on Ticonderoga and Mount Independence the next day. Since the battery on Sugar Loaf exposed the boom and bridge to enemy fire, neither garrison could support the other during a heavy attack. According to St. Clair, cooperation between Fort Ticonderoga and Mount Independence was absolutely necessary because the entire American army consisted of only 2,089 Continental troops, a corps of artillery, 900 raw militia troops, and 124 unarmed workmen. When St. Clair asked Brigadier Generals Roche de Fermoy, Enoch Poor, John Patterson, and Colonel Pierce Long for their opinion on what should be done, each officer recommended the immediate evacuation of both posts to prevent the army from falling into British hands.[35]   St. Clair agreed.

Controversy still rages over the reasons why Schuyler and Gates failed to fortify Sugar Loaf Mountain. There can be no doubt that they knew of its strategic value and accessibility. Colonel John Trumbull emphasized this while he was stationed at Mount Independence in 1776. He and Major Ebenezer Stevens loaded a long double fortified French brass gun (a 12-pounder) with a "proof charge of the best powder . . . ." A shell fired from this weapon struck at "more than half the height of the hill." Then they repeated the experiment from Fort Ticonderoga with similar results.[36]

To prove Sugar Loaf could also be climbed without difficulty, Trumbull, Arnold, and Wayne also scrambled to its highest point in a short time. From there they saw how easily artillery could be brought up from the Lake George side.[37]   Later Colonel Trumbull suggested that a permanent fort be constructed on the summit because he thought such a position, manned by a garrison of five hundred men with twenty-five heavy cannon and a year's supply of ammunition, pay, and provisions, would make other positions around Ticonderoga unnecessary. Trumbull claimed he submitted these observations to Gates, to Schuyler, and to the Continental Congress, but no action was taken.[38]

Although Horatio Gates did nothing about Sugar Loaf himself, he tried to warn General St. Clair of its potential danger. He told St. Clair the occupation of this hill would decide the fate of Fort Ticonderoga. Gates claimed he wanted to take possession of it the previous year "but Schuyler thought it wrong to throw away labor in preventing an evil that could never happen. . . ."[39] He insisted no army could carry 18- or 24-pounders up its sides. Gates agreed with this argument, but then he told of what he had learned from Trumbull. Eighteen and 24-pounders were unnecessary because "howitzers could easily be carried up . . ." the hill. From this location, he believed they could drive off the enemy from either Ticonderoga or Mount Independence should British troops gain possession of one or both of them. Furthermore, Gates considered howitzers better than guns because they could "throw either *shot* or shells and put an end to any attempts" by the enemy shipping to destroy the bridge across Lake Champlain.[40] Unfortunately, St. Clair had neither the time nor the men to take Gates's advice. So on July 5, American troops withdrew from Fort Ticonderoga and Mount Independence without a struggle.

Although the sight of British artillery on Sugar Loaf weighed heavily on General St. Clair's decision to abandon Ticonderoga, other deep-rooted considerations must have helped to shape his thinking. For example, eighteenth century military conventions recommended the evacuation of a post once enemy artillery could enfilade it. When Washington's army occupied Dorchester Heights in 1775, the British left Boston. Obviously this may also have significantly influenced St. Clair. In addition to this, propaganda about British strength in Canada helped to confuse American leaders before the campaign started. The gossips said most Canadian troops had joined Howe for a campaign in the southern colonies. After this information had apparently been confirmed, Continental and militia units originally scheduled to report to Schuyler were reassigned elsewhere. Large numbers of troops and supplies were detained in the eastern states because Howe's fleet continued to lurk off the New England coast.When Schuyler and St. Clair added this information to recent reports of a mutiny in Canada, sickness in the army, and an exaggerated account of a fire in the enemy's magazines at St. Johns, it is no wonder that they believed there was little or nothing to fear from Canada.[41]

Thus when the invasion began, Schuyler and St. Clair were surprised to learn Burgoyne had a powerful expeditionary force ready to strike at Ticonderoga. To further complicate matters, early information placed his strength at five thousand men.[42] Just prior to his attack, however, a new estimate credited Burgoyne with at least ten thousand troops. This figure made resistance appear hopeless once communication over Lake George was severed. After all, how could supplies and reinforcements be brought through woods swarming with savages when Schuyler had been unsuccessful in his attempts to strengthen Ticonderoga during the previous eight months? St. Clair knew there was even less of a chance then. He had little confidence in Schuyler's ability to save him from defeat, so he saw no other course open to him except that of surrender or retreat.

One can always argue that St. Clair's decision to withdraw was premature. His council of war on July 5, may have overlooked several important points. First, General Schuyler was known to be on his way to Ticonderoga with sizable reinforcements. Because of their numbers they probably could have broken through enemy forces investing Ticonderoga and Mount Independence. Although British artillery had been put into position on Sugar Loaf Mountain, it would have been difficult at best for the gunners to bring enough ammunition to the top of the hill to effectively bombard two posts fourteen and fifteen hundred yards distant.[43] Since preparations for a concentrated strike were inadequate, St. Clair's well-entrenched soldiers probably could have held out for weeks.[44]   By abandoning Fort Ticonderoga and Mount Independence, he permitted huge quantities of powder, food, supplies, and cannon to fall into enemy hands. Worst of all, British troops were greatly encouraged by this totally unexpected turn in events. Finally, there appears to be some question about St. Clair's strength. Most reports place his troops at 2,200 to 3,500 men, but Major General William Heath had a document in his possession placing St. Clair's force at 5,612 men when he ordered the retreat.[45] If this were true, then General St. Clair should have remained to fight Burgoyne's army.

St. Clair's decision to evacuate Ticonderoga was kept secret until after nightfall. As dusk settled over Lake Champlain's silent waters, American guns opened fire to cover patrols as they pushed out toward enemy positions to maintain contact during the night. On the surface, everything appeared normal. Behind the lines, however, confusion reigned as officers and enlisted men were awakened just before midnight and told to prepare to leave. Fires were smothered and heavy guns were spiked. Since the nights were short, practically no supplies or provisions could be removed. To be sure, British sentries heard unusual activity behind the American lines, and they half expected an attack. When none came, they grew suspicious. Were their opponents trying to retreat? They listened and wondered. But the Americans had concealed their intentions well, and everything went smoothly. At two o'clock on the morning of July 6, St. Clair's main body of troops crossed to Vermont and marched into the woods toward Hubbardtown. The sick, the wounded, and the women escaped by water to Skenesborough, thirty miles away, protected by six hundred of Colonel Pierce Long's New Hampshire troops. When the rear guard set fire to the bridge and General Roche de Fermoy's residence around 4 a.m., enemy troops realized what had happened. Almost immediately, two deserters confirmed their suspicions — Ticonderoga and Fort Independence had been abandoned.[46]

British officers reacted swiftly. In minutes, General Fraser's grenadiers and light infantry plunged into the woods after St. Clair's army. As dawn broke, some of General Riedesel's Hessians occupied Mount Independence while others hurried off to support Fraser. Before 9 o'clock, Burgoyne's fleet succeeded in smashing through the massive chain and log boom near the fort and with the aid of a northerly wind, his vessels rapidly closed in on the Americans sailing leisurely up South Bay. Since the channel between Ticonderoga and Mount Independence was blocked by a boom, Colonel Long and his party thought any pursuers would be at least a full day behind them. Instead of being depressed, they took this

opportunity to celebrate their good fortune in escaping Burgoyne's trap by drinking the wine they found in the hospital
stores. It was not until shortly after noon that Long's fleet
finally reached Skenesborough. Much to the Americans'
amazement, British ships were sighted on the horizon a few
minutes later. Sensing an opportunity for a quick victory,
Phillips' troopers rushed ashore in an attempt to envelop
Long, while Captain John Carter, a courageous British
artillery officer, captured and blew up five American gunboats. Long, seeing the hopelessness of his situation, set fire
to the stockade and nearby buildings and fled toward Fort
Anne.[47]

Meanwhile, General Fraser used a forced march to try to
overtake St. Clair, whose ragged army stretched six miles
from Hubbardtown to Castleton. Both sides pushed through
the hot, sticky forest all day. That night they slept on their
arms. Fraser was determined to catch St. Clair, however,
and ordered his men to get underway again at 3 a.m. on
July 7. Contrary to St. Clair's orders, three American regiments had encamped six miles to the rear of the main
column and at 5 o'clock they were surprised at breakfast by
Fraser's men.[48]

After recovering from the initial shock which routed most
of Colonel Jonathan Hale's militia regiment, the remaining
seven hundred Americans fought back with great courage.
The colonial marksmen were extremely effective in firing
from behind fallen trees and logs. So savage was their
counterattack that they almost succeeded in putting to flight
Fraser's grenadiers, who were finding it difficult to maneuver
in the tangled underbrush. The American riflemen outflanked
the enemy infantry, poured on a steady fire, and momentarily
forced it to give way. But their advantage was shortlived.
Moments later a blast of bugles, the sound of fifes, cheers,
and a band playing German battle hymns, announced General Riedesel's arrival. The Americans panicked and fled into
the woods, bringing to an end the bloody Battle of Hub-

bardtown. Three hundred and twenty-four Americans were either killed, wounded or captured, while British losses were placed at 198 dead or wounded.[49] As a result of the American defeats at Hubbardtown and Skenesborough, St. Clair was left with only a few of the troops he had withdrawn from Ticonderoga and Fort Independence. He had no other choice than to avoid further contact with enemy units by heading east toward Rutland with his battered forces. From Rutland, St. Clair hoped to join General Schuyler at Fort Edward by taking a much longer but safer route.

Schuyler always maintained that he never expected St. Clair to abandon Fort Ticonderoga. When Deputy Quartermaster General Udney Hay brought him the bad news, he could hardly believe his ears.[50] St. Clair's troop returns of several days before had listed four thousand men at the lake posts and they were supposed to have been reinforced by fifteen hundred New England militia troops. Since Ticonderoga had on hand a 39-day supply of meat, plenty of cannon and ammunition, and a two-month supply of flour, Schuyler thought Burgoyne had little chance for a quick victory. "What," he asked, "could induce General St. Clair and the general officers with him, to evacuate Ticonderoga..." when "Not a battery...was opened against it?"[51]

General St. Clair's whereabouts remained unknown and no one knew whether he and Fort Ticonderoga's garrison had escaped or not. To make matters worse, Schuyler could count upon no more than fifteen hundred troops to block Burgoyne's advance. When Burgoyne did not immediately press his advantage, the Americans thought that he might choose to push unopposed into New England instead of continuing toward Albany. Because of this possibility, Yankee militia units then marching toward New York were ordered to join Colonel Seth Warner's Green Mountain Boys in the New Hampshire Grants until Burgoyne committed himself.[52] The lack of information about enemy movements worried Schuyler, but he thought Burgoyne might

still be stopped if America organized and rallied to his
support. Once again he urged his countrymen to send troops,
tents, camp kettles, provisions, cannon, ammunition, artillerymen, horses, and workmen. The next move was up to
Burgoyne.

Chapter Ten

THE SUMMER OF DISCONTENT

News of Fort Ticonderoga's evacuation spread quickly. Exaggerated accounts of what took place were brought back by stragglers from St. Clair's army, and many Americans living in the enemy's path panicked at the possibility of Indian outrages. Some decided to accept Burgoyne's guarantee of safety and placed themselves under British protection, while others fled toward Albany. Even in Albany, however, fear so gripped the people that many hid furniture and household goods in the country for safekeeping until the danger ended. As the crisis deepened, a few militia troops felt duty-bound to return home and protect their families. Others showed how angry they were by throwing away their rifles, saying they would not fight under an officer who sold out to British leaders. Then there were several units which had been moving toward Albany that turned back in disgust upon hearing that Ticonderoga had been abandoned on orders from General Schuyler.[1]

To Americans from Boston to Charleston, Ticonderoga had appeared indestructible. Even though Schuyler had repeatedly warned of the danger facing it, not many Americans believed the fortress would ever fall.[2] Only a few days before, General Washington had said, upon hearing that a large supply of provisions had reached the fort, he "could see no reason for apprehending that it can possibly fall into the hands of the Enemy in a short time, even..." if they brought their whole force to bear on the post.[3] Suddenly Ticonderoga was in enemy hands and no one could understand why. Overnight it became the chief topic of conversation and General Schuyler the target of every complaint. Wild rumors, describing how he had ordered Ticonderoga's heavy artillery to be replaced with light guns, spread like wildfire. He supposedly had been paid for his treason with British gold and silver fired into American lines in hollow cannon balls. Although few people believed such tales, they helped, nonetheless, to discredit Schuyler because they led others to believe he was only interested in getting rich.

To make matters worse, Schuyler had been at Albany when Ticonderoga fell and did not know what had happened to St. Clair. This placed him in an embarrassing position in the eyes of Congress. "It is indeed droll," said Sam Adams, "...to see a general not knowing where to find the main body of his army!" Again and again Adams hammered at this point.[4] Even Albany's usually friendly citizens complained because Schuyler had not been at the fortress when it fell.[5] William Whipple leveled the same charge from Portsmouth, New Hampshire, and Paul Revere echoed it in Boston.[6] In a remark directed at Schuyler and St. Clair, Revere said he could see no hope for an American victory as long as Continental generals ran "away from such Fortresses as Ticonderoga."[7]

As discontent grew, Schuyler tried to placate Congress by relaying news as quickly as possible, but most of his letters were tinged with defeatism. On one occasion, while particularly depressed, he lashed out at New England for its failure to support him. "I cannot help remarking," he wrote, "that of the few Continental Troops we have had to the Northward, one-third part is composed of Men too far advanced in Years for Field Service; of Boys, or rather Children, and mortifying barely to mention, of Negroes."[8] There may have been some validity to these charges but Schuyler should never have made them. Such remarks accomplished nothing and left him open to bitter attacks. As a result, his critics pressed their demands for an investigation and clamored to have him recalled.

As debate over the fall of Ticonderoga increased, Schuyler redoubled his efforts to delay Burgoyne's advance. On July 8, 1777, he ordered Colonel Henry Van Rensselaer to rush his 440 New York militia troops to Fort Anne and reinforce Colonel Long's retreating New Hampshire Continentals. Van Rensselaer arrived just in time to assist Long in repulsing advance English units. For a while the Americans appeared to have the enemy trapped, but Long's men ran out of ammunition and the British escaped. Gunpowder was so scarce that the troops did not have bullets to use for guard duty that night.[9]

At Skenesborough, Burgoyne halted to rest his troops and await Governor Carleton's reply to his request for reinforcements. Carleton said he could not spare any troops, so Burgoyne had to leave 910 regulars behind on garrison duty. This delay helped the Americans. Schuyler had not expected the invaders to hesitate and wondered what "Gentleman Johnny" had in mind. He feared the British might have decided to strike eastward into New England instead of pressing toward Albany for a junction with St. Leger and Howe. But Burgoyne was merely taking stock of the situation.[10]

The British failure to renew the attack immediately gave Schuyler time to withdraw cannon, troops, and supplies from Fort George, a post that could not be defended. Once Schuyler learned Burgoyne had decided to move south on the east side of Lake George, he regrouped his forces at Fort Edward directly in the enemy's path. At the same time, he sought more support from the local citizens with a proclamation designed to minimize Burgoyne's guarantee of safety for those who placed themselves under British protection.[11] While thus encouraging frontier settlers to resist and retard the enemy advance, he sent hundreds of workmen into the woods to ravage the countryside. They cut up corduroy roads, felled great hemlocks and pines, burned bridges, and blocked streams with logs and rocks to make them impassable at strategic points. Cattle and horses were driven off and wagons were removed. Every possible measure was taken to impede Burgoyne's advance through New York.

When British forces began cutting their way through the heavily wooded country, General Schuyler's tactics started to pay off. More than fifty burned bridges needed repair. At one point, a huge man-made swamp forced the enemy to construct a two-mile causeway where dampness and the stifling heat brought out millions of black insects called "punkies," which made conditions almost unbearable. British and Canadian workmen cut through mile after mile of forest only to find devastation at every clearing. Some farmers had burned unharvested grain to keep it out of British hands and set fire to dwellings to make the desolation complete. When Burgoyne's scouts arrived, they were unable to find horses or draft animals for most of the artillery as they had expected. This forced the British to leave their heavy guns at Ticonderoga or ship them with the supplies over Lake George. Schuyler's strategy worked so well that Burgoyne could not reach Fort Anne until July 25, 1777, almost three weeks after the British first occupied Skenesborough only twenty miles away. Even then, his workmen needed four additional days to clear the road to Fort Edward.[12]

When Schuyler rushed to Fort Edward from Albany to direct operations on July 7, he found the fort in ruins. A man on horseback could jump over ramparts that had been allowed to deteriorate since the French and Indian War. Schuyler told Washington he had often done so himself. A few cannon remained, but they were scattered on the ground because there were no carriages on which to mount them. The condition of the one-hundred-man garrison was no better. Its members were so discouraged and out of hand that they did not hesitate to ravage the countryside when it suited them; and, like most American troops, they had only five musket cartridges per man.[13]

With the arrival of Long's detachment and the remnants of St. Clair's force, which reported on July 12, came Brigadier General John Nixon from Peekskill with six hundred Continentals. These reinforcements increased Schuyler's forces to approximately 4,500 men, yet they were hardly enough to stop a well-trained, well-equipped, and well-supplied army reported to be three times their size. General Washington tried to help in another way by making the "damned Dutchman" more acceptable to recalcitrant New England troops. He sent two popular major generals from those states to assist Schuyler — Benedict Arnold of Connecticut and Benjamin Lincoln of Massachusetts.[14]   Schuyler liked Arnold because he was a brave, daring, and spirited officer whose presence pleased the militia; and Lincoln handled affairs well in the Hampshire Grants.

In spite of these reinforcements, Fort Edward was untenable, and Schuyler issued orders to fall back to Moses Creek and Snook Hill five miles below. The fort, barracks, stores, and houses around Fort Edward were burned in keeping with Schuyler's intention to leave only waste and devastation in Burgoyne's path. From Moses Creek the little army moved to Saratoga for several days. Positions there were no easier to defend because heavy woods surrounded the area and Indians constantly cut off picket guards, so Schuyler retreated again.[15]   He wanted to draw Burgoyne deeper into New York to make him vulnerable to a flank attack by General Lincoln's troops in the Hampshire Grants. On August 3, Schuyler's troops occupied defensive positions at Stillwater designed by the Polish engineering expert, Thaddeus Kosciusko, but again they did not remain there long because reinforcements and supplies failed to arrive in great numbers as expected. Finally, Schuyler's army crossed the Mohawk River near Loudon's Ferry to take up positions at the mouth of the river on Van Schaak's Island.

These continual retreats, accompanied by hardships, shortages, and vicious rumors, almost completely undermined
confidence in Schuyler. The Connecticut troops were especially critical and many of them accused him of incompetence and treasonable conduct.[16]   As a result, desertions
became commonplace. Between July 20 and July 24, two
hundred men abandoned their units. Although a few reinforcements arrived to replace these troops, the New England
states were slow in sending help, and Schuyler's strength
did not increase to any great extent.[17]

Aside from their dislike of Schuyler, New Englanders
were deeply concerned about the threat of an invasion by
sea. It was well known that General William Howe had
embarked from New York City during the first days of July
with fifteen thousand troops, and late in the month his
destination still remained a mystery. Many New Englanders
momentarily expected a landing on their shores, so they
hesitated to send militia troops to New York and leave their
own villages unprotected.[18]

Lookouts along the Atlantic Coast watched to see where
Howe would land, but by August 3, Burgoyne already knew
the answer.[19]   Howe had informed him that he had proceeded with his original plan to take Philadelphia. "If,
according to my expectations we may succeed rapidly . . . the
enemy having no force of any consequence there, I shall,
without loss of time, proceed to cooperate with you in the
defeat of the Rebel army. . . . " Since Howe apparently did
not expect an American army to pursue him, he left Major
General Henry Clinton at New York City "to amuse Washington and Putnam" and keep them from reinforcing Schuyler.[20]   This left Burgoyne with one hope for assistance:
Colonel Barry St. Leger advancing down the Mohawk Valley.
Although Howe later received instructions to advance to
Albany, he considered it impossible to comply because
operations in Chesapeake Bay were about to get underway.
New Englanders and New Yorkers, on the other hand, were

General Sir Guy Carleton

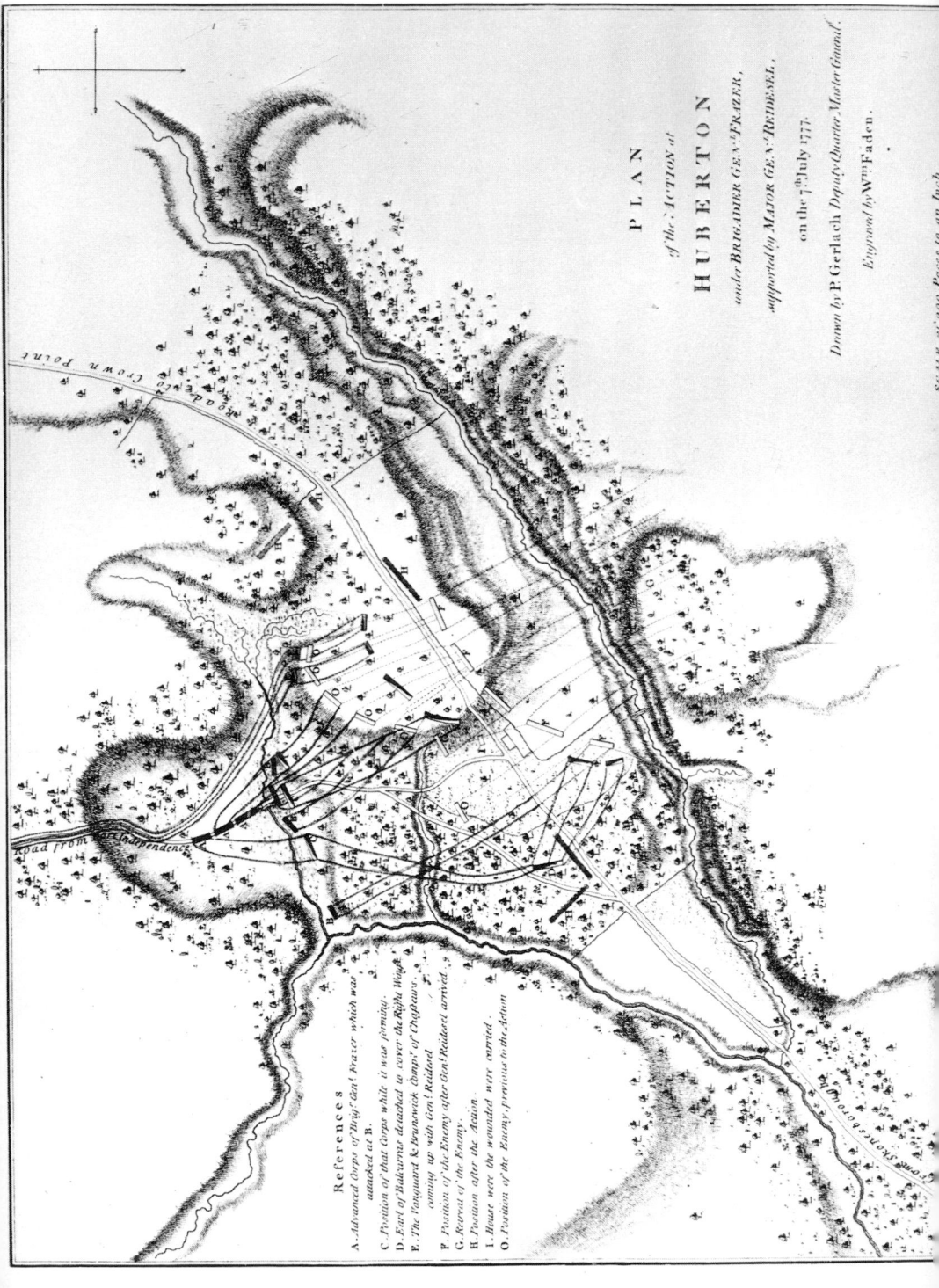

greatly relieved to learn Howe had been sighted off the coast of Delaware.[21]   They no longer had to fear a coastal invasion or a quick thrust up the Hudson; now all their attention could be focused on Burgoyne.

For some reason, the British had paused again for an undue length of time after reaching Fort Edward. This may have been due to Burgoyne's failure to obtain transportation for his artillery and supplies; or perhaps he wished to give St. Leger a chance to attack and divide Schuyler's little army. Whatever his reasons were for the delay, it gave the Americans an opportunity to prepare for him. There was no respite, however, for Schuyler. People were angry and upset at the abandonment of Fort Ticonderoga; some cried treachery, and some cowardice. Sam Adams was particularly bitter. "I confess it is no more than I expected when He (Schuyler) was again appointed to the Command there."[22]   Pierre Van Cortlandt said that New York's inhabitants were "disgusted, disappointed and alarmed," yet the New York Council could not give Schuyler much help since five counties were controlled by the enemy and three others were threatening to revolt.[23]   Jonathan Trumbull, Jr. told his father the troops were not at fault. "Our Men will fight," he said, "if officers will lead them."[24]

Although General St. Clair tried to absolve Schuyler of all blame in Ticonderoga's loss, agitation for Schuyler's removal failed to subside. Roger Sherman of Connecticut believed New York would not be defended unless General Gates returned to command the Northern Department.[25]   Sam Adams agreed: "Gates is the Man of my Choice. He is honest and true and has the Art of gaining the love of his soldiers, particularly because he is always present and shares with them in Fatigue and Danger."[26]   By late July, many colonists shared the same opinion. They could not understand how Schuyler could possibly have reported the fortress's strength at over five thousand troops just before it fell. If the fort were that strong, why had resistance collapsed so easily? Even General Washington could hardly believe the news. "The whole affair is so mysterious," he wrote, "it even baffles conjecture."[27]   Although Schuyler explained why he misjudged Ticonderoga's numbers, too much damage had been done to his reputation. When criticism did not abate, Schuyler's removal became inevitable.

The New England delegates spearheaded the drive to replace Schuyler. John Adams, Sam Adams, William Williams, Elbridge Gerry, and James Lovell openly ridiculed his letters.[28]   Sam Adams said he saw in the whole affair "the evident Marks of (a) Design," while young James Lovell sought to discredit both Schuyler and New York with a biting satire.[29]   He told Congress, "Schuyler was beloved by the Eastern States, especially by the officers from thence — that he was the Key to the Militia of Albany County, and that the Indians called him father." This brought on jeers and laughter. Lovell then turned toward Schuyler's New York friends to tell them he had been "told so six weeks ago by a gentleman (James Duane) of intelligence, veracity and honor." Again the delegates roared with laughter.[30]

By July 29, demands for an investigation were so strong that Congress passed a resolution to examine the incident. This gave the New Englanders a chance to tell Congress their militia might not fight unless the "damned Dutchman" was replaced. Since this feeling had become widespread, there was little opposition to their move to relieve the General. "Washington and Congress were assured," wrote John Jay, "that unless another general presided in the Northern Department the militia of New England would not be brought into the field."[31]   Congress thus exchanged Schuyler for militia support from New England. Members of the New York delegation were chagrined but they could do nothing to stop their colleagues. They did, however, attempt to prevent Gates from being named as Schuyler's successor by insisting that General Washington make the choice.[32]   Washington refused to be drawn into the controversy, so on August 4 Congress resolved, by a vote of eleven to one, to make Gates commander of the Northern Department.[33] New York cast the lone dissenting vote because of its loyalty to Schuyler.

The Congressional decision to replace General Schuyler was regrettable. He had nothing to do with Ticonderoga's abandonment, but he had to accept responsibility for its loss. At the same time, the General had done everything in his power to strengthen the Northern Department with almost inexhaustible energy. By persevering after the disaster at Ticonderoga, he expertly slowed Burgoyne's advance with a series of brilliant delaying tactics that were probably decisive in the end. Yet sectional jealousies, frustrations, defeats, and Schuyler's own discouraging letters to Congress undermined his leadership. An aroused nation demanded scapegoats, so Schuyler and St. Clair had to be removed to restore confidence. Strange though it may seem, this whole affair had a supremely ironic quality. Before General Gates could take over on August 19, the military situation significantly improved. A tragedy and two decisive victories over British troops — one near Bennington and the other at Fort Stanwix — helped bring about the change, far more than Schuyler's removal from command of the Northern Department.

The tragedy involved the murder of reputedly beautiful Jane McCrea. Her patriot brother had urged her to accompany his family to Albany as Burgoyne's forces approached Fort Edward, but Jane declined. She wished to stay behind to marry her former neighbor, David Jones, who was returning to New York with one of Burgoyne's units. While Jane waited for her lover on July 27, hostile Indians siezed her and a Mrs. Sarah McNeil. The Indians quarreled over Jane and one of them shot her, then scalped and mutilated her naked body.[34]

Jane McCrea's death had a tremendous impact on the country, and news of it flashed through New York and New England as the savages spread terror before Burgoyne's advance. Americans began to realize for the first time that there was little or no safety in Burgoyne's protection. Panic gripped the countryside and men rushed to join Schuyler's army to prevent a similar fate from happening to their own families. To be sure, the importance of Jane McCrea's murder has probably been over-emphasized. Yet it apparently did help to shock Americans into action against Burgoyne while Schuyler was still in command of the Northern Department, and thousands of men headed toward Albany to fight the British.

Several units of fresh militia troops under General John Stark of New Hampshire made their presence felt almost immediately. On August 18, Stark's forces routed a band of Germans and Tories under Colonel Friedrich Baum at Bennington, Vermont. That same day, they defeated a relief column led by Col. Heinrich Breymann rushing to Baum's assistance. In these engagements nearly 907 enemy troops were captured, killed, or wounded, compared to only seventy American casualties.[35]   The Americans were elated. Burgoyne's troops had been defeated and New England militia units were rushing to join Schuyler to finish the job. They knew the time had come to throw their full weight against the deadly menace descending from Canada.

Meanwhile, Schuyler had learned that advance units of Colonel Barry St. Leger's expedition were laying siege to Fort Schuyler in western New York. This endangered the entire Mohawk Valley. If Fort Schuyler fell, St. Leger might well be able to link his forces with Burgoyne's near Saratoga. At a hurriedly-called council of war on August 12, 1777, Schuyler proposed to send a relief expedition at once. Much to his surprise, several officers opposed him because they were reluctant to weaken the army in the face of Burgoyne's advance. In the midst of the discussion, Schuyler heard one of his officers say: "He means to weaken the army." With this General Schuyler flew into a rage, biting his pipe in two in the process. "Gentlemen," he said, "I shall take the responsibility upon myself; where is the brigadier that will take command of the relief? I shall beat up for volunteers tomorrow." General Benedict Arnold stepped forward. He would lead the expedition and 950 volunteers joined him.[36] They never engaged the British, however, for a clever ruse by Arnold caused the Indians to abandon St. Leger. Without them, St. Leger was powerless, so he gave up his hope of joining Burgoyne and returned to Oswego.[37]

General Schuyler's judgment had paid off just as General Horatio Gates arrived to assume command of the Northern Department on August 20, 1777. "I have done all that could be done...." he told Gates, "to inspire confidence in the soldiers of our own army..., but the palm of victory is denied me, and it is left to you, General, to reap the fruits of my labours." Then without a trace of bitterness in his voice he said: "I will not fail, however, to second your views; and my devotion to my country, will cause me with alacrity to obey all your orders."[38] With this statement, Schuyler's active military career came to an end, because Gates refused to call on him for assistance or advice.

Chapter Eleven

"NOT GUILTY"

After Schuyler relinquished command of the Northern Department, he returned to the relative quiet of his home in Albany to await the congressional inquiry into his conduct. He was by no means inactive and spent a great deal of his time conferring with the Six Iroquois Nations to make them honor their pledge of neutrality during the campaign. He also managed to stay abreast of operations on the battlefront through correspondence with his former aide-de-camp, Colonel Henry B. Livingston, and his former secretary, Colonel Richard Varick.

Although the Continental Congress selected a committee of three on August 27, 1777, to conduct an inquiry into the evacuation of Ticonderoga, little progress was made. This irritated Schuyler because he wanted to settle the issue quickly. Until official charges were made against him, suspicions and rumors would continue to damage his reputation in every corner of the colonies. Yet he heard nothing from Congress other than a description of its instructions directing the committee to recommend a court-martial if it uncovered evidence indicating that the post had been lost due to neglect or misconduct.[1] One month passed, and then another, without any action being taken; and Schuyler became increasingly bitter. Occasionally he sent letters to Congress requesting a statement of the charges against him, but they brought no positive results. Finally on December 29, he urged Congress to act. "I have suffered so much in public life," he wrote, "that it cannot create surprise if I anxiously wish to retire and pay that attention to my private affairs which the losses I have sustained . . . have occasioned, and yet the impropriety of resigning . . . before the inquiry had taken place or the committee reported my innocence is too striking to need dwelling on."[2] By this time, the knowledge that he had been widely branded as a traitor throughout the New England states, coupled with the congressional failure to announce the charges against him, had deepened Schuyler's bitterness. He became so depressed he would fly into a rage at the mere mention of New England. It was a matter of honor, one that should be settled without delay. Once this was done he would end his military career, relax, smoke his beloved pipe, and criticize "those Fellows of the Congress for abridging . . . American liberties."[3]

Several statements made by Schuyler at this time indicate that he had given up completely on America's chances of defeating British arms. In spite of Burgoyne's surrender at Saratoga, an end to the war appeared to be a long way off as General Washington desperately struggled to keep his army together in winter quarters at Valley Forge. Since Schuyler had never really accepted the idea of independence, he told William Smith "he would take almost any risk to end independence if Britain would cede its taxing power to the colonies."[4] This statement probably did not surprise Smith because Schuyler had expressed the same idea before, but with much less conviction. According to Peter Schaak, Schuyler told several of Burgoyne's officers shortly after they surrendered at Saratoga that Congress would renounce independence if Britain explicitly agreed to surrender the power of taxation. He also proposed a toast to reconciliation with Major John Ackland, one of the captured officers.[5] Other evidence suggests that many Americans shared Schuyler's sentiments, but they did not dare to express them publicly. If the General had attempted to do so before his court-martial, he might have been convicted. Therefore he chose the safe course, that of judicious silence.

When Congress received Schuyler's plea for a trial late in December, it finally ordered the committee of inquiry to report its conclusions. On February 8, 1778, the committee presented the evidence it had gathered and sent it to General Washington for implementation; but Washington refused to appoint a court-martial because no charges had been made.[6] He thought it would be improper to make the charges himself, particularly in Schuyler's case, since he did not know what instructions Congress had given the commander of the Northern Department.[7] Washington suggested, therefore, that Congress state the charges itself in the interests of justice. This forced Congress to reopen its investigation with an entirely new committee.[8] Late in March, the new group, composed of William Ellery, Eliphalet Dyer, James Lovell, and James Smith, asked permission to report its findings, but Schuyler's friend, William Duer, demanded another delay.[9] It is difficult to ascertain why Duer did this. Perhaps he wanted to make a deal for Schuyler, or perhaps he insisted on a statement of charges against the General before the committee went further to avoid any more postponements. The latter conclusion is more plausible because the committee appears to have staunchly refused to present charges despite Duer's insistence. According to Gouverneur Morris, the men gathering evidence intended merely to collect and present their findings, and nothing more. In an attempt to end the impasse, Morris asked to have an additional committee appointed especially to state the charges against General Schuyler, but he could not do this until Duer missed a meeting.[10]   This move by Morris finally broke the impasse.

Several weeks went by while the charges were being prepared by the new committee. During this time, New York elected Schuyler to a seat in the Continental Congress since the state had been unrepresented there for many weeks. After Schuyler learned of this, he urged Congress to act on his case immediately so the affair could be settled before he arrived.[11]   In reality, however, Schuyler probably did not want to attend Congress or even serve the public any longer; he merely wanted to use the opportunity to prod the delegates a little. This is apparent from his reply to Governor George Clinton's official announcement of Schuyler's election and from advice given to him by Walter Livingston.[12] He told Clinton his personal affairs in Albany prevented him from leaving, especially in view of the threat of an Indian raid, and insisted on staying with his family while negotiating with the savages to prevent a possible massacre.[13]   Livingston saw through these excuses and warned Schuyler he would lose most of the support he had in Congress if he did not report there soon. "I am tolerably well acquainted with the disposition of the part of the Representatives with respect to yourself...." wrote Livingston, "that many who voted for you last March will not do so again unless you repair to Congress speedily. They will take no denial."[14]   In spite of this warning, Schuyler steadfastly refused to attend until he was cleared.

On Friday, June 12, 1778, after ten months of delay, Congress finally announced the formal charge against Schuyler — "neglect of duty." The report said he failed to stay at Ticonderoga "to expedite the works on Mount Independence, and to cause a retreat to be made, when it became no longer possible to maintain the posts, consistent with the safety of the troops and stores...."[15]   Because Fort Ticonderoga and Mount Independence were posts of great importance, the committee believed Schuyler should have remained at the fort when an enemy attack became imminent. Schuyler's failure to do so resulted, in the opinion of the committee, not only in the loss of the fortress, but of its sick, ammunition, cannon, provisions, clothing, and the sacrifice of many lives. On the basis of this evidence, Congress charged Schuyler "With neglect of duty in not being present at Ticonderoga to discharge the functions of his command from the middle of June, 1777, until it was no longer possible to maintain Ticonderoga and Mount Independence." [16]

This was good news for the General. The charges would not be easy to prove because Congress's own instructions had permitted him freedom of movement. As a result, he became more certain than ever of his innocence in the loss of Ticonderoga. When one also considers his wish to bring the matter into the open at the earliest possible date, there can be no doubt about Schuyler's confidence of being acquitted. His nine letters to Congress urging a trial attest to this. Had there been any doubt in his own mind, he obviously would not have continued to demand a hearing for ten months.

The court-martial of Generals Charles Lee and Arthur St. Clair held precedence, so General Washington could not set the judicial machinery in motion for Schuyler's trial until early in the autumn. [17]   Three months later, on September 30, 1778, Washington directed the court-martial to convene. [18]   He ordered Benjamin Lincoln to serve as president and Brigadier Generals John Nixon, James Clinton, Anthony Wayne, and Peter Muhlenberg to sit with him. [19]   John Laurance served as Judge Advocate General, to complete the court, and he personally presented the charges against Schuyler on behalf of the United States. [20]   With one exception, the court remained exactly the same as the one which acquitted General Arthur St. Clair. [21]   In view of St Clair's acquittal, Schuyler felt certain that the prevailing air of suspicion about his own actions would be removed. He neither objected to any member of the court, nor did he request any changes in its composition since the case against General St. Clair had been much stronger than the one against himself — and St. Clair had been cleared.

When General Lincoln called the court to order on October 1, 1778, a few observers were surprised to learn the General would defend himself. [22]   Once he took the floor, however, it became clear that he was well prepared to protect his reputation in spite of the evidence presented by the prosecution. In his opening move for the prosecution, Laurance presented the charges against Schuyler and sought to strengthen his case by introducing as evidence significant congressional resolutions and several letters from General St. Clair. By doing this, Laurance tried to prove that Schuyler knew all about Burgoyne's plans and strength before the latter attacked Fort Ticonderoga and Mount Independence. He also pointed out that Schuyler had been fully informed of the great danger threatening Fort Ticonderoga, and, despite these warnings, he did not stay there to direct defensive preparations. According to Laurance, it was "General Schuyler's duty to have been at the head of the army, and to have remained there..." when the enemy attacked because Ticonderoga was one of the most strategic posts in the United States.[23]

Although Laurance admitted Congress had released Schuyler from all previous orders in establishing his headquarters in May of 1777, he said it had expected him to stay at the fortress to repulse the enemy attack. Because of this somewhat contradictory approach and the overall weakness of the case, Laurance apparently had no hope of getting a conviction, or perhaps he never intended to try for one. He appears to have gone through the motions of a trial for the government to give Schuyler an opportunity to go on record publicly in his own defense. If there had been any doubt of Schuyler's innocence, it was quickly removed and the outcome of the trial never appeared to be in question.

Upon taking the floor, Schuyler admitted he had been informed of the great danger to Fort Ticonderoga and he knew of its shortage of troops and provisions. He also agreed that it was a post of great importance, but he considered the prosecution's statement about his absence when Burgoyne attacked to be the weak link in the case against him. Therefore he centered his attention on this point. As witnesses for the defense, Schuyler asked to have Richard Varick and John Lansing, his secretaries, sworn in. They were both extremely intelligent young men. Lansing had studied law with Robert Yates and James Duane, and, just before fighting broke out in the colonies, he had been admitted to practice law in Albany. Varick, like Lansing, was of Dutch parentage and a friend and admirer of Schuyler. For months they had copied official military letters and orders in large books after they had been carefully checked against the originals. These letters were now presented as evidence of Schuyler's unremitting efforts to strengthen the Northern Department. Since both men had served with Schuyler throughout the war, they tried hard to defend him because they felt he had been victimized by sectional jealousies.

After questioning them, Schuyler delivered a carefully prepared statement designed to reveal the weakness in the case against him. Although he admitted he had been absent from Ticonderoga when the attack took place, he attempted to prove his absence had been necessary and helpful to the Northern Department. With the use of numerous letters, orders, and related documents as evidence, he described his conduct prior to the evacuation; then he explained why his absence had been necessary. After that he described his actions from the time of the evacuation and told how he had served his country even after being superseded by General Gates in "the moment when there was a prospect of acquiring a great reputation."[24] In questioning his third and final witness, Major General Arthur St. Clair, Schuyler cleared himself beyond all reasonable doubt. The former commandant of Ticonderoga said the entire Northern Department would have suffered had Schuyler remained at the fortress. His post, declared St. Clair, "ought to have been at or near Albany, to have collected the necessaries, and to have urged on the militia for the aid of the whole. Ticonderoga was at a corner of the department, in an uninhabited part of the country, and the communication to it from any part of the country (except New England) (was) across (a) Lake."[25]

After these statements, John Laurance did not press the government's case further. No witnesses for the prosecution were called to testify, and Laurance made no attempt to summarize his arguments against the defendant. Schuyler, on the other hand, fought to the end. In a strong closing statement, he showed why he returned to Albany after being reinstated on May 22, 1777, and how he used every available means at his command to prepare for the campaign ahead. He told the court he had visited Fort Ticonderoga within eight days after returning to Albany to learn what could be done to improve its defenses, and he had also made plans to inspect Fort Schuyler until news of the enemy's advance down Lake Champlain prevented him from going there. Upon hearing of the British approach, he sought to raise troops and personally bring a small relief force to Ticonderoga just before news of its evacuation arrived. Finally, he told of his attempts to prevent and retard the enemy advance, an action which probably helped make possible Gates's victory at Saratoga.[26] Three days after the trial convened, General Lincoln announced the verdict: "The court, having considered the charge against Major General Schuyler, the evidence, and his defense, are unanimously of the opinion that he is NOT GUILTY of any Neglect of Duty in not being at Ticonderoga, as charged, and the Court therefore do acquit him with the highest honour."[27]

When the truth came to light at the trial, there could no longer be any question about Schuyler's conduct. Even those who had been bent on discrediting him knew it could not be done. A fight-or-die order to General St. Clair would have been impractical if not impossible, so St. Clair, not Schuyler appears to have been at fault in the loss of Fort Ticonderoga. If Schuyler were clearly innocent of any misconduct at Ticonderoga, it is only natural to ask why he was tried at a court-martial. First, a great deal of confusion had occurred. Most reports were incorrect or exaggerated and rumors predominated, so no one could be certain of the strength of the opposing armies. Furthermore, sectional prejudices largely motivated thinking in this affair, and they had to be cleared up to restore at least the semblance of harmony between the states involved. Above all else, General Schuyler wanted to be court-martialed so he could publicly clear himself and promote a better understanding of the events surrounding the abandonment of Fort Ticonderoga. He also, apparently, attempted to show by implication that it was New England's well-known friendship toward General Horatio Gates which brought about the change of command, and not his own failure as an officer.

Although the court-martial cleared Schuyler, he has gone down in history a rather questionable character. This may be due in a large part to the early influence of George Bancroft, the great New England historian. To the extremely nationalistic Bancroft, everything was either black or white. Since Philip Schuyler failed to measure up to Bancroft's standards of patriotism because of his reluctance to break with Great Britain, he attacked the General unmercifully. According to Bancroft: "The British were never harried by the troops with Schuyler, against whom public opinion was rising.... To screen his popularity, he insisted that the retreat was made without the least hint from himself, and was ill-judged and not warranted from necessity." [28] Later, he accused Schuyler of losing his courage.[29] But Bancroft was far more sympathetic to General St. Clair who, "With manly frankness...assumed the sole responsibility of the praise-worthy act which saved the country many of its bravest defenders."[30] This statement about St. Clair is in striking contrast to the general opinion expressed by New Englanders in July of 1777.

There is really little truth to Bancroft's reasoning, engaging as it may appear. Few of the soldiers who retreated from Ticonderoga stayed around long enough to fight at Saratoga; indeed, many of them went directly home. The evidence suggests that General St. Clair sacrificed an important post without a fight, dispersed his own army, permitted badly-needed supplies and ammunition to fall into enemy hands, and by so doing he gave the invaders considerable encouragement. Worst of all, the evacuation practically demoralized the American soldiers and panicked inhabitants living in the path of the advancing enemy. Although the court-martial brought this out, it never succeeded in removing the traitorous image of General Schuyler that months of gossip, slander, and abuse had created.

Chapter Twelve

THE COMMITTEE AT HEADQUARTERS

On October 18, 1779, Schuyler agreed to return to Congress as one of New York's representatives. He accepted the position with mixed feelings, however, since it would be difficult to work with men who had once clamored to have him stripped of his command in the Northern Department. A court-martial had removed that stigma, to be sure, but Schuyler never again placed much faith in the Philadelphia statesmen. Partially in protest of their actions, and also for personal reasons, he had retired from active military duty after the court-martial, explaining that he preferred to keep the Six Iroquois Nations at peace and look after private affairs at home. But close friends knew better. They said Schuyler had lost faith in America's struggle for independence.

Even while Schuyler served as a Continental officer, he never really believed independence would work. A permanent break with Great Britain appeared economically unwise for America, not only because of the loss of trade with England, but because Congress had proved itself incapable of governing a loose confederation of thirteen states. In Schuyler's opinion, the only logical culmination of the war would be an amicable settlement with the mother country. Until other Americans arrived at the same conclusion, he preferred to stay out of national politics. Notwithstanding, close friends, particularly James Duane, had urged him to return to the legislative arena. "It is a mark of respect which is due to you," Duane told Schuyler after the General had agreed to serve again, "and, however indifferent you may be, it affords your friends much satisfaction. But this is not the principal reason why I wished for it — your country required your service."[1]

Schuyler reached the Quaker City on November 15, 1779, just as preparations were being made to obtain stronger support for Washington's army during the impending campaign against British forces in the South.[2] This was not unusual, for such activity had been commonplace each autumn ever since fighting broke out in the colonies. Washington would submit strategic recommendations with requests for well-supplied troops and Congress would debate his needs far into the winter; but bureaucratic haggling, shortages, and emergencies generally stifled action. By spring, little was accomplished. Troops had shuffled in and out of the army and valuable stores had been gathered only to be stolen or squandered, thus leaving General Washington poorly prepared to cope with the well-equipped, well-supplied, and well-trained British forces.

The main reason for Congress's inability to act appears to have been the weak monetary structure within which it attempted to work. Congress never had enough money to satisfy current demands because the Continental treasury was empty most of the time. This created an exceptionally critical situation since funds were needed for bounties to stimulate recruiting. "Our finances," wrote Schuyler, "are deranged to a most alarming degree...;" and to make matters worse, the delegates appear unequal to the task at hand.[3] In an effort to end this impasse, several members proposed a program of military retrenchment and reform to ease the money shortage. By reducing the Continental army from eighty-eight to sixty battalions, they believed an equally effective and better-equipped force could be put in the field at less expense.[4] General Washington staunchly opposed them since the plan might prolong the war. He reminded Congress that false ideas about peace had already caused recruiting to lag, and urged its members to consider the ramifications of their suggestion. "There is nothing so likely to produce peace," he insisted, "as to be well prepared to meet an enemy."[5]

French Foreign Minister Chevalier de la Luzerne also showed concern and wished to know how many troops Congress could put into the field if such a program were enacted. How well would they be supplied? And where would these supplies come from? Although these questions were somewhat embarrassing to Congress, it responded almost boastfully. Luzerne was told that the United States could easily put 25,000 well provisioned troops in the field at any time and also guaranteed ample supplies and provisions to any additional French or Americans who took the field. They would be supported with tax money collected from the individual states and also through internal loans.[6] On the surface, the plan appeared sound and Luzerne accepted it at face value, but members of Congress knew they could not live up to their boast. To save face, they discarded plans for cutbacks in personnel and equipment on February 9, 1780, and approved a long-debated recruiting measure.[7] Once the controversy had been settled, Congress redoubled its efforts to find other methods of solving America's financial crisis without weakening its military establishment.

Continental currency had been rapidly sinking in value for many months. In an attempt to stop this decline, Congress urged state officials to collect taxes and meet their contribution quotas to the Continental treasury because funds continued to fall short of demands, and money trickled in too slowly to meet current needs.[8] Without adequate working capital, American officers had to struggle to keep troops in the field as Congress frantically searched for a solution to the dilemma. When expected domestic loans failed to materialize, Congress tried another solution, this time one involving the direct transfer of supplies and stores from various states without the use of money. Each state had to contribute its most abundant resource on a voluntary basis under a so-called direct requisition plan.[9] In theory it appeared to have merit; in practice, however, it operated poorly. Some areas of the country were flooded with supplies, while others had none, and provision and fodder quotas often fell far below minimum daily needs even at headquarters; yet Congress could not comprehend why this happened. Its members expected the situation to improve soon. When it grew worse, Washington became extremely worried. He told Schuyler ruin would follow if Congress's latest innovation went unchallenged.[10] The delegates, on the other hand, had great hopes for their plan since it promised, if successful, to reduce demands on the Continental treasury and thus help to stabilize the Continental currency. In the past, the ratio of the Continental dollar to sterling had fluctuated between forty and sixty to one, but recent sharp rises so worsened the situation that Congress was now threatened with bankruptcy.[11] The delegates knew inflation had to be stopped because congressional authority rested on the nation's confidence, and America's hopes for victory and the army's morale rested on the value of the Continental dollar.

With Robert Morris absent from Congress, Schuyler was looked upon as the best-informed member on financial affairs then present. The General had created quite a stir the year before with a pamphlet entitled *Causes of Depreciation of the Continental Currency*.[12] Although it irritated several delegates, most of them respected his forthright approach to money problems, so they named him (March 5, 1780) to a committee of six to develop a plan to restore the value of Continental currency.[13] Much to Schuyler's surprise, the other committee members readily followed his suggestions and adopted a plan which called for an end to further issues of unsecured paper money and the reissuance of a limited amount of Continental currency at a ratio of forty to one.

At the same time, Congress as a whole began to consider

several measures aimed at making the army more effective
while also strengthening its own authority. On May 28,
1779, it had appointed a committee to study ways of reforming military staff departments.[14] The committee failed to
make satisfactory progress, however, so on January 20, 1780,
almost eight months later, Congress selected another committee to see what it could do.[15] General Schuyler was
included on the latter committee but he refused to serve,
arguing that it would be improper to act in a capacity which
implied that he was a servant to Congress. "I could not,"
he wrote, "consistently with my honor and reputation accept
of any employment under Congress in a Station either less
honorable or less Important than that which I once had the
honor to hold."[16] On the other hand, there may have been
a more significant reason for his refusal. General Thomas
Mifflin and Colonel Timothy Pickering, the two other committee members, were known to be unfriendly toward General Washington, and Schuyler probably wanted no part of
any plan detrimental to his former chief. He did offer,
however, to serve on the committee "to Consult with the
Commander-in-Chief and the heads of the several civil departments of the Army and to Adopt such Measures as will
have a probable tendency to complete the great Object of
the resolution of the 21st of January."[17]

By the end of winter, conditions in the Continental army
had become critical. Washington urged Congress to send help
at once as dissatisfaction among the troops had seldom been
worse. If Congress hesitated too long before acting, America's struggle to attain independence might disintegrate. One
head will gradually change into thirteen, he warned, and one
army will branch "into thirteen, which instead of looking
up to Congress as the supreme controlling power of the
United States..." will consider themselves as dependent
upon their own states.[18] There were many reasons for poor
morale. Most complaints, however, centered on the disparity
in provisions supplied to various units, the unequal bounties,

the differing terms of enlistments, and the six-months back pay most soldiers had never received.[19] Washington sought to correct most of these abuses by putting the entire army on one standard directly under Congress. This appeared all the more desirable because the direct requisition system showed signs of failing.

Congress shared General Washington's concern and turned its attention to a new proposal calling for a committee of three to work out solutions to these problems at headquarters with General Washington. The measure was approved on April 6, 1780, but only after a long debate caused by several influential delegates who were reluctant to strengthen the army's power at Congress's expense. They sought to stop approval of the committee's instructions by demanding the establishment of a grand committee composed of at least one member from each state. Opponents of the grand committee plan quickly pointed out that such a cumbersome body could not possibly be effective, so Congress rejected the suggestion and approved (April 12, 1780) instructions to reform the staff departments with the three-man committee.[20] The following day it selected John Mathews, the outspoken delegate from South Carolina, Nathaniel Peabody of New Hampshire, and New York's Philip Schuyler as its Committee at Headquarters.[21]

The new committee had almost complete freedom to recommend changes to General Washington, institute regulations in various departments, and supervise the implementation of reforms. These things could be done with Washington's cooperation at the committee's discretion and without prior consent so long as it kept Congress informed. This meant a lot to Washington since it assured him of a quick decision when needed. Most important perhaps was the new line of communications with Congress. That body became better informed on military problems than ever before and Washington believed this would bring about closer cooperation. Indeed, Congress had made great concessions, yet

Washington thought it had not given the committee enough power.[22]   Even so, he welcomed its members when they arrived at headquarters in Morristown, New Jersey, late in April, and guards were ordered to show them the same respect accorded the Commander-in-chief, a gesture which genuinely pleased Philip Schuyler who still enjoyed the forms of convention observed in military life.

Soon after Schuyler arrived at headquarters, Lafayette brought General Washington news from France of his country's intention to send military and naval support to the United States. These reinforcements could be decisive, so Washington, Schuyler, Mathews, and Peabody pushed everything aside to discuss the most effective manner of cooperating with the French. They even urged Congress to be more imaginative by setting a new and daring course for the country. Washington soon revealed what they had in mind. The Committee at Headquarters wanted Congress to give it what amounted to almost dictatorial powers.[23]   Since the committee had the same idea, John Mathews went to Congress to see if he could generate support for this proposal. At the same time, unexpected support came from French Minister Luzerne who urged Congress to give the committee extraordinary powers to deal with any emergency.

This pressure caused considerable agitation. Finally, on May 19, 1780, Congress reluctantly gave the committee additional, although rather insignificant powers—far short of what Schuyler and the others asked for.[24]   The committee decided, therefore, to try to push Congress a little further. Robert R. Livingston told Schuyler the chances of obtaining more concessions were slim because Congress had acted with great reluctance on the original proposal.[25] James Duane, on the other hand, was more optimistic. "The powers," he told Schuyler, "fell vastly short of your views and my efforts, but it is the fate of deliberate bodies to move with caution...the obstacles to a committee plenipo(tentiary)... are deep-rooted in the human passions, and not to be surmounted on the first impression." This is why Duane believed Congress would still support every reasonable measure General Washington considered necessary.[26]

While debate raged over the issue of surrendering more power to a group working closely with the Commander-in-chief, the Committee at Headquarters took a careful look at its original assignment — suggesting and initiating military organizational reforms. Before it could make any progress, however, supply problems reached critical proportions as the state requisition system began to break down. The source of trouble appeared to lay in the act itself. The various states had been directed to stockpile supplies within their borders without any provisons to transport these badly-needed supplies to the army. As the committee members considered various alternatives open to them, they appealed to the states on May 25, 1780, to use their own resources to transport supplies until a new system could be started.[27] Several days later, they repeated their request and also urged Congress to give them more support in language that must have shocked that body. They bluntly told Congress it had to shake its lethargy and do more than just make recommendations. If Congress did not act soon, its members would risk the loss of their army and thereby the loss of an empire.[28] The committee appears to have been implying that Congress should not wait until the states granted it certain powers, it should take the initiative and assume those powers for the good of all concerned. Washington added his support in a letter dated May 27, by telling Congress how desperate the army had become. He said some troops had mutinied and others threatened to follow unless they were given the six-months back pay which Congress owed them.[29] Yet this appeared impossible, because only the worthless Continental currency was available.

As unrest in the army increased, the Committee at Headquarters became for a time a real center of activity in the colonies in spite of Congress's reluctance to give it power.

Congress did relent a little on June 21, when it adopted several resolutions designed to encourage the states to cooperate with the committee.[30] But it only appeared to do so because Luzerne reminded its members of their assurances in January, when they guaranteed supplies and a sizable army to fight alongside any French forces which came to America. Luzerne pointed out that such a force was on its way. Schuyler, Peabody, and Mathews thus had an excellent opportunity to focus attention on the chaotic military situation, for in mid-July Admiral Chevalier de Ternay arrived with ten French warships and six thousand of France's finest troops under Comte de Rochambeau. The committee told Congress the eyes of Europe generally, and those of all America were intently turned to Congress, and to the operations of their army in the campaign ahead. "We cannot contemplate without horror," it warned, "the Effect of disappointment" if Congress fails to act with vigor.[31]

Congress's lack of effectiveness prompted many Americans to talk of making General Washington a dictator as the only means of saving the colonies from destruction. This gossip took definite form in September, 1780, when John Mathews presented a detailed motion in Congress asking that it confer dictatorial powers on Washington.[32] Congress ignored this proposal, however, because affairs suddenly appeared to take a turn for the better as one state after another sent assurances that large numbers of supplies and troops were rapidly being assembled. Since the improved military situation made the committee's work less important, its members contented themselves with their original task of reforming the military staff department.

The most troublesome had been the Quartermaster Department. Various plans to improve it had been suggested to Congress for months, most notably one drawn up by Thomas Mifflin and Timothy Pickering in March, 1780. Although Congress instructed the committee to pay particular attention to this plan, Schuyler disapproved of it, so the other committee members refused to consider it. Instead they followed Schuyler's lead in working closely with General Nathaniel Greene and General Washington to develop an entirely new proposal. When they completed their own plan in mid-June, Schuyler brought it to Philadelphia to introduce it to Congress, but he was disheartened to see it amended beyond recognition during almost a month of debate.[33] General Greene agreed. "Congress always destroys with the left hand," he complained, "what they begin with the right. People that will not learn Wisdom by suffering and experience cannot be saved."[34]

The question of Quartermaster General Greene's responsibility appeared to be the main point at issue. Since Greene could not agree with Congress on the manner in which the department should be handled, he resigned on July 26, 1780. He did not choose to attempt an experiment of so dangerous a nature where it appeared physically impossible to perform the duties required of him. The Committee at Headquarters sided with General Greene, much to the displeasure of Congress, and thus incurred a reprimand for interfering with congressional authority.[35] By this time, however, Schuyler had left for New York and Peabody had been taken ill, so the burden of answering for the committee fell to John Mathews. In a rather bold letter dated August 6, Mathews defended the committee's stand in a manner which further annoyed his colleagues in Philadelphia.[36] As a result, Congress passed a motion to discharge the committee by a vote of ten to two, with Virginia divided.[37]

The Committee at Headquarters had clearly outlived its usefulness to Congress or it would not have been dropped. Schuyler and the others had done their best, but they could not have succeeded where Congress had already failed. Even so, General Washington was sorry to learn the committee had been dismissed. "I feel myself under the greatest obligations to them," he wrote, "for having done all in their power to accomplish the objects of their appointment."[38]

Schuyler, Mathews, and Peabody had seen the end coming in view of their constant disagreements with Congress, but they were still so displeased with the move that neither Schuyler nor Peabody ever attended another meeting of Congress. John Mathews, on the other hand, did return to Philadelphia to resume his seat and carry on the fight.

Schuyler remained in or around Albany for the rest of the war, but he was by no means inactive. As President of the Board of Commissioners of Indian Affairs he worked hard to keep informed of enemy activities by hiring two men in Canada for this purpose. With the aid of these agents, conferences with the Indians, and an extensive correspondence with individuals living on the frontier, he watched for suspicious enemy movements to the North. This intelligence network soon paid off handsomely, for on October 1, 1780, he told Governor George Clinton he had learned of enemy plans to invade New York over the Lake Champlain route.[39] Ten days later the enemy attacked. Several British units moved against Fort Anne, Fort Edward, Fort George, and Ballston, while a second force struck settlements along the Connecticut Valley. On October 17, a third enemy army almost a thousand strong, ravaged the Scoharie Valley settlements on New York's western frontier. These forays appear to have been part of a large-scale plan to draw attention away from the lower Hudson Valley where British leaders expected to step up activity after Benedict Arnold turned over West Point to them. After achieving limited success, the enemy temporarily withdrew to Canada to regroup for further raids.

The following summer, they renewed their attacks and attempted to kidnap Schuyler himself during a daring move into the heart of Albany. Colonel John McKenstrey had suspected something like this as early as August 5, 1781, and warned Schuyler that a band of marauders planned to intercept him on his way to Saratoga.[40] The British apparently hoped to upset Indian relations and throw a scare into the countryside by seizing Schuyler, so the General remained on constant alert with six soldiers on guard at his home. In spite of these precautions, the enemy almost succeeded. John Meyer, once an officer with Barry St. Leger, led a party of renegades into Albany late in August and surrounded Schuyler's home. The General bolted the door and hurried his family to safety in an upper bedroom where he attempted to attract attention by firing a pistol from the window. By this time, the savages had forced their way into the house and overcome the guards. Suddenly, Mrs. Schuyler realized they had forgotten her baby in a cradle downstairs. She was restrained from leaving, but her daughter Margaret slipped down the darkened stairs to bring the child to safety. Meanwhile, the General attempted to frighten off the intruders by pretending to direct a group of rescuers who were approaching the house. It worked. The raiders fled into the night taking with them three captives and the Schuyler silver.[41] The General immediately issued instructions to the Indians to track down Meyer and his gang, but they could not be found.[42] This incident indicates, however, that Schuyler still exerted a great deal of influence among Indians on the frontier in 1781. Otherwise, he could not have called on them to help find Meyer's raiders. It is also improbable that the enemy would have gone to so much trouble to kidnap him if he had not still been considered a powerful American leader.

Chapter Thirteen

EPILOGUE

After leaving Congress in June, 1780, Schuyler ceased to play an active role in the American Revolution. From then on, he remained at home to observe from the sidelines while attending to his personal affairs. Occasionally, he would give advice and encouragement to his former comrades in arms, especially when New York's frontier was threatened, but on the whole he preferred to remain in the background whenever possible. As the war drew to a close, Schuyler appears to have finally accepted the idea of independence, a rather difficult concession for a man who had been a reluctant rebel from the beginning, and for one who always hoped America would remain within the economic framework of the British Empire. Parliament's misuse of its power of taxation, however, initially forced him to join the opposition in New York's Provincial Assembly in 1768; then his irritation was heightened by the unyielding support given Parliament by the DeLancey majority in the Assembly. This state of affairs eventually drove him to a point where he willingly accepted a seat in the Second Continental Congress and took an active military role in the war.

Most of Schuyler's activities bear out the above statements. As a young officer under Colonel John Bradstreet, Schuyler tried to gain recognition and wealth while serving in the British army during the Seven Years War. After those hostilities, he acquired and enlarged his landholdings in New York to establish himself as an influential landlord and one of the colony's leading entrepreneurs. His flax mill, fishing fleet, and lumber mills attest to this. Once he had accumulated considerable wealth, Schuyler turned to politics in 1768, to extend his influence and thereby protect and enhance his aristocratic and economic position in New York.

Election to the New York Provincial Assembly suddenly placed him in the middle of America's struggle with Britain. Since the legislature was dominated by the ultra-conservative DeLancey faction that supported Parliament without question, Schuyler sided with the Livingston minority, which wanted Parliament to cede its taxing powers to the colonies. Within a short time, he became a leader of this opposition and supported the principles laid down by the First Continental Congress in its attempt to reach a compromise with the mother country.

When the Second Continental Congress convened in Philadelphia in 1775, Schuyler played an active role in spelling out American policies toward Great Britain. Because of his business, political, social, and military background in New York, Congress appointed him a major general to command the Northern Department in spite of considerable opposition from New England. Although he regretted the necessity of having to take up arms, he accepted the post determined not to fight for independence, but to force Parliament to relinquish its power of taxation to the thirteen colonies. Even when many Americans began to speak of independence, as the war progressed, Schuyler still harbored hopes for reconciliation. As a result of this attitude many of his enemies suspected him of Tory sympathies, especially New Englanders whom he had vigorously opposed in the Hampshire Grants boundary controversy.

Reverses on the battlefield, poor health, and Indian negotiations throughout the war made his position untenable and often left him open to abuse and ridicule. In July and August, 1775, for example, he concentrated on building an army to invade Canada, but just as an attack was launched,

illness forced him to return to Fort Ticonderoga. Unfortunately, these efforts had been foredoomed to failure anyway
in view of the multitude of problems he encountered. By
December, 1775, the army had been reduced to a ragged,
almost undisciplined mob in spite of all efforts to send it
support. This made most people overlook his Herculean
effort to put any army in the field before Sir Guy Carleton
could seize the initiative, and they remembered instead his
sicknesses and defeats. Had it not been for Schuyler, however, this same army might well have perished that autumn.
Yet all he could do was postpone Montgomery's and Arnold's fate. After the disaster at Quebec, Schuyler organized
Lake Champlain's defenses and successfully blocked Carleton's attempt to seize Fort Ticonderoga in October, 1776.
Still the military picture did not brighten.

Any notion Schuyler might have had that independence
could work in America was destroyed by his unhappy relations with Congress. Not only did its members misunderstand
the situation in northern New York, they permitted themselves to use it to further their own selfish ambitions at one
another's expense. New Englanders jealously guarded and
sought to extend their influence, so Schuyler became the
object of their scorn and abuse. Defeat, sickness, shortages
of troops, lack of equipment, and inadequate provisions were
all blamed on him, and New England demanded his dismissal. Meanwhile, Fort Ticonderoga had become practically
defenseless (January, 1777).

Because the Northern Department had fallen into such a
critical state, Schuyler believed America had exhausted its
resources and could no longer raise or support an army on
the pretense of fighting for independence. While he agreed
that active French assistance might help, he even thought
this was doubtful. Therefore, he decided to visit the New
York Convention and to promote, if possible, reconciliation
with Great Britain; but the Convention refused to listen to
him. Shortly thereafter, Congress replaced him as com

mander of the Northern Department as New England finally succeeded in putting Horatio Gates in command of the Northern army. Although the New York delegation managed to get Schuyler reinstated several weeks later, it proved to be a costly victory, for many New Yorkers had lost faith in the General, and he lost his bid to be elected the state's first governor. To make matters worse, Ticonderoga fell several weeks later, and Gates returned to the helm in northern New York even though Schuyler was not to blame. In fact, Schuyler's delaying tactics slowed Burgoyne's advance long enough to permit a huge army to gather and defeat the invading British troops.

Schuyler was incensed with Congress by his removal; he also resented its failure to support him while he commanded the Northern Department. These experiences strengthened his conviction that America would never prosper under a legislative body that had proved itself incapable of governing thirteen colonies, and encouraged him to speak of reconciliation with Burgoyne's officers after the battle of Saratoga. Once he had done this, he said little on the subject because of his impending trial for neglect of duty. Such statements might have led to a conviction.

Although the trial proved the allegations against him were groundless, he decided to leave the service and return to civilian life. Friends urged him to return to Congress, but he refused, thinking it a senseless task until more Americans realized independence would not work. Later, he relented for a while and returned to Congress, where he performed a valuable service with the Committee at Headquarters. Yet this, too, ended in a disagreement with Congress and another disappointing experience. As a result, Schuyler returned home to sit out the remainder of the war. It had been a bitter experience. His reputation had suffered because he could never let himself become a patriot fighting for an independent America. Thus he remained true to his principles to the end, and struggled to preserve aristocratic rights and privileges, and an'American economy, within the British Empire.

LIST OF ABBREVIATIONS

The following is a list of most frequently used abbreviations for sources cited in the footnotes:

NYHS	New York Historical Society
NYPL	New York Public Library
Public Record Office, C.O.	British Public Record Office, Colonial Office
Public Record Office, S.P.	British Public Record Office, State Papers

NOTES AND REFERENCES

Chapter One

1. Francis J. Hudleston, *Gentleman Johnny Burgoyne* (Indianapolis, 1927), p. 217.
2. Cuyler Reynolds, ed., *Hudson-Mohawk Genealogical and Family Memoirs* (4 vols., New York, 1911), I, pp. 28 ff. See Edmund Burke O'Callaghan and Berthold Fernow, eds., *Documents Relative to the Colonial History of the State of New York* (15 vols., Albany, 1853-1887), IV, p. 406. Hereafter cited as *Docs. Rel. Col. Hist. N.Y.*
3. Benson J. Lossing, *The Life and Times of Philip Schuyler* (2 vols., New York, 1872), I, pp. 65-66. Hereafter cited as Lossing, *Philip Schuyler.*
4. Anne Grant, *Memoirs of an American Lady* (2 vols., New York, 1901), I, p. 280. Hereafter cited as Anne Grant, *Memoirs.*
5. Lossing, *Philip Schuyler,* I, p. 66.
6. Dorothy Rita Dillon, *The New York Triumvirate* (New York, 1949), p. 95.
7. Anne Grant, *Memoirs,* I, p. 281.
8. Philip Schuyler to James DeLancey, June, 1775, E.B. O'Callaghan, ed., *Calendar of Historical Manuscripts in the Office of the Secretary of State,* Albany, N.Y. (2 parts, Albany, 1865-1866), II, p. 638.
9. Inscription in the Schuyler family Bible, Schuyler Mansion, Albany, New York. Schuyler's date of birth (November 10, 1733) as recorded in the family Bible is based on the old style calendar entry. The new style date would be November 21, 1733. With the proper adjustment, which he would have had to make after 1752, the entry made on his wedding day would be correct.
10. Anne Grant, *Memoirs,* I, p. 281.
11. George W. Schuyler, *Colonial New York: Philip Schuyler and His Family* (2 vols., New York, 1885), II, pp. 259-260. Hereafter cited as Schuyler, *Colonial New York.*
12. E.B. O'Callaghan, *Calendar of New York Colonial Commissions, 1680-1770* (New York, 1929), pp. 47, 50, 71.
13. John Bradstreet to Philip Schuyler, July 7, 1760, Schuyler Papers, NYPL. See also John Bradstreet to Philip Schuyler, July 6, 1760, Miscellaneous Papers, NYHS.
14. Don R. Gerlach, *Philip Schuyler and the American Revolution in New York, 1733-1777* (Lincoln, 1964), pp. 30-31. Hereafter cited as Gerlach, *Schuyler.*

15. "Invoice of Sundries sent from London to Col. Bradstreet," Schuyler Papers, NYPL. See also Anna K. Cunningham, *Schuyler Mansion a Critical Catalogue of the Furnishings & Decorations,* (Albany, 1955), pp. 6-8.
16. "Certified Copies of Land Grants," and a "List of Divisions of the Saratoga Patent, Jan. 3, 1763," Schuyler Papers, NYPL. See also Schuyler, *Colonial New York,* I, p. 203, and II, pp. 150, 242, 257.
17. John Bradstreet to Philip Schuyler, Nov. 17, 1768, Schuyler Papers, NYPL.
18. Testimony of Lt. Gen. John Burgoyne to the House of Commons, May 26, 1778, *The Parliamentary Register; or, History of the Proceedings and Debates of the House of Commons: Series One,* VIII, p. 311.
19. *Ibid.*
20. Lewis A. Leonard, *Life of Charles Carroll of Carrollton* (New York 1918), pp. 282, 284.
21. William Johnson to Philip Schuyler, Feb. 29, 1768, Schuyler Papers, NYPL.
22. Gerlach, *Schuyler,* p. 173.
23. See George Dangerfield, *Chancellor Robert R. Livingston of New York, 1746-1813* (New York, 1960), p. 41.
24. Gerlach, *Schuyler,* p. 170.
25. *Ibid.,* p. 171.
26. Lossing, *Philip Schuyler,* I, p. 250.
27. *Ibid.,* p. 246.
28. Philip Schuyler to Charles Gould (copies), Oct. 2, 1774, Schuyler Papers, NYPL.
29. Gerlach, *Schuyler,* p. 248.
30. *Ibid.,* p. 250.
31. Bayard Tuckerman, *Life of General Philip Schuyler, 1733-1804* (New York, 1903), pp. 83-84.
32. R.M. Keith to (?) Chamier, April 13, 1775, British Museum, Add. Mss. 35509, Hardwick Papers, Transcripts, Library of Congress.
33. *Journals of the Provincial Congress, Provincial Convention, Committee of Safety and Council of Safety of the State of New York, 1775-1776-1777* (2 vols., Albany, 1842), I, p. 1. Hereafter cited as *Journals of the Provincial Congress of New York.*
34. *Ibid.,* I, pp. 4-5.

Chapter Two

1. Edmund Burnett, *Letters of Members of the Continental Congress* (8 vols., Washington, D.C., 1921-36), I, ivii. Hereafter cited as Burnett, *Letters of Cont. Cong.*
2. *Ibid.,* p. 90 n.
3. Worthington C. Ford, et al., eds., *The Journals of the Continental Congress, 1774-1789* (34 vols., Washington, 1904-1937), II, p. 52. Hereafter cited as *Journ. of Cont. Cong.*
4. *Ibid.*
5. *Ibid.,* pp. 55-56.
6. Benedict Arnold to the Massachusetts Committee of Safety, May 14, 1775, Peter Force, ed., *American Archives,* Fourth Series (6 vols., Wash-

ington, 1837-1846), II, pp. 584-585. Hereafter cited as 4 *Amer. Arch.*

7. Benedict Arnold reported that 400 British regulars had arrived at St. Johns on May 19, 1775, and they were preparing to cross the lake. He said the enemy also intended to use Indians in their plan to control the lakes. See Benedict Arnold to the Continental Congress, May 23, 1775, *Journ. of Cont. Cong.*, II, pp. 73-74.

8. Silas Deane to Mrs. Silas Deane, June 18, 1775, *Collections* of the New-York Historical Society (38 vols., New York, 1886), I, p. 61. Schuyler and Deane also secretly plotted to seize a vessel in New York Harbor, probably the man-of-war *Asia*. When the British became suspicious, the plan was dropped. See Philip Schuyler to Silas Deane, July 3, 1775, J. Hammond Trumbull, ed., *Collections* of the Connecticut Historical Society (Hartford, 1870), II, pp. 251-252.

9. *Journ. of Cont. Cong.*, II, pp. 55-56.

10. *Ibid.*, p. 64. See also Benedict Arnold to the Continental Congress, May 29, 1775, 4 *Amer. Arch.*, II, pp. 734-735; Benedict Arnold to the Massachusetts Committee of Safety, May 29, 1775, 4 *Amer. Arch.*, II, p. 735; Ethan Allen to the Continental Congress, May 29, 1775, 4 *Amer. Arch.*, II, p. 733.

11. *Journ. of Cont. Cong.*, II, p. 67. Other members of the committee included merchant Thomas Mifflin; lawyer Silas Deane; Samuel Adams; and Lewis Morris, one of New York's large landowners. Schuyler also served on a committee to find ways of introducing the manufacture of saltpetre into the colonies.

12. Eliphalet Dyer to Jonathan Trumbull, Sr., June 16, 1775, Burnett, *Letters of Cont. Cong.*, I, p. 127.

13. Joseph Warren to the Continental Congress, May 3, 1776, *Journ. of Cont. Cong.*, II, pp. 24-25.

14. *Ibid.*, p. 25.

15. *Ibid.*, p. 89.

16. *Ibid.*, p. 80.

17. *Ibid.*, p. 90. The committee modeled the Articles of War for the Continental Army after the British Mutiny Act, and Congress adopted its recommendation on June 30, 1775, Hugh Hastings, comp., *Public Papers of George Clinton* (10 vols. Albany, 1899-1914), I, p. 103.

18. Lyman H. Butterfield, ed., *The Adams Papers* (4 vols., Cambridge, 1961), 1st. Series, III, p. 321 ff.

19. John Adams to James Warren, June 20, 1775, Warren-Adams Papers, Mass. Historical Society. "Nothing has given me more Torment," wrote Adams, "than the scuffle we have had in appointing the General Officers ...there were prejudice enough among the weak and fears enough among the timid as well as other obstacles from the cunning; but the great Necessity for officers of skill and experience, prevailed."

20. The New York Delegates to the New York Provincial Congress, June 3, 1775, Burnett, *Letters of Cont. Cong.*, I, pp. 110-111.

21. Eliphalet Dyer to Jonathan Trumbull, June 16, 1775, Burnett, *Letters of Cont. Cong.*, I, p. 127. He said New York's cautious men were saving "for themselves and the Province a safe retreat if possible."

22. Eliphalet Dyer to Joseph Trumbull, June 20, 1775, Joseph Trumbull Collection, Connecticut State Library. See also Richard Montgomery to Robert R. Livingston, June 3, 1775, Robert R. Livingston Papers, NYHS. Montgomery appears to have had doubts about Schuyler. "His

consequence in the province makes him a fit subject for an important trust," he wrote, "but has he strong nerves?"

23. George Washington to the President of Congress, June 24, 25, 1775, John C. Fitzpatrick, ed., *The Writings of George Washington* (39 vols. Washington, D.C., 1931-44), III, pp. 301-302. Hereafter cited as Fitzpatrick, *Writings of Washington.*

24. Philip Schuyler to Peter Van Brugh Livingston, June 24, 1775, *Journals of the Provincial Congress of New York*, II, pp. 10-11.

25. I.N. Phelps Stokes, *The Iconography of Manhattan Island: 1498-1909* (6 vols., New York, 1922), I, pp. 894-895.

26. John Cruger to Peter Van Schaak, June 26, 1775, Misc. John Cruger Papers, NYHS.

27. *Ibid.*

28. *Ibid.*

29. Fitzpatrick, *Writings of Washington*, III, pp. 301-302.

30. *Ibid.*, pp. 302-304.

31. Philip Schuyler to David Wooster, June 28, 1775, Schuyler Papers, NYPL. See also David Wooster's General Orders, June 30, 1775, Schuyler Orderbook, Henry Huntington Library. General Orders for Battery Guard, June 30, 1775, Schuyler. Orderbook, Henry Huntington Library.

32. Philip Schuyler to the Continental Congress, June 28, 1775, 4 *Amer. Arch.*, II, pp. 1123-1124.

33. Philip Schuyler to William (?) Douglas, June 30, 1775; Philip Schuyler to Benjamin Hinman, June 28, 1775, Schuyler Orderbook, Henry Huntington Library.

34. Philip Schuyler to the Continental Congress, June 30, 1775, 4 *Amer. Arch.*, II, pp. 1138-1139. Philip Schuyler to Walter Livingston, June 30, 1775, Schuyler Orderbook, Henry Huntington Library.

35. John Hancock to Philip Schuyler, June 28, 1775, Peter Force Papers, Library of Congress. Hereafter cited as Force Transcripts, Library of Congress.

Chapter Three

1. A General monthly Return of the Army of the Associated Colonies in the Colony of New York, under the command of Major-General Philip Schuyler, July 1, 1775, 4 *Amer. Arch.*, II, p. 1667.

2. Jonathan Trumbull, Jr. to Joseph Trumbull, July 17, 1775, Joseph Trumbull Collection, Conn. State Library. See also Affidavit of John MacPherson, Aug. 2, 1775, Papers of the Continental Congress, National Archives.

3. Philip Schuyler to John Hancock, July 2, 1775, Schuyler Papers, NYPL.

4. Philip Schuyler to John Hancock, July 3, 1775, Schuyler Papers, NYPL. See also Philip Schuyler to George Washington, July 15, 1775, 4 *Amer. Arch.*, II, p. 1668.

5. Philip Schuyler to George Washington, July, 1775, Schuyler Papers, NYPL.

6. Philip Schuyler to John Brown, July 23, 1775, Schuyler Orderbook, Henry Huntington Library; Philip Schuyler to James Smith, July 31, 1775, Schuyler Orderbook, Henry Huntington Library.

7. George Washington to Philip Schuyler, June 25, 1775, Fitzpatrick, *Writings of Washington*, III, p. 303.

8. John Brown to Jonathan Trumbull, Sr., Aug. 14, 1775, 4 *Amer. Arch.,* III, p. 136. See also Eliphalet Dyer to Joseph Trumbull, Aug. 17, 1775, Joseph Trumbull Collection, Conn. State Library.

9. Philip Schuyler to John Hancock, July 15, 1775, Schuyler Papers, NYPL.

10. *Ibid.*

11. *Journ. of Cont. Cong.,* II, pp. 175-183.

12. William H.W. Sabine, Ed., *Historical Memoirs of William Smith: 1763-1778* (2 vols., New York, 1956), I, p. 232. Hereafter cited as Sabine, *Memoirs of William Smith.*

13. General Orders, July 7, 1775, Schuyler Orderbook, Henry Huntington Library.

14. Resolved, Aug. 1, 1775, *Journ. of Cont. Cong.,* II, p. 237. See also James Duane to Philip Schuyler, Aug. 4, 1775, Schuyler Papers, NYPL.

15. Benjamin Franklin to Philip Schuyler, Aug. 8, 1775, Jacob Bigelow Papers, Mass. Hist. Soc.

16. Nathaniel Hazard to Joseph Trumbull, July 5, 1775, Joseph Trumbull Collection, Conn. Hist. Soc.

17. Resolved, July 17, 1775, *Journ. of Cont. Cong.,* II, p. 186.

18. Nathaniel Hazard to Joseph Trumbull, July 5, 1775, Joseph Trumbull Collection, Conn. Hist. Soc.

19. Philip Schuyler to Morgan Lewis, Nov. 9, 1776, Schuyler Papers, NYPL.

20. Philip Schuyler to the Continental Congress, July 21, 1775, Schuyler Papers, NYPL.

21. Philip Schuyler to George Washington, July 18, 1775, Schuyler Papers, NYPL.

22. Philip Schuyler to Jonathan Trumbull, Sr., July 21, 1775, Schuyler Papers, NYPL.

23. Clarence E. Bennett, *Advance and Retreat to Saratoga in the Revolution* (Schenectady, 1927), pp. 15-16.

24. Jonathan Trumbull, Jr. to Joseph Trumbull, Aug. 9, 1775, Joseph Trumbull Collection, Conn. State Library.

25. Henry B. Carrington, *Battles of The American Revolution: 1775-1781* (New York, 1876), p. 139.

26. Jonathan Trumbull, Jr. to Joseph Trumbull, July 17, 1775, Joseph Trumbull Collection, Conn. State Library.

27. *Ibid.* See also Jonathan Trumbull, Sr. to Philip Schuyler, July 17, 1775, 4 *Amer. Arch.,* II, pp. 1676-1677.

28. Philip Schuyler to Jonathan Trumbull, Sr., Aug. 3, 1775, 4 *Amer. Arch.,* III, p. 17.

29. Affidavit of John Shatforth, Aug. 2, 1775, Papers of the Continental Congress, National Archives.

30. Philip Schuyler to George Washington, July 31, 1775, Schuyler Papers, NYPL.

31. *Ibid.*

32. *Ibid.*

33. Richard Montgomery to Robert R. Livingston, Aug. 6, 1775, Robert R. Livingston Papers, NYPL.

34. *Ibid.*

35. Benjamin Trumbull's Journal of the Expedition Against Canada: 1775, Fort Ticonderoga Library.

36. Philip Schuyler to George Washington, Aug. 6, 1775, 4 *Amer. Arch.,* III, pp. 50-51. See also Philip Schuyler to the Continental Congress

Aug. 6, 1775, Papers of the Continental Congress, National Archives.

37. Samuel Chase to Philip Schuyler, Aug. 10, 1775, Schuyler Papers, NYPL.

38. George Washington to Philip Schuyler, Aug. 20, 1775, Schuyler Papers, NYPL.

39. Philip Schuyler to the Continental Congress, July 26, 1775, Papers of the Continental Congress, National Archives.

40. Philip Schuyler to Benjamin Franklin, Aug. 23, 1775, 4 *Amer. Arch.*, III, pp. 242-243. See also Philip Schuyler to the Continental Congress, Aug. 6, 1775, Papers of the Continental Congress, National Archives; An Estimate of Military Stores, Provisions, etc. To Be Sent to Albany, July 3, 1775, 4 *Amer. Arch.*, II, pp. 1536-1537.

41. Richard Montgomery to Philip Schuyler, Aug. 25, 1775, Schuyler Papers, NYPL.

42. John Brown to Richard Montgomery, Aug. 23, 1775, 4 *Amer. Arch.*, III, p. 468.

43. James Livingston to Philip Schuyler, Aug. 23, 1775, Schuyler Papers, NYPL.

44. Philip Schuyler to George Washington, Aug. 27, 1775, Schuyler Papers, NYPL.

45. A Hearing Held at Ticonderoga, Aug. 25, 1775, 4 *Amer. Arch.*, III, pp. 670-671. A soldier named Peter Griffin said he saw two vessels fifty to sixty feet long at St. Johns "planked up to the wales, and pitched black...." Griffin also stated that the inhabitants along the lake were impatient to have the Americans arrive. Furthermore these people said they would supply the army with greens and sauce.

46. Philip Schuyler to George Washington, Aug. 27, 1775, Schuyler Papers, NYPL. Schuyler told Washington: "I learn with pleasure that he (Montgomery) has since the Receipt of Griffin's Information, ordered the Cannon to be embarked and he will probably be off from Ticonderoga so soon, that I shall only be able to join him at Crown Point, such being my Intentions and from the Ideas I had formed of the Necessity of penetrating into Canada without Delay."

47. *Ibid.*

Chapter Four

1. Distribution of His Majesty's Forces in North America on 19 July 1775, P.R.O., W.O., 1. 11., pp. 143-144, Transcripts, Library of Congress. Two companies from the Royal Regiment of Artillery were stationed in Canada, one at Montreal and the other on the lakes. There were two companies of the 65th Regiment: one at Halifax, Nova Scotia, and one at St. Johns. Ten companies from the 7th Foot Regiment were at Quebec, and four companies of the 8th Foot at Niagara, three at Detroit, two at Mackinac, and one at Oswegatchie. Nine companies of the 26th Foot Regiment were stationed at Montreal, Three Rivers, Chambly, and St. Johns. One company from this regiment had been captured at Fort Ticonderoga by Ethan Allen.

2. *Ibid.*

3. *Ibid.*

4. Précis of Operations on the Canadian Frontier, S.P., America and the West Indies, Vol. 269, Transcripts, Library of Congress.

5. John McPherson's Notes Before Quebec 1775, Misc. Richard Montgomery Papers, NYHS.

6. Précis of Operations on the Canadian Frontier, S.P., America and the West Indies, Vol. 269, Transcripts, Library of Congress. On July 26, 1775, a group of 1,664 Canadian Indians met at Montreal to pledge themselves to keeping open and protecting the water communications between New York and Canada.

7. *Ibid.*

8. *Ibid.*

9. *Ibid.*

10. Eliphalet Dyer to Joseph Trumbull, Aug. 17, 1775, Joseph Trumbull Collection, Conn. State Library.

11. Precis of Operations on the Canadian Frontier, S.P., America and the West Indies, Vol. 269, Transcripts, Library of Congress.

12. Richard Montgomery to Philip Schuyler, Aug. 2, 1775, Schuyler Papers, NYPL. Schuyler had long suffered from gout, so much so that his physician Samuel Stringer had questioned Schuyler's ability to stand the rigors of a campaign when he learned of Schuyler's appointment as a major general.

13. A Proclamation to the Inhabitants of Canada, Sept. 5, 1775, Schuyler Papers, NYPL.

14. Simon Metcalf's Book, Fort Ticonderoga Library.

15. Benjamin Trumbull, "A Concise Journal or Minutes of the Principle Movements Towards St. John...in 1775," *Collections* of the Connecticut Historical Society (Hartford, 1899), VII, pp. 140 ff.

16. Philip Schuyler to John Hancock, Sept. 8, 1775, Schuyler Papers, NYPL.

17. *Ibid.*

18. *Ibid.*

19. *Ibid.*

20. "An account of The Manoeuvres and Movements of the Army in Canada, Under General Montgomery," Sept 10, 1775, George Washington Papers, Library of Congress.

21. Catherine V.R. Bonney, *A Legacy of Historical Gleanings* (2 vols., Albany, 1875), I, p. 44.

22. Philip Schuyler to the Continental Congress, Sept. 19, 1775, Schuyler Papers, NYPL.

23. Extract of a Letter To a Gentleman in New-York from an Officer at Isle-Aux-Nois, Sept. 17, 1775, 4 *Amer. Arch.,* III, p. 726. Thirty British regulars died in this encounter.

24. Philip Schuyler to James Livingston, John Brown, and Ethan Aller, Sept. 9, 1775, Schuyler Papers, NYPL.

25. *Ibid.*

26. Philip Schuyler to the Continental Congress, Sept. 19, 1775, Schuyler Papers, NYPL.

27. Philip Schuyler to John Hancock, Sept. 8, 1775, Schuyler Papers, NYPL.

28. Philip Schuyler to George Washington, Sept. 20, 1775, George Washington Papers, Library of Congress.

29. Jonathan Trumbull, Sr. to Philip Schuyler, Sept. 29, 1775, 4 *Amer. Arch.,* III, pp. 841-842. Because he was anxious to continue at Ticonderoga, Schuyler asked Dr. Samuel Stringer to come to see him. "I am very far from being as well as when you left...a continual lax and insolent Sweating Every night with a troublesome cough weaken and seduce me." Philip Schuyler to Samuel Stringer, Oct. 20, 1775, C.P. Greenough Papers, Massachusetts Historical Society.

30. Philip Schuyler to George Washington, Sept. 20, 1775, Schuyler Papers, NYPL.
31. Richard Montgomery to Philip Schuyler, Sept. 24, 1775, Schuyler Papers, NYPL.
32. Philip Schuyler to Walter Livingston, Sept. 26, 1775, Schuyler Orderbook, Henry Huntington Library.
33. General Orders, Sept. 25, 1775, Schuyler Orderbook, Henry Huntington Library. An officer was ordered to accompany each scow, and either a sergeant or corporal in each batteau.
34. Philip Schuyler to Walter Livingston, Sept. 26, 1775, Schuyler Orderbook, Henry Huntington Library.
35. Philip Schuyler to the Continental Congress, Sept. 29, 1775, Papers of the Continental Congress, National Archives.
36. Philip Schuyler to John Hancock, Oct. 18, 1775, Schuyler Papers, NYPL.
37. Philip Schuyler to John Hancock, Oct. 21, 1775, Schuyler Papers, NYPL.
38. James Lockwood to Silas Deane, Oct. 16, 1775, The Deane Papers: 1774-1777, *Collections* of the New-York Historical Society (New York, 1886), I, p. 83.
39. Francis V. Greene, *The Revolutionary War and the Military Policy of the United States* (New York, 1911), p. 23.
40. *Ibid.* See also George Washington to Philip Schuyler, Oct. 4, 1775, Schuyler Papers, NYPL. An intercepted letter indicated Quebec would surrender without a shot if the Americans attacked before Governor Carleton returned.
41. Philip Schuyler to Walter Livingston, Sept. 26, 1775, Schuyler Orderbook, Henry Huntington Library.
42. Report of the Committee Appointed to confer with General Philip Schuyler, Dec. 23, 1775, 4 *Amer. Arch.*, IV, pp. 442-446.
43. Philip Schuyler to George Washington, Nov. 22, 1775, Schuyler Papers, NYPL.
44. Richard Montgomery to Philip Schuyler, Dec. 5, 1775, 4 *Amer. Arch.*, IV, pp. 188-190. See also James Livingston to Timothy Bedel, Oct. 5, 1775, Timothy Bedel Papers, New Hampshire His. Soc. Livingston said: "The Canadians are far from being content, and unless they can be supplied with provisions they will drop off by degrees...."
45. Richard Montgomery to Philip Schuyler, Dec. 18, 1775, Schuyler Papers, NYPL.
46. Philip Schuyler to John Hancock, Nov. 20, 1775, 4 *Amer. Arch.*, III, p. 1617. See also Richard Montgomery to Philip Schuyler, Dec. 16, 1775, Schuyler Papers, NYPL.
47. Richard Montgomery to Philip Schuyler, Dec. 5, 1775, 4 *Amer. Arch.*, IV, pp. 188-190.
48. *Journ. of Cont. Cong.*, IV, pp. 70-71.
49. Jonathan Trumbull to Joseph Trumbull, Jan. 24, 1776, Joseph Trumbull Collection, Conn. State Library.
50. The Tryon County Committee to Philip Schuyler, Jan. 11, 1776, Miscellaneous Mss., MYHS.
51. Affidavit of Jonathan French, Jan. 11, 1776, 4 *Amer. Arch.*, pp. 667-668.
52. Philip Schuyler to John Hancock, Jan. 23, 1775, 4 *Amer. Arch.*, pp. 818-829.
53. *Ibid.*
54. *Ibid.*
55. *Ibid.*

56. Philip Schuyler to Robert Treat Paine, Jan. 29, 1776, Robert Treat Paine Papers, Massachusetts Historical Society.

Chapter Five

1. James Van Rensselaer to Philip Schuyler, Feb. 22, 1776, Lossing, *Philip Schuyler*, II, p. 29.
2. Clarence E. Bennett, *Advance and Retreat to Saratoga*, p. 52.
3. Willard M. Wallace, *Appeal to Arms* (New York, 1951), p. 84. Hereafter cited as Wallace, *Appeal to Arms*.
4. David Wooster to Roger Sherman, Feb. 11, 1776, Misc. Papers, Mass. Hist. Society.
5. Philip Schuyler to John Hancock, Feb. 20, 1776, Schuyler Papers, NYPL.
6. David Wooster to Roger Sherman, Feb. 11, 1776, Misc. Papers, Mass. Hist. Society.
7. See Fitzpatrick, *Writings of Washington*, IV, p. 165 n.
8. John Hancock to Philip Schuyler, Feb. 20, 1776, Schuyler Papers, NYPL.
9. On February 17, 1776, Congress resolved "That Major General [Charles] Lee be directed immediately to repair to Canada and take command of the Army...;" "That Major General Schuyler be directed to repair, as soon as his health would permit, to New York to take command of the forces...," there. Congress soon reversed itself, however, and sent Major General John Thomas to Canada, kept Schuyler in Albany, and placed Lee in command of the Southern Department, *Journ. of Cont. Cong.*, IV, pp. 157, 175, 180-181, 186-187.
10. Precis of Operations on the Canadian Frontier, S.P., American West Indies, vol. 269, Transcripts, NYPL.
11. *Ibid.*
12. *Ibid.*
13. Resolved, Feb. 15, 1776, *Journ. of Cont. Cong.*, IV, pp. 151-152.
14. Benjamin Franklin, Samuel Chase, and Charles Carroll to John Hancock, May 8, 1776, 4 *Amer. Arch.*, V, p. 1237.
15. Resolved, May 22, 1776, *Journ. of Cont. Cong.*, IV, pp. 375-377.
16. Wallace, *Appeal to Arms*, p. 85.
17. Christopher Ward, edited by John Richard Alden, *The War of the Revolution* (2 vols., New York, 1952), I, p. 197. Hereafter cited as Ward, *War of the Revolution*.
18. *Ibid.*
19. Wallace, *Appeal to Arms*. p. 85.
20. John Sullivan to George Washington, June 19, 1776, 4 *Amer. Arch.*, VI, pp. 1103-1104. See also Diary of Maj[or] Henry Blake, New Hampshire Historical Society.
21. Resolved, June 17, 1776, *Journ. of Cont. Cong.*, V, p. 448.
22. Memorandum: A Conversation With General Gates, June 30, 1776, Philip Schuyler Papers, Henry Huntington Library. See also Lossing, *Philip Schuyler*, II, pp. 94-95.
23. Resolved, July 8, 1776, *Journ. of Cont. Cong.*, V, p. 526.
24. Elbridge Gerry to Horatio Gates, Aug. 24, 1776, 5 *Amer. Arch.*, I, pp. 1146-1147.
25. Minutes of a Council of War, July 7, 1776, 5 *Amer. Arch.*, I, p. 233.
26. *Ibid.*
27. Lossing, *Philip Schuyler*, II, pp. 117-119.

28. Horatio Gates to George Washington, July 29, 1776, 5 *Amer. Arch.*, I, p. 650.
29. Samuel Adams to Joseph Trumbull, Aug. 3, 1776, Samuel Adams Papers, NYPL. See also Joseph Trumbull to Samuel Adams, Aug. 12, 1776, Samuel Adams Papers, NYPL. John Hancock to George Washington, June 21, 1776, George Washington Papers, Library of Congress.
30. Robert Morris to Horatio Gates, July 25, 1776, 5 *Amer. Arch.*, I, p. 572.
31. Ward, *War of the Revolution*, I, pp. 386 ff.
32. *Ibid.*
33. Horatio Gates to John Hancock, July 29, 1776, 5 *Amer. Arch.*, I, p. 649.
34. Arthur St. Clair to James Wilson, July 22, 1776, Simon Gratz Collection, Historical Society of Philadelphia.
35. Memorandum of An Agreement Made By General Schuyler for Carpenters, Mar. 1, 1776, New York Genealogical and Biographical Society.
36. See 5 *Amer. Arch.*, I, pp. 303, 474, 563, 630, 649, 682.
37. See 5 *Amer. Arch.*, I, pp. 350, 399-400, 620, 623-624, 932.
38. General Return of...the Northern Department..., Aug. 24, 1776, 5 *Amer. Arch.*, I, pp. 1199-1200.
39. Philip Schuyler to Horatio Gates, Sept. 7, 1776, Schuyler Papers, NYPL.
40. Lossing, *Philip Schuyler*, II, pp. 107-113.
41. Philip Schuyler to George Washington, Aug. 6, 1776, Schuyler Papers, NYPL. Philip Schuyler to John Hancock, Aug. 7, 1776, Schuyler Papers, NYPL.
42. Philip Schuyler to John Hancock, Sept. 9, 1776, Schuyler Papers, NYPL.
43. Resolved, Oct. 2, 1776, *Journ. of Cont. Cong.*, V, p. 841.
44. Lossing, *Philip Schuyler*, II, pp. 127-128.
45. Ward, *War of the Revolution*, I, p. 393.
46. *Ibid.*, pp. 395 ff.
47. *Ibid.*
48. Benedict Arnold to George Washington, Nov. 6, 1776, *The Bulletin of the Fort Ticonderoga Museum*, V (No. 1, Jan., 1939), p. 26.
49. Horatio Gates to Philip Schuyler, Nov. 8, 1776, *The Bulletin of the Fort Ticonderoga Museum*, V (No. 1, Jan., 1939), p. 28.

Chapter Six

1. Philip Schuyler to Richard Stockton and George Clymer, Nov. 6, 1776, 5 *Amer. Arch.*, III, pp. 1585-1587.
2. Philip Schuyler to Jonathan Trumbull, Sr., Dec. 3, 1776, 5 *Amer. Arch.*, III, p. 1063. See also Jonathan Trumbull, Sr. to Philip Schuyler, Dec. 12, 1776, 5 *Amer. Arch.*, III, p. 1194.
3. Philip Schuyler to Pierre Van Cortlandt, Nov. 11, 1776, Schuyler Papers, NYPL.
4. Horatio Gates to Caleb Hide, Nov. 9, 1776, *The Bulletin of the Fort Ticonderoga Museum*, V (No. 1, Jan. 1939).
5. Col. William Maxwell, of the Second New Jersey Regiment: Col. William Winds, of the First New Jersey Regiment: Col. John Philip de Haas, of the Second Pennsylvania Regiment; Philip Schuyler to Robert H. Harrison, Nov. 13, 1776, 5 *Amer. Arch.*, III, p. 665; State of Troops at Ticonderoga, Nov. 17, 1776, *The Bulletin of the Fort Ticonderoga Museum*, V (No. 1, Jan., 1939), pp. 29-30; Horatio Gates to

John Hancock, Nov. 27, 1776, *The Bulletin of the Fort Ticonderoga Museum*, V (No. 1, Jan., 1939), pp. 31-32.

6. When reports arrived of Crown Point's evacuation, Capt. Richard Varick suggested that militia units be discharged to save their credit. Richard Varick to Philip Schuyler, Nov. 6, 1776, Schuyler Papers, NYPL: State of Troops at Ticonderoga, Nov. 17, 1776, *The Bulletin of the Fort Ticonderoga Museum*, V (No. 1, Jan., 1939), pp. 31-32.

7. Philip Schuyler to Horatio Gates, Nov. 26, 1776, Horatio Gates Papers, NYHS.

8. Philip Schuyler to Jonathan Trumbull, Jr., Nov. 26, 1776, Jonathan Trumbull, Jr. Papers, Conn. Historical Society.

9. Philip Schuyler to Pierre Van Cortlandt, Dec. 11, 1776, *The Bulletin of the Fort Ticonderoga Museum*, VI (No. 4, July, 1942), p. 150.

10. Philip Schuyler, Horatio Gates, Benedict Arnold, and James Bricket, at a Council of War, Saratoga, Nov. 21, 1776, 5 *Amer. Arch.*, III, p. 797; Philip Schuyler to John Hancock, Nov. 21, 1776, 5 *Amer. Arch.*, III, pp. 796-797.

11. Josiah Bartlett to Anonymous, Nov. 25, 1776, *Letters by Josiah Bartlett, William Whipple and Others* (Philadelphia, 1889), p. 58.

12. *Ibid.*

13. Anthony Wayne to Horatio Gates, Dec. 1, 1776, *The Bulletin of the Fort Ticonderoga Museum*, VI (No. 4, July, 1942), p. 149.

14. Wood also said that: "One-third at least of the poor wretches is now barefoot, and in this condition obliged to do duty. This is shocking to humanity. It cannot be viewed in any milder light than black murder." Joseph Wood to Thomas Warton, Jr., Dec. 4, 1776, *The Bulletin of the Fort Ticonderoga Museum*, V (No. 1, Jan., 1939), p. 36.

15. "Journal of Lieutenant Ebenezer Elmer," New Jersey Historical Society, *Proceedings*, XIII (Newark, 1848), p. 93.

16. *Ibid.*, p. 92.

17. Cornelius Wynkoop to Horatio Gates, Nov. 6, 1776, *The Bulletin of the Fort Ticonderoga Museum*, V (No. 1, Jan., 1939), p. 25.

18. The Committee in Philadelphia to John Hancock, Jan. 2, 1777, Papers of the Continental Congress, National Archives.

19. David Rittenhouse to the President of Congress, Dec. 22, 1776, *The Bulletin of the Fort Ticonderoga Museum*, V (No. 1, Jan., 1939), p. 36.

20. Robert R. Livingston believed this "ill judged defeat...sacrificed the flower" of the American army and "encouraged the enemy who would otherwise have had very little reason to be satisfied with the issue of the campaign..." Robert R. Livingston to Philip Schuyler, Dec., 1776, Robert R. Livingston Papers, NYPL.

21. William H. Smith, ed., *The Life and Public Service of Arthur St. Clair* (2 vols., Cincinnati, 1882), I, pp. 378-379. Hereafter cited as Smith, *Arthur St. Clair*.

22. Robert H. Harrison to Philip Schuyler, Nov. 26, 1776, 5 *Amer. Arch.*, III, pp. 854-855.

23. Horatio Gates to John Hancock, Nov. 27, 1776, 5 *Amer. Arch.*, III, pp. 874-875.

24. Four New Hampshire regiments — Stark's, Poor's, Reed's, and Bedel's, and four Massachusetts regiments — Peterson's, Bond's, Porter's, and Greaton's, 2,441 troops in all, were dispatched by Schuyler. Philip

Schuyler to Horatio Gates, Nov. 26, 1776, 5 *Amer. Arch.*, III, pp. 861-862.

25. Philip Schuyler to Pierre Van Cortlandt, Dec. 11, 1776, Schuyler Papers, NYPL.

26. Philip Schuyler to Jonathan Trumbull, Sr., Dec. 29, 1776, *The Bulletin of the Fort Ticonderoga Museum*, VI (No. 4, July, 1942), p. 151.

27. Report of the Committee Sent to the Northern Department, Nov. 27, 1776, 5 *Amer. Arch.*, III, pp. 1584-1588.

28. Resolved, Nov. 28, 1776, *Journ. of Cont. Cong.*, IV, pp. 988-991.

29. Resolved, Dec. 7, 1776, *ibid.*, p. 1009.

30. Later he said: "I would repair to Congress, but if I quit this quarter before the garrison of Ticonderoga is relieved, and the accident I dread should happen, the misfortune will be imputed to me." Philip Schuyler to Horatio Gates, Nov. 27, 1776, 5 *Amer. Arch.*, III, p. 879. See also Philip Schuyler to John Hancock, Dec. 10, 1776, Papers of the Continental Congress, National Archives; Philip Schuyler to Robert R. Livingston, Dec. 20, 1776, Robert R. Livingston Papers, NYPL.

31. Smith, *Arthur St. Clair*, I, p. 62.

32. John Lansing, Jr. to Philip Schuyler, Jan. 7, 1777, Schuyler Papers, NYPL.

33. Report of the Committee Sent to the Northern Department, Nov. 27, 1776. 5 *Amer. Arch.*, III, pp. 1584-1588.

34. Philip Schuyler to Pierre Van Cortlandt, Dec. 11, 1776, Schuyler Papers, NYPL.

35. Philip Schuyler to John Hancock, Dec. 30, 1776, Papers of the Continental Congress, National Archives. These troop dispositions were first reported on Nov. 25, 1776, but American officers expected a further withdrawal when the weather became more inclement. Anthony Wayne to James (?) Hurd, Nov. 25, 1776, *The Bulletin of the Fort Ticonderoga Museum*, VI (No. 4, July, 1942), p. 148.

36. Resolved, Dec. 24, 1776, *Journ. of Cont. Cong.*, IV, p. 1038.

37. Samuel Adams to James Warren, Dec. 25, 1776, Mellen Chamberlain Collection, Boston Public Library.

38. John Lansing, Jr. to Philip Schuyler, Jan. 9, 1777, Schuyler Papers, NYPL.

39. Nathaniel Buel to Philip Schuyler, Jan. 22, 1777, Papers of the Continental Congress, National Archives. See also Samuel Van Vechten to Philip Schuyler, Jan. 25, 1777, Schuyler Papers, NYPL.

40. "Journal of Lieutenant Ebenezer Elmer," New Jersey Historical Society *Proceedings*, XIII (Newark, 1848), p. 54.

41. Anthony Wayne to Philip Schuyler, Jan. 22, 1777, Papers of the Continental Congress, National Archives.

42. "What the Enemy have hitherto not been able to do by force," wrote Schuyler, "...they will be enabled to accomplish by our own infernal Divisions." Philip Schuyler to John Hancock, Jan. 25, 1777, Papers of the Continental Congress, National Archives.

43. Sabine, *Memoirs of William Smith*, p. 62.

44. *Ibid.*, p. 64.

45. *Ibid.*, pp. 63-64, 70.

46. Pierre Van Cortlandt to Philip Schuyler, Feb. 9, 1777, Fort Ticonderoga Museum.

47. Sabine, *Memoirs of William Smith*, p. 73.
48. Philip Schuyler to Nicholas Gilman, Feb. 17, 1777, Schuyler Papers, NYPL.
49. Philip Schuyler to the Continental Congress, Feb. 15, 1777, Schuyler Papers, NYPL.
50. Jonathan Trumbull, Sr. to Philip Schuyler, Dec. 12, 1776, 5 *Amer. Arch.*, III, p. 1194.
51. New York Provincial Congress to the Continental Congress, Jan. 22, 1777, Papers of the Continental Congress, National Archives.
52. James Warren to Samuel Adams, Feb. 2, 1777, Samuel Adams Papers, NYPL.
53. New York Provincial Congress to the Continental Congress, Jan. 22, 1777, Papers of the Continental Congress, National Archives.
54. Jonathan Trumbull, Sr. to Philip Schuyler, Dec. 12, 1776, 5 *Amer. Arch.*, III, p. 1194.
55. Philip Schuyler to John Hancock, Jan. 25, 1777, Papers of the Continental Congress, National Archives. A week later, smallpox again broke out among the eastern troops. Anthony Wayne to Philip Schuyler, Feb. 2, 1777, Papers of the Continental Congress, National Archives.
56. Philip Schuyler to Meshech Weare, Jan. 23, 1777, Pierpont Morgan Library.
57. George Washington to Philip Schuyler, Jan. 27, 1777, Schuyler Papers, NYPL.
58. Philip Schuyler to George Washington, Feb. 15, 1777, Schuyler Papers, NYPL.
59. Anthony Wayne to Philip Schuyler, Feb. 4, 1777, Fort Ticonderoga Museum.
60. Anthony Wayne to Philip Schuyler, Feb. 13, 1777, Papers of the Continental Congress, National Archives.

Chapter Seven

1. Philip Schuyler to the Continental Congress, Jan. 13, 1777, Papers of the Continental Congress, National Archives. Twenty weeks before Burgoyne launched his invasion in June, 1777, Schuyler's agents told him "The Enemy intend[ed] to open the next Campaign by an Attempt to penetrate up Hudson's River, whilst General Carleton will press" upon New York from "The Northward, and cause a Diversion to be made by the way of Oswego and another on the Sea Coast of Massachusetts Bay to draw the Attention of that and the Eastern States."
2. Philip Livingston and James Duane to the New York Convention, May 9, 1777, Burnett, *Letters of Cont. Cong.*, II, pp. 357-358.
3. When John Hancock sent Schuyler the congressional resolves of February 6, 1777, he added that he had "delivered a duplicate" to General Gates. Since Gates no longer commanded troops in the Northern Department, this incident had an ominous ring for Schuyler. John Hancock to Philip Schuyler, Feb. 6, 1777, Schuyler Papers, NYPL.
4. Sabine, *Memoirs of William Smith*, II, pp. 199-201. James Duane told Smith the New York Convention was "high spirited for maintaining the N.Y. Jurisdiction, and a Man under the New England Influence was considered as an Enemy. Our Maxim is Property first and then Liber-

ty." "Aye," replied Smith, "Liberty with nothing else, is of little worth...."

5. Committee of Safety of New York to the Continental Congress, April 2, 1777, Papers of the Continental Congress, National Archives.

6. Philip Schuyler to Jonathan Trumbull, Sr., March 16, 1777, Schuyler Papers, NYPL. During the winter, two men from the Albany area purchased four or five sled loads of rum, sugar, salt, and other commodities in Massachusetts for their own use and that of some neighbors who shared expenses. When they went to get these items, permission was refused until they obtained a permit. This considerably increased the cost of the goods.

7. Edmund D. Burnett, "New York in the Continental Congress," Alexander Flick, ed., *History of New York State* (10 vols., New York, 1933), III, pp. 307 ff. Hereafter cited as Flick, *History of New York.*

8. *Journ. of Cont. Cong.,* V, pp. 808, 822-823. Schuyler became angry when he learned the committee had been directed to confer with Gates at Ticonderoga before it met with him. Congress repeated this insult on March 13, 1777.

9. Philip Schuyler to Jonathan Trumbull, Sr., Dec. 29, 1776, *The Bulletin of the Fort Ticonderoga Museum,* VI (No. 4, July, 1942), p. 151.

10. John Adams to Abigail Adams, Feb. 21, 1777, Burnett, *Letters of Cont. Cong.,* II, p. 269.

11. James Sullivan, ed., *Minutes of the Albany Committee of Correspondence: 1775-1778* (Albany, 1923), I, p. 675. On Feb. 5, 1777, a few days after conferring with General Schuyler the Committee "Resolved That the Deputies of this County in Convention be instructed to use their Influence to have General Schuyler appointed one of the Delegates to represent this State in [the] Continental Congress."

12. Philip Schuyler to Robert R. Livingston, Dec. 20, 1776, Robert R. Livingston Papers, NYPL. Edward Rutledge to John Jay, Nov. 24, 1776, 5 *Amer. Arch.,* III, pp. 825-826.

13. *Ibid.*

14. Philip Schuyler to the Continental Congress, Mar. 8, 1777, Schuyler Papers, NYPL.

15. Lossing, *Philip Schuyler,* II, p. 45.

16. Samuel Adams to John Adams, Jan. 8, 1777, Burnett, *Letters of Cont. Cong.,* II, pp. 209-210.

17. Philip Schuyler to the Continental Congress, Feb. 4-5, 1777, Papers of the Continental Congress, National Archives. The Trumbull letter referred to, was published in the *New-York Mercury.* It said Schuyler had detained a commission for Trumbull.

18. *Journ. of Cont. Cong.,* VII, pp. 180-181. Resolved, Mar. 15, 1777.

19. Samuel White Patterson, *Horatio Gates: Defender of American Liberties* (New York, 1941), p. 118. Hereafter cited as Patterson, *Horatio Gates.*

20. *Journ. of Cont. Cong.* VII, p. 202, Resolved, Mar. 25, 1777.

21. Sabine, *Memoirs of William Smith,* II, p. 136. On May 13, John Trumbull said he found out that John Hancock kept back his appointment and not General Schuyler. Joseph Trumbull said he "applied to Col. Hancock several Times in person and by Writing to know when the Commission was sent — he had not, and will not do it... I am Convinced he [neve]r Sent it, and I fancy he never intended to."

22. Philip Schuyler to Richard Varick, Mar. 30, 1777, Schuyler Papers,

NYPL. Dr. Jonathan Potts had just returned from Philadelphia with this information.

23. *Ibid.*
24. Sabine, *Memoirs of William Smith*, II, p. 137.
25. *Ibid.*, p. 138.
26. *Ibid.*
27. Philip Schuyler to Richard Varick, Mar. 30, 1777, Schuyler Papers, NYPL.
28. Horatio Gates to George Washington, April 19, 1777, Papers of the Continental Congress, National Archives. General Gates arrived in Albany on April 18, 1777. He reported that "One Briga[d]ier Gen[eral], a Col[onel], and several Captains" had been taken into "Custody with about Seventy others. The Influence of Bribery and Fear have had this surprising Effect...." John Pierce, Jr. to Jonathan Trumbull, Jr., Apr. 18, 1777, Force Transcripts, Library of Congress.
29. Patterson, *Horatio Gates*, p. 123 ff. John Pierce, Jr. to Jonathan Trumbull, Jr., April 18, 1777, Force Transcripts, Library of Congress. Horatio Gates to the President of Congress, April 22, 1777, Force Transcripts, Library of Congress.
30. Horatio Gates to the President of Congress, Apr. 2, 1777, Horatio Gates Papers, NYHS.
31. Patterson, *Horatio Gates*, pp. 121 ff. It is worth noting that several of Schuyler's critics accused him of staying too close to Albany in spite of his insistence that it was absolutely necessary to promote the war effort. When Gates arrived, he realized Schuyler had acted wisely in working out of Albany. In fact, affairs there kept Gates so busy he never had a chance to visit Fort Ticonderoga during this tour of duty.
32. Jonathan Trumbull, Sr. to Horatio Gates, Apr. 25, 1777, Horatio Gates Papers, NYHS.
33. Jonathan Trumbull, Sr. to John Hancock, Mar. 3, 1777, Papers of the Continental Congress, National Archives.
34. George F. Scheer and Hugh F. Rankin, *Rebels and Redcoats*, (New York, 1959), p. 289.
35. Horatio Gates to Joseph Trumbull, Apr. 29, 1777, Joseph Trumbull Collection, Conn. State Library. Josiah Bartlett reported great difficulties in raising New Hampshire Regiments in spite of the enormous bounty promised. Of those that had been enlisted, none were over half full. Josiah Bartlett to William Whipple or Matthew Thornton, Mar. 1, 1777, Josiah Bartlett Papers, New Hampshire Historical Society.
36. Philip Schuyler to Richard Varick, Apr. 16, 1777, Lossing, *Philip Schuyler*, II, p. 168.
37. *Ibid.*, p. 169.
38. James Duane to Robert R. Livingston, June 24, 1777, Robert R. Livingston Papers, NYPL.
39. *Ibid.*
40. *Ibid.*
41. Lossing, *Philip Schuyler*, II, p. 168
42. *Ibid.*, pp. 168-169 n.
43. See Schuyler Letterbook, Apr. 10 to May 15, 1777, Schuyler Papers, NYPL. See also *Journ. of Cont. Cong.*, VII, pp. 273 ff.
44. *Ibid.*
45. Philip Livingston, James Duane and William Duer to Abraham Ten

Broeck, Apr. 21, 1777, Burnett, *Letters of Cont. Cong.*, II, p. 337.
46. *Ibid.*
47. James Lovell to Horatio Gates, May 1, 1777, Force Transcripts, Library of Congress.
48. *Journ. of Cont. Cong.*, VII, pp. 279-280. The committee consisted of Matthew Thornton of New Hampshire, James Lovell of Massachusetts, William Ellery of Rhode Island, Oliver Wolcott of Connecticut, William Duer of New York, Jonathan Elmer of New Jersey, George Clymer of Pennsylvania, James Sykes of Delaware, William Smith of Maryland, Mann Page, Jr., of Virginia, Thomas Burke of North Carolina, Thomas Heywood of South Carolina, and Nathan Brownson of Georgia.
49. Philip Schuyler to Richard Varick, April 26, 1777, Schuyler Papers, NYPL.
50. *Ibid.*
51. Philip Schuyler to the Treasury Board, Apr. 27, 1777, Schuyler Papers, NYPL. Philip Livingston and James Duane to the New York Convention, May 9, 1777, Burnett, *Letters of Cont. Cong.*, II, p. 358. The Treasury Board had sent a sharply-worded message to Schuyler in response to his letter of April 11, 1777. They believed statements about the misuse of the money-chest had been directed at them. "If the unfeeling Villains who contrived and assiduously propagated the Report that I detained the Specie designed for Canada were capable of feeling they must be overwhelmed with Shame and Confusion," wrote Schuyler, "and those who lent a willing Ear to such an improbable Tale must come in for a Share of the Reproach." Philip Schuyler to the Continental Congress, Feb. 24, 1777, Papers of the Continental Congress, National Archives.
52. Philip Schuyler to George Washington, April 30, 1777, Schuyler Papers, NYPL.
53. *Journ. of Cont. Cong.*, VII, pp. 326-327.
54. James Lovell to Horatio Gates, May 1, 1777, Force Transcripts, Library of Congress.
55. Philip Livingston and James Duane to the New York Convention, May 9, 1777, Burnett, *Letters of Cont. Cong.*, II, p. 358.
56. *Ibid.*, John Lansing, Jr. to Richard Varick, April 26, 1777, Pierpont Morgan Library.
57. Philip Schuyler's Memorial to the Continental Congress, May 6, 1777, Schuyler Papers, NYPL.
58. *Ibid.*
59. *Ibid.*
60. *Ibid.*
61. *Ibid.*, Joseph Trumbull accused Schuyler of detaining the commission of Deputy Adjutant-General of the Northern Department which was supposed to have been sent to his brother, Colonel John Trumbull. The letter was printed in *The New-York Mercury*, published by Hugh Gaine.
62. Philip Schuyler's Memorial to the Continental Congress, May 6, 1777, Schuyler Papers, NYPL.
63. *Ibid.*
64. *Journ. of Cont. Cong.*, II, p. 336.
65. James Lovell to Horatio Gates, May 22, 1777, Burnett, *Letters of Cont. Cong.*, II, p. 370.
66. *Ibid.*

67. James Lovell to Horatio Gates, May 1, *ibid.*, p. 351. Philip Livingston and James Duane said: "The Revolt in our states cannot be considered as a dangerous and alarming Example.... Every Country is plagued with profligate and ambitious men who in Times like the present may find it [in] their Interest, or be led by their Passions to bring on Revolutions." Philip Livingston and James Duane to the New York Provincial Congress, May 23, 1777, James Duane Papers, NYHS.
68. James Lovell to Horatio Gates, May 1, 1777, Burnett, *Letters of Cont. Cong.*, II, p. 370.
69. James Lovell to Horatio Gates, May 22, 1777, *ibid.* p. 380.
70. *Journ. of Cont. Cong.*, VII, p. 347.
71. *Ibid.*, p. 364. See also Philip Schuyler to George Washington, May 18, 1777, George Washington Papers, Library of Congress.
72. Resolved, May 23, 1777, *Journ. of Cont. Cong.*, VII, p. 376.
73. William Duer to Robert R. Livingston, May 28, 1777, Robert R. Livingston Papers, NYHS. Duer's description is the most complete, but others report the vote as being five to four and two divided. See James Lovell to Horatio Gates, May 22, 1777, Gates Papers, NYHS; Joseph Trumbull to Horatio Gates, May 24, 1777, Gates Papers, NYHS; James Lovell to Oliver Wolcott, June 7, 1777, Oliver Wolcott Papers, Conn. Historical Society.
74. Resolved, May 22, 1777, *Journ. of Cont. Cong.*, VII, p. 375.
75. William Duer to Robert R. Livingston, May 28, 1777, Robert R. Livingston Papers, NYHS.
76. Roger Sherman to Jonathan Trumbull, Sr., May 26, 1777, Force Transcripts, Library of Congress.
77. Philip Livingston and James Duane to the New York Provincial Congress, May 23, 1777, James Duane Papers, NYHS.
78. Lossing, *Philip Schuyler*, II, p. 180.

Chapter Eight

1. Sabine, *Memoirs of William Smith*, II, p. 151.
2. John Jay to John Ten Broeck, June 6, 1777, George Bancroft Transcripts, NYPL.
3. Robert R. Livingston to William Duer, June 12, 1777, Robert R. Livingston Papers, NYHS.
4. Dangerfield, *Chancellor Livingston*, pp. 94-95.
5. William Duer to Philip Schuyler, June 19, 1777, Schuyler Papers, NYPL.
6. John Jay, *et al* to Egbert Benson, June 2, 1777, Washington's Headquarters Museum, Newburgh, New York.
7. *Ibid.*
8. Sabine, *Memoirs of William Smith*, II, p. 157.
9. Philip Schuyler to Philip Livingston, James Duane, and William Duer, June 9, 1777, Schuyler Papers, NYPL.
10. Gerlach, *Schuyler*, p. 306.
11. Christopher Tappen to George Clinton, May 27, 1777, Hastings, *Public Papers of George Clinton*, I, pp. 848-850.
12. *Journals of the Provincial Congress of New York*, II, pp. 947 ff.
13. *Ibid.*, p. 948.
14. *Ibid.*, p. 957.

15. *Ibid.*, pp. 957-958.
16. Flick, Alexander. (ed.), *History of the State of New York* (10 vols., New York, 1933-1937), IV, p. 169.
17. Sabine, *Memoirs of William Smith,* II, pp. 151 ff.
18. *Ibid.*
19. *Ibid.*
20. Gerlach, *Schuyler,* p. 308.
21. Philip Schuyler to John Jay, June 30, 1777, Johnston, *Public Papers of John Jay,* I, p. 144.
22. The summary of votes cast in Albany, Charlotte, Dutchess, Tryon, Ulster, and Westchester Counties shows: 1,012 for Schuyler, 865 for George Clinton, 368 for John Morin Scott, 367 for Jay, 11 for Philip Livingston, and 7 for Robert R. Livingston.
23. Philip Schuyler to William Duer, July 3, 1777, George Bancroft Transcripts, NYPL.
24. Philip Schuyler to John Jay, July 14, 1777, Johnston, *Public Papers of John Jay,* I, pp. 146-147.
25. Gerlach, *Schuyler,* p. 310.

Chapter Nine

1. "Sir William Howe's Campaign of 1777," Public Record Office, C.O., 5: pp. 253, 273, Transcripts, Library of Congress.
2. *Ibid.*, p. 274.
3. *Ibid.*, p. 277.
4. *Ibid.*, p. 281.
5. *Ibid.*, p. 286.
6. *Ibid.*, p. 289.
7. Horatio Gates to Joseph Trumbull, Apr. 29, 1777, Joseph Trumbull Collection, Conn. State Library.
8. See John Welles to Philip Schuyler, Apr. 21, 1777, Schuyler Papers, NYPL. He said the service had been static since Schuyler's departure. Arthur St. Clair to James Wilson, June 18, 1777, Simon Gratz Collection, Historical Society of Pennsylvania. When St. Clair returned to Fort Ticonderoga he found the situation worse than it had been the previous year. Arthur St. Clair (?) to Horatio Gates, May 16, 1777, Horatio Gates Papers, NYHS. The writer stated that the "department had degenerated incredibly...."
9. Horatio Gates to the President of Congress, Apr. 22, 1777, Horatio Gates Papers, NYHS. Gates said: "General Wayne had endeavored to quicken the march of the Eastern troops, ...but the general apathy seems to have pervaded our whole system, which I am very apprehensive, nothing but the cannon of the Enemy will awaken."
10. Jonathan Trumbull, Sr. to John Hancock, Mar. 3, 1777, Papers of the Continental Congress, National Archives. Jonathan Trumbull, Sr. to Horatio Gates, Apr. 25, 1777, Horatio Gates Papers, NYHS. Orders from Josiah Bartlett to Colonels on the Connecticut River, May 3, 1777, Josiah Bartlett Papers, New Hampshire Historical Society.
11. Philip Schuyler to the Continental Congress, June 25, 1777, Schuyler Papers, NYPL.

12. Arthur St. Clair to James Wilson, June 18, 1777, Simon Gratz Collection, Historical Society of Pennsylvania.
13. James Wilkinson, *Memoirs of My Own Times* (3 vols., Philadelphia, 1816), I, p. 169 n. Hereafter cited as Wilkinson, *Memoirs.*
14. "Canada: 1777," Public Record Office, C.O., 5: pp. 253, 339, Transcripts, Library of Congress. Sir Guy Carleton retained 3,723 troops in Canada.
15. Philip Schuyler to the Continental Congress, June 25, 1777, Schuyler Papers, NYPL.
16. Council of General Officers, Held at Ticonderoga, June 20, 1777, Smith, *Arthur St. Clair,* I, pp. 404-405.
17. George Washington to Philip Schuyler, June 20, 1777, *Writings of Washington,* VIII, pp. 273-274.
18. Philip Schuyler to George Washington, June 25, 1777, Schuyler Papers, NYPL.
19. Philip Schuyler to George Washington, June 28, 1777, Schuyler Papers, NYPL.
20. Brockholst Livingston to William Livingston, June 30, 1777, William Livingston Papers, Mass. Historical Society.
21. Arthur St. Clair to Philip Schuyler, June 25, 1777, Philip Schuyler Papers, Henry Huntington Library.
22. Ward, *War of the Revolution,* I, pp. 409 ff.
23. Hoffman Nickerson, *The Turning Point of the Revolution* (Boston, 1928), pp. 141-142.
24. Andrew Hodges Tracy, July 3, 1777, George Washington Papers, Library of Congress.
25. Ward, *War of the Revolution,* I, p. 409.
26. Schuler Von Senden Journal, 1776-1777, Morristown National Historic Park, Morristown, New Jersey.
27. Diedrick Brehm's Report, 1759, Thomas Gage Papers, William L. Clements Library. Brehm said: "Artillery can be brought to the Top of the Mountain, though none but Royal Howitzers and Mortars."
28. Ward, *War of the Revolution,* I, p. 410.
29. Wilkinson, *Memoirs,* I, p. 184.
30. Philip Schuyler to William Heath, July 3, 1777, William Heath Papers, Mass. Historical Society.
31. See also Arthur St. Clair to Philip Schuyler, July 2, 1777, Schuyler Papers, NYPL.
32. Samuel Brewer to William Heath, July 3, 1777, William Heath Papers, Mass. Historical Society.
33. Journal of a British Officer: 1776-1777, p. 41, United States Military Academy Library. "The Evening of the 4th a Detachment of ours took post on Sugar Hill, which looked down upon, and entirely commanded the Enemy's works, from the Steepness of the Hill, they had thought it impossible to draw Cannon up it, had therefore not thought it necessary to establish a Post there. This movement of ours seemed to Alarm the Enemy much, when upon repeated trials, they found, their shot could not reach the Height."
34. *Ibid.*
35. Council of War, July 5, 1777, George Washington Papers, Library of Congress.
36. Theodore Sizer, ed., *The Autobiography of Colonel John Trumbull* (New Haven, 1953), pp. 29-31.

37. *Ibid.*

38. *Ibid.*

39. Horatio Gates to Arthur St. Clair, (copy), (June 12, 1777 (?)), Horatio Gates Papers, NYPL.

40. *Ibid.*

41. Horatio Gates to John Patterson, May 8, 1777, Horatio Gates Papers, NYHS. Jonathan Trumbull, Jr. to Jonathan Trumbull, Sr., June 10, 1777, Force Transcripts, Library of Congress.

42. George Washington to Philip Schuyler, June 20, 1777, Fitzpatrick, *Writings of Washington*, VIII, p. 273.

43. "John Brown and the Dash for Ticonderoga," *The Bulletin of the Fort Ticonderoga Museum,* II (No. 7, Jan., 1930), pp. 23 ff.

44. Schuler Von Senden Journal, 1776-1777, Morristown National Historic Park, Morristown, New Jersey. Von Senden thought it surprising "that the enemy gave up those two strong fortifications on his own free will.... A few years ago, during the Seven Years War, they stood up to the siege for a long time for which the English paid with 2,000 dead. This time our losses, with 7 dead and 20 wounded, are as small as thinkable. At the fort we got hold of 72 guns and some provisions."

45. Memorandum of the State of the Army at Ticonderoga Before the Evacuation (July 5, 1777), William Heath Papers, Mass. Historical Society.

46. Samuel Savage to William Heath, July (8), 1777, William Heath Papers, Mass. Historical Society.

47. Ward, *War of the Revolution,* I, pp. 414-415.

48. Wilkinson, *Memoirs,* I, pp. 186-187.

49. Ward, *War of the Revolution,* I, p. 414.

50. Lossing, *Philip Schuyler,* II, p. 214.

51. Philip Schuyler to Pierre Van Cortlandt, July 9, 1777, *Journals of the Provincial Congress of New York,* II, p. 514.

52. George Washington to William Heath, July 13, 1777, Fitzpatrick, *Writings of Washington,* VIII, pp. 394-395. General Washington "ordered the Men belonging to Putnam's, Greaton's, Alden's, and Nixon's Regiments..." to join Schuyler as quickly as possible. See also Leonard Gansevoort to Peter Gansevoort, July 2, 1777, Gansevoort-Lansing Collection, NYPL. Leonard Gansevoort said: "New England seems roused from the Lethargy she was imperceptibly involved in and resumes the Character she sustained in the beginning of this contest."

Chapter Ten

1. See Pierre Van Cortlandt to the New Hampshire Committee of Safety, July 27, 1777, Meschech Weare Papers, New Hampshire Historical Society. Jonathan Trumbull, Jr. to Horatio Gates, July 22, 1777, Horatio Gates Papers, NYHS.

2. John Glover to Anonymous, June 14, 1777, John Glover Papers, NYPL. Glover said "we may conclude our army will have but little to do at the Northward."

3. George Washington to Philip Schuyler, July 2, 1777, Fitzpatrick, *Writings of Washington,* VIII, pp. 331-332.

4. Samuel Adams to Richard Henry Lee, July 22, 1777, Samuel Adams Papers, NYPL.
5. Jonathan Potts to Horatio Gates, July 28, 1777, Horatio Gates Transcripts, Library of Congress.
6. William Whipple to James Lovell, Aug. 12, 1777, Force Transcripts, Library of Congress. Paul Revere to Samuel Adams, Aug. 24, 1777, Samuel Adams Papers, NYPL.
7. *Ibid.*
8. Philip Schuyler to the President of the State of Massachusetts Bay, July 28, 1777, Mass. Archives Division, State House.
9. Ward, *War of the Revolution,* I, pp. 415-416.
10. Burgoyne analyzed the advantages and disadvantages of several courses of action open to him and then chose to move his troops overland by way of Skenesborough and Wood Creek. This would avoid the appearance of even a temporary withdrawal, which might encourage the Americans. On the other hand, supplies were sent forward by way of Lake George. Had Burgoyne also chosen the latter route for his infantrymen, it would have been necessary to transport 400 batteaux over the portage between Lake Champlain and Lake George. This would have taken two weeks longer than the route they actually used. Although Colonel Philip Skene, Burgoyne's Loyalist advisor and himself the owner of considerable property east of Lake George, may have influenced his chief, the Skenesborough-Wood Creek route was the quickest way to Albany. That Skene stood to profit by a road through the forest was probably only incidental to the decision.
11. Ward, *War of the Revolution,* I, pp. 404-405.
12. Philip Schuyler to George Washington, July 10, 1777, George Washington Papers, Library of Congress. See also Narrative of Joseph Gray: A Revolutionary Soldier, New Hampshire Historical Society.
13. Philip Schuyler to George Washington, July 9, 1777, George Washington Papers, Library of Congress.
14. George Washington to the President of Congress, July 10, 1777, Fitzpatrick, *Writings of Washington,* VIII, pp. 376-378. See also George Washington to Philip Schuyler, July 24, 1777, *ibid.,* pp. 456-459.
15. Benedict Arnold to George Washington, July 27, 1777, George Washington Papers, Library of Congress.
16. Walter Stewart to Horatio Gates, Aug. 13, 1777, Horatio Gates Papers, NYHS. Anonymous to Jonathan Trumbull, Sr., July 15, 1777, Jonathan Trumbull, Sr. Papers, Conn. State Library. He said: "Many of the Continental Soldiers when they were fleeing for their lives threw their Guns away and Solomly (sic) declared they would not fight no more under their officers for they were sold to their enemies by them."
17. Benjamin Harrison to George Washington, Aug. 20, 1777, George Washington Papers, Library of Congress.
18. Eliphalet Dyer to Joseph Trumbull, July 15, 1777, Joseph Trumbulll Papers, Conn. Historical Society. Dyer said: "Enemy ships are all along the sea coast giving alarm then to divert them [the New England states] from giving aid to other parts . . . ."
19. John Burgoyne to George Germain, Aug. 20, 1777, Meschech Weare Papers, New Hampshire Historical Society.
20. William Howe to John Burgoyne, July 20, 1777, George Washington Papers, Library of Congress.

21. Howe was finally sighted off the capes of Delaware on July 31, 1777.
22. Samuel Adams to Richard Henry Lee, July 15, 1777, Samuel Adams Papers, NYPL.
23. Pierre Van Cortlandt to Jonathan Trumbull, Sr., July 27, 1777, Force Transcripts, Library of Congress.
24. Jonathan Trumbull, Jr. to Jonathan Trumbull, Sr., July 23, 1777, *ibid.*
25. Roger Sherman to Samuel Adams, July 11, 1777, Samuel Adams Papers, NYPL.
26. Samuel Adams to Richard Henry Lee, July 15, 1777, *ibid.*
27. George Washington to Philip Schuyler July 13, 1777, Fitzpatrick, *Writings of Washington,* VIII, pp. 392-393.
28. Jonathan Potts to Horatio Gates, July 28, 1777, Horatio Gates Papers, NYHS. Samuel Adams to Richard Henry Lee, July 22, 1777, Samuel Adams Papers, NYPL.
29. Samuel Adams to Roger Sherman, Aug. 11, 1777, *ibid.*
30. James Lovell to William Whipple, July 21, 1777, Force Transcripts, Library of Congress. Lovell was undoubtedly alluding to the remarks made on Schuyler's behalf several weeks before during the Schuyler-Gates command controversy.
31. John Jay to Philip Schuyler, Sept. 12, 1777, Lossing, *Philip Schuyler,* II, p. 306.
32. William Williams to Jonathan Trumbull, Sr., August 5, 1777, Burnett, *Letters of Cont. Cong.,* II, pp. 440-441.
33. Resolved, Aug. 4, 1777, *Journ. of Cont. Cong.,* VIII, p. 604.
34. Robert O. Bascom, *The Fort Edward Book* (Fort Edward, 1903) pp. 43 ff.
35. Ward, *War of the Revolution,* I, pp. 424 ff.
36. Lossing, *Philip Schuyler,* II, pp. 287-288.
37. Ward, *War of the Revolution,* II, pp. 489-490.
38. Alexander Garden, *Anecdotes of the American Revolution* (2 vols., Brooklyn, 1865).

Chapter Eleven

1. *Journ. of Cont. Cong.,* VIII, pp. 684-686. The committee consisted of Henry Laurens, Richard Henry Lee, and John Adams. On December 26, 1777, Francis Dana, John Witherspoon, and William Ellery were added to the committee. Later, James Lovell was substituted for Dana, and on January 27, 1778, James Smith became a committee member.
2. Lossing, *Philip Schuyler,* II, pp. 313-314.
3. Sabine, *Memoirs of William Smith,* II, p. 306.
4. *Ibid.,* p. 287.
5. *Ibid.,* p. 406.
6. *Journ. of Cont. Cong.,* X, p. 66.
7. George Washington to The President of Congress, Feb. 27, 1778, Fitzpatrick, *Writings of Washington,* X, pp. 518-519.
8. All three members of the original committee had been replaced. John Adams was in France; Richard Henry Lee did not resume his seat until May 1; and Henry Laurens had been excused.
9. Henry Laurens to George Washington, April 4, 1778, George Washington Papers, Library of Congress.

10. Gouverneur Morris to John Jay, April 28, 1778, Johnston, *Public Papers of John Jay*, I, p. 177. Morris intimates that Duer had been using the wrong approach. "This was unanimous," he wrote, "and yet I would have undertaken to argue for it in a style which would absolutely have ruined the measure." The committee consisted of Roger Sherman, Francis Dana, and William Drayton.
11. Philip Schuyler to Henry Laurens, May 9, 1778, Henry Laurens Letterbooks, South Carolina Historical Society.
12. Walter Livingston to Philip Schuyler, July 4, 1778, Schuyler Papers, NYPL.
13. *Ibid.* William Smith said Schuyler slept with a loaded gun at this time.
14. *Ibid.*
15. *Journ. of Cont. Cong.*, X, pp. 601-602.
16. *Ibid.* The charges were made under Article 5, Section 18, of The Rules and Articles of War.
17. George Washington to Philip Schuyler, July 22, 1778, Fitzpatrick, *Writings of Washington*, XII, pp. 200-201.
18. General Orders, Sept. 30, 1778, Fitzpatrick, *Writings of Washington*, XII, p. 526.
19. *Ibid.* Congress selected John D. Sergeant, Attorney General of the State of Pennsylvania, and William Patterson, Attorney General of New Jersey, to assist the judge advocate in the trial. The other members of the court were Colonels Samuel Willis, John Greaton, Rufus Putnam, Mordecai Gist, William Russell, William Grayson, Walter Stewart, and Return Jonathan Meigs. One change became necessary when Colonel Willis suddenly became ill. Washington replaced him with Colonel Francis Johnston.
20. *Ibid.* Five of the officers came from New England (Lincoln, Nixon, Greaton, Putnam, and Meigs); one from New York (Clinton); four from Pennsylvania (Wayne, Muhlenberg, Johnson, and Stewart); one from Maryland (Gist); and two from Virginia (Russell and Grayson).
21. See "The Trial of Major General St. Clair, August, 1778," Collections of the New York Historical Society (New York, 1881), pp. 1-72.
22. The trial was held at the home of Reed Ferris in Pawling, New York. The site had been near Washington's headquarters at Quaker Hill before Washington moved to Fredericksburgh, New York.
23. "The Trial of Major General Schuyler, October, 1778," *Collections* of the New-York Historical Society (New York, 1880), pp. 7-24.
24. *Ibid.*, p. 148.
25. *Ibid.*, p. 208.
26. *Ibid.*, pp. 209-210.
27. *Ibid.*, pp. 210-211.
28. Lossing, *Philip Schuyler*, II, p. 325.
29. *Ibid.*, p. 327.
30. George Bancroft, *History of the United States of America, From The Discovery of The Continent* (6 vols., New York, 1896), V, p. 161.

Chapter Twelve

1. James Duane to Philip Schuyler, Oct. 30, 1779, Schuyler Papers, NYPL.

2. Philip Schuyler to George Clinton, Nov. 29, 1777, Burnett, *Letters of Cont. Cong.*, IV, pp. 528-529.

3. Philip Schuyler to George Washington, Nov. 18, 1779, George Washington Papers, Library of Congress. Samuel Huntington feared the army would not be well supplied although supplies were plentiful. "Individuals seem to have laid aside all thought of danger, and are pursuing their private gains in oppositions to public." Samuel Huntington to Jonathan Trumbull, Sr., Dec. 20, 1779, Samuel Huntington Papers, Conn. Historical Society.

4. Burnett, *The Continental Congress*, p. 442. Robert R. Livingston of New York made the motion to have General Washington release all troops whose enlistments expired in April, 1780. It was seconded by John Penn of North Carolina.

5. George Washington to Elbridge Gerry, Jan. 29, 1780, Fitzpatrick, *Writings of Washington*, XVII, p. 463.

6. Burnett, *The Continental Congress*, p. 443.

7. Resolved, Feb. 25, 1780, *Journ. of Cont. Cong.*, XVI, pp. 196-197. The states were to furnish, according to their resources, provisions, hay, short fodder, salt, rum, and tobacco. For example, New Hampshire was supposed to contribute 34,000 gallons of rum, and Virginia six thousand hogsheads of tobacco.

8. Burnett, *The Continental Congress*, p. 444.

9. Resolved, Feb. 25, 1780, *Journ. of Cont. Cong.*, XVI, pp. 196 ff.

10. George Washington to Philip Schuyler, Mar. 22, 1780, Fitzpatrick, *Writings of Washington*, XVIII, pp. 137-138.

11. John Morin Scott, William Floyd, Philip Schuyler, Robert R. Livingston, and Ezra L'Hommedieu to George Clinton, Mar. 21, 1780, Burnett, *Letters of Cont. Cong.*, V, pp. 87-89.

12. John C. Miller, *Alexander Hamilton: Portrait In Paradox* (New York, 1959), p. 52.

13. Douglas Southall Freeman, *George Washington: A Biography* (5 vols., New York, 1948-1952) V, pp. 153-154 n.

14. Resolved, May 28, 1779, *Journ. of Cont. Cong.*, XIV, pp. 661-662.

15. Resolved, May 28, 1779, *Journ. of Cont. Cong.*, XVI, pp. 75-76.

16. Philip Schuyler to the President of Congress, Mar. 6, 1780, Burnett, *Letters of Cont. Cong.*, V, pp. 60-61.

17. *Ibid.*

18. George Washington to Joseph Jones, May 31, 1780, Fitzpatrick, *Writings of Washington*, XVIII, p. 453.

19. George Washington to The President of Congress, Apr. 3, 1780, Fitzpatrick, *Writings of Washington*, XVIII, pp. 207-211.

20. Burnett, *The Continental Congress*, p. 446.

21. *Ibid.*, p. 447.

22. *Ibid.*, p. 446.

23. George Washington to Joseph Jones, May 14, 1780, Fitzpatrick, *Writings of Washington*, XVIII, pp. 356-358. See also George Washington to James Duane, May 14, 1780, *ibid.*, p. 358.

24. Resolved, May 19, 1780, *Journ. of Cont. Cong.*, XVII, pp. 438-439.

25. Robert R. Livingston to Philip Schuyler, May 26, 1780, Schuyler Papers, NYPL.

26. James Duane to Philip Schuyler, May 26, 1780, Burnett, *Letters of Cont. Cong.*, V, pp. 170-171.

27. The Committee at Headquarters to the Several States, May 25, 1780, George Washington Papers, Library of Congress.

28. The Committee at Headquarters to the President of Congress, May 28, 1780, Papers of the Continental Congress, National Archives.

29. George Washington to the President of Congress, May 28, 1780, Fitzpatrick, *Writings of Washington,* XVIII, pp. 428-432.

30. Resolved, June 21, 1780, *Journ. of Cont. Cong.,* XVIII, pp. 538 ff.

31. Burnett, *The Continental Congress,* p. 460.

32. *Ibid.*

33. *Ibid.,* p. 461.

34. *Ibid.*

35. Resolved, Aug. 2, 1780, *Journ. of Cont. Cong.,* XVII, p. 686.

36. John Mathews to the President of Congress, Aug. 6, 1780, Papers of the Continental Congress, National Archives.

37. John Mathews to Philip Schuyler, Aug. 23, 1780, George Bancroft Transcripts, NYPL.

38. George Washington to The President of Congress, Aug. 28, 1780, Fitzpatrick, *Writings of Washington,* XIX, p. 463.

39. Philip Schuyler to George Clinton, Oct. 3, 1780, Hastings, *Public Papers of George Clinton,* VI, pp. 275-276.

40. John McKenstrey to Philip Schuyler, Aug. 5, 1781, Schuyler Papers, NYPL.

41. See the Albany *Knickerbocker News,* Oct. 27, 1942.

42. Philip Schuyler to Henry Glen, Aug., 1781, Philip Schuyler Papers, New York State Library. The poor spelling and punctuation in this letter indicate that Schuyler was shaken by the attempt to seize him.

BIBLIOGRAPHY

PRIMARY SOURCES

MANUSCRIPTS

Albany Institute of History and Art
    Philip Schuyler Papers
American Antiquarian Society
    Miscellaneous Papers
American Philosophical Society
    Benjamin Franklin Papers
    Richard Henry Lee Papers
Biblioteque Municipale, Ville de Nantes, France
    Labouchere Collection
Boston Public Library
    Mellen Chamberlain Collection
John Carter Brown Library, Brown University
    Miscellaneous Papers
William L. Clements Library, University of Michigan
    Henry Clinton Papers
    Thomas Gage Papers
    George Germain Papers
    Nathanael Greene Papers
Columbia University
    John Jay Collection
    Gouverneur Morris Papers
Connecticut Historical Society
    Jonathan Trumbull, Sr. Papers
    Jonathan Trumbull, Jr. Papers
    Joseph Trumbull Collection
    Jeremiah Wadsworth Papers
    Oliver Wolcott, Sr. Papers
Connecticut State Library
    Joseph Trumbull Collection
Cornell University
    Harmanus Schuyler Papers
Dartmouth College
    Josiah Bartlett Papers
    Eleazer Wheelock Papers
Fort Ticonderoga Library
    Benjamin Trumbull's Journal of the Expedition Against Canada: 1775

Simon Metcalf's Book
    This tiny volume contains good drawings and descriptions of most of
    the strategic posts and waterways near the New York-Canadian
    border.
Harvard University
    Jared Sparks Papers
Historical Society of Pennsylvania
    Ferdinand Dreer Collection
    Simon Gratz Collection
    Robert Morris Papers
    Anthony Wayne Papers
    James Wilson Papers
Henry Huntington Library
    Philip Schuyler Orderbook
        From this source, one can begin to understand the problems Schuyler
        faced in putting an army into the field and how he tried to solve
        them.
    Philip Schuyler Papers
Library of Congress
    John Adams Papers
    Samuel Adams Papers (photostats)
    British Museum, London: Additional Manuscripts (transcripts)
    British Public Record Office, London (transcripts)
        These papers tell what British officials were doing in North America.
        One can get an accurate picture of British strategy, an aspect often
        neglected by historians of the American Revolution who have written
        about the fighting in northern New York.
    Peter Force Papers (transcripts)
        Because Force only published material dated between 1774 and De-
        cember 31, 1776, this is an extremely valuable collection. Transcripts
        of several items found here have either been lost or destroyed by fire
        in their original repository, so in many cases Force's copies are
        unique.
    Horatio Gates Papers (transcripts)
    Alexander Hamilton Papers
    Robert Morris Papers
    George Washington Papers
        Together with the journals and papers of the Continental Congress,
        this is one of the best and most complete sources on the war.
Massachusetts Historical Society
    Jeremy Belknap Papers
    Jacob Bigelow Papers
    Bowdoin — Temple Papers
    C. E. French Papers
    Elbridge Gerry Papers
    C. P. Greenough Papers
    William Heath Papers
    Henry Knox Papers
    William Livingston Papers
    Miscellaneous Papers
    Robert Treat Paine Papers
    Joseph Palmer Papers

Timothy Pickering Papers
Samuel P. Savage Papers
Theodore Sedgwick Papers
John Sullivan Papers
John Thomas Papers
Artemas Ward Papers
Warren — Adams Papers
Meschech Weare Papers
Massachusetts State Archives, State House, Boston, Massachusetts
Revolutionary War Papers
Morristown National Historical Park
Lord Francis Napier, "Journal of the Burgoyne Campaign."
Lloyd Wadell Smith Collection
Smith collected many documents related to the war which have sel-
dom been used because of their location.
Schuler Von Senden Journal
This is a partially translated journal kept by a Hessian officer during
the campaigns of 1776 and 1777.
Anthony Wayne Papers
National Archives
Papers of the Continental Congress
One could write almost any history of the war from these papers.
They are excellent.
National Library of Scotland, Edinburgh
Charles Cochrane Papers
New Hampshire Historical Society
Josiah Bartlett Papers
Timothy Bedel Papers
Jeremy Belknap Papers
Diary of Major Henry Blake
Narrative of Joseph Gray: A Revolutionary Soldier
John Langdon Papers
Samuel Livermore Papers
Morris — Stark Papers
John Sullivan Papers
Meschech Weare Papers
New Jersey Historical Society
Miscellaneous Papers
New York Geneological and Biographical Society
Memorandum of an Agreement Made by General Schuyler for Carpen-
ters, March 1, 1776.
New-York Historical Society
William Alexander Papers
Benedict Arnold Papers
John Cruger Papers
William Duer Papers
As a staunch Schuyler supporter, Duer often described his efforts to
defend and aid the General during the Gates command controversy.
James Duane Papers
Since Schuyler often confided in Duane, their correspondence is par-
ticularly revealing on occasion.
Horatio Gates Papers

Robert R. Livingston Papers
William Livingston Papers
Alexander McDougall Papers
Miscellaneous Papers
Gouverneur Morris Papers
Joseph Reed Papers
Philip Schuyler Papers
George Smyth Papers
Ebenezer Stevens Papers
Walter Stewart Papers
Marinus Willett Papers
New York Public Library
Samuel Adams Papers
The New England animosity toward New York and Schuyler is ex-
emplified by Adams, so his papers are useful in the controversy
between the states involved.
Benedict Arnold Papers
George Bancroft Collection
Like Peter Force, George Bancroft had others transcribe documents
for him. This makes the collection useful, especially since many of
the transcripts are from British collections.
Samuel Chase Papers
George Clinton Papers
Thomas A. Emmet Collection
Horatio Gates Papers (transcripts)
Mordecai Gist Letterbook (transcripts)
Henry Glen Papers
John Glover Papers
Lansing-Gansevoort Collection
This collection is rich in information about the war on New York's
western frontier.
Benjamin Lincoln Papers
Robert R. Livingston Papers (transcripts)
Theodorus B. Meyers Collection
Robert Morris Papers
Philip Schuyler Papers
This collection contains approximately ten thousand documents. It
includes letterbooks of incoming and outgoing correspondence up to
July, 1777. In addition there are troop returns, journals, and diaries
covering Schuyler's long and active career, as well as considerable
incoming correspondence.
William Smith Diaries, 7 vols., 1732-1783
Although a Loyalist, Smith remained a close friend to Schuyler
throughout the war. His journals contain considerable source material
which historians have still not used.
Van Cortlandt — Van Wyck Papers
Artemas Ward Diary
Abraham Yates, Jr. Papers
As an active participant in the writing of New York's first constitution, Yates made numerous comments on the problems involved. His
papers indicate that he, and not John Jay, probably wrote this
document.

New York State Library
    John Burgoyne Order Book, 1777
    Morgan Lewis Papers
    Philip Schuyler Papers
    John Williams Papers
Pierpont Morgan Library
    Miscellaneous Papers
Princeton University
    Andre de Coppet Collection
Public Archives of Canada, Ottawa
    Haldimand Papers
Rhode Island Historical Society
    Jeremiah Olney Papers
Schuyler Mansion, Albany, New York
    Schuyler Family Bible
South Carolina Historical Society
    Henry Laurens Letter Books
United States Military Academy
    "Anonymous Journal of the Burgoyne Campaign"
        This journal has apparently been overlooked by historians. It gives
        some of the best descriptions of fighting in northern New York that
        one can find anywhere.
Washington's Headquarters Museum, Newburgh, New York
    John Burgoyne Order Book, 1777
    Miscellaneous Papers
Yale University
    John Trumbull Papers

COLLECTED DOCUMENTS, LETTERS, AND WORKS

A Reply to General Burgoyne's Letter to His Constitutents. London, Printed
    for J. Wilkie, 1779.
Bouton, Nathaniel (ed.), *Provincial Papers of New Hampshire,* Vols. VII &
    VIII. Nashua, Orren C. Moore, 1873.
Burnett, Edmund C. (ed.), *Letters of Members of the Continental Congress,*
    8 vols. Washington, The Carnegie Institution of Washington, 1921-1936.
Butterfield, Lyman H. *et al.* (eds.), *Diary & Autobiography of John Adams,*
    4 vols. Cambridge, Belknap Press, 1961.
*Calendar of Historical Manuscripts relating to the War of the Revolution in
    the office of the Secretary of State.* Albany, Weed, Parsons & Co., 1864.
Collections of the New York Historical Society, 38 vols. New York, The
    New York Historical Society, 1868-1906.
Collections of the Connecticut Historical Society, 24 vols. Hartford, The
    Society, 1944.
Cushing, Harry Alonzo (ed.), *The Writings of Samual Adams,* 4 vols. New
    York, G. P. Putnam's Sons, 1904-1908.
Fitzpatrick, John C. (ed.), *The Writings of George Washington, 1745-1799,*
    39 vols. Washington, U. S. Government Printing Office, 1931-1944.
Force, Peter (ed.), *American Archives,* Fourth Series, 6 vols. Washington,
    M. St. Clair Clarke & Peter Force, 1837-1846; and Fifth Series, 3 vols.
    Washington, M. St. Clair Clarke & Peter Force, 1848-1853.

Ford, Worthington, C., *et al.* (eds.), *The Journals of the Continental Congress, 1774-1789,* 34 vols. Washington, U.S. Government Printing Office, 1904-1937.

Hamilton, Stanislaus Murray (ed.), *Letters to Washington and Accompanying Papers,* 5 vols. Boston, Houghton, Mifflin & Co., 1902.

Hammond, Otis G. (ed.), *Letters and Papers of Major-General John Sullivan: Continental,* 3 vols. Concord, New Hampshire Historical Society, 1930.

Hastings, Hugh (comp.), *Public Papers of George Clinton,* 10 vols. Albany, The State of New York, 1899-1914.

Heitman, Francis B., *Historical Register of Officers of the Continental Army During The War of the Revolution.* Washington, The Rare Book Publishing Co., 1914.

Johnston, Henry P. (ed.), *The Correspondence and Public Papers of John Jay,* 4 vols. New York, G. P. Putnam's Sons, 1890-1903.

Journal of the Legislative Council of the Colony of New York, 1691-1775, 2 vols. Albany, Weed, Parsons & Co., 1961.

Journals of the Provincial Congress, Provincial Convention, Committee of Safety and Council of Safety of the State of New York, 1775-1776-1777, 2 vols. Albany, Thurlow Weed, 1842.

Kirkland, Frederic R. (ed.), *Letters on the American Revolution in the Library at "Karolfred."* Philadelphia, Privately Printed, 1941.

Letters by Josiah Bartlett, William Whipple and Others. Philadelphia, 1889.

Lodge, Henry Cabot (ed.), *The Works of Alexander Hamilton.* New York, G. P. Putnam's Sons, 1904.

Moore, Frank, *Diary of the American Revolution,* 2 vols. New York, Charles Scribner, 1860.

Munsell, Joel, Collections of the History of Albany from its Discovery to the Present Time, 4 vols. Albany, J. Munsell, 1865-1871.

Munsell, Joel, *The Annals of Albany,* 10 vols. Albany, J. Munsell, 1850-1959.

O'Callaghan, E. B. (ed.), *Calendar of Historical Manuscripts in the Office of the Secretary of State, Albany, N.Y.* Two parts. Albany, Weed, Parsons & Co., 1865-1866.

O'Callaghan, E. B. (ed.), *Calendar of New York Colonial Commissions, 1680-1770.* New York, The New York Historical Society, 1929.

O'Callaghan, Edmund B. and Berthold Fernow (eds.), *Documents Relative to the Colonial History of the State of New York,* 15 vols. Albany, Weed, Parsons & Co., 1853-1857.

O'Callaghan, E. B. (ed.), *Orderly Book of Lieutenant General John Burgoyne.* Albany, Joel Munsell, 1860.

O'Callaghan, E. B. (ed.), *The Documentary History of the State of New York,* 4 vols. Albany, Weed, Parsons & Co., 1849-1851.

Paltsits, Victor Hugo (ed.), *Minutes of the Commissioners for Detecting and Defeating Conspiracies in the State of New York, Albany County Sessions: 1778-1781.* Albany, State of New York, 1909.

The Parliamentary Register; or, History of the Proceedings and Debates of the House of Commons, 17 vols. London, J. Walker, R. Lea and J. Nunn, 1802.

Report of the Regents' Boundary Commission Upon the New York and Pennsylvania Boundary. Albany, Weed, Parsons & Co., 1886.

Report of the Regents of the University on the Boundaries of the State of New York, Vol. II. Albany, The Argus Co., 1884.

Reynolds, Cuyler (ed.), *Hudson-Mohawk Genealogical and Family Memoirs,* 4 vols. New York, Lewis Historical Publishing Co., 1911.

Smith, William H. (ed.), *The Life and Public Service of Arthur St. Clair,* 2 vols. Cincinnati, R. Clarke & Co., 1882.

Sparks, Jared (ed.), *Correspondence of the American Revolution,* 4 vols. Boston, Little, Brown & Co., 1853.

Stevens, Benjamin Franklin, *Facsimiles of Manuscripts in European Archives. Relating to America: 1773-1783,* 25 vols. London, Chiswick Press, 1889-1898.

Stokes, I. N. Phelps (comp. & ed.), *The Iconography of Manhattan Island: 1498-1909,* 6 vols. New York, Robert H. Dodd, 1895-1928.

Sullivan, James (ed.), *Minutes of the Albany Committee of Correspondence, 1775-1778,* 2 vols. Albany, The University of the State of New York, 1923-1925.

Sullivan, James *et al.* (eds.), *Sir William Johnson Papers,* 12 vols. Albany, The University of the State of New York, 1921-1957.

Syrett, Harold C. (ed.), *The Papers of Alexander Hamilton,* Vols. I & II. New York, Columbia University Press, 1961.

The State of the Expedition from Canada, as Laid Before the House of Commons, by Lieut. Gen. Burgoyne. London, Printed for J. Almon, 1780.

Werner, Edgar A., *Civil List and Constitutional History of the State of New York.* Albany, Weed, Parsons & Co., 1884-1888.

AUTOBIOGRAPHIES AND REMINISCENCES

Anburey, Thomas, *Travels Through the Interior Parts of America,* 2 vols. Boston, Houghton Mifflin, 1923.

Baxter, Katherine Schuyler, *A Godchild of Washington.* New York, F. Tennyson Neely, 1897.

(Becker, John P.), *The Sexagenary or Reminiscences of the American Revolution.* Albany, W. C. Little & O. Steele, 1833.

(Bradstreet, John), *An Impartial Account of Lieut. Col. Bradstreet's Expedition to Fort Frontenac.* Toronto, Rous & Mann Ltd., 1940.

Bonney, Catherine V. R. (comp.), *A Legacy of Historical Gleanings,* 2 vols. Albany, J. Munsell, 1875.

De Chastellux, Marquis, *Travels in North America in the Years 1780, 1781, and 1782,* 2 vols. London, 1787.

De Riedesel, Madam, *Letters and Memoirs Relating to the War of American Independence and the Capture of the German Troops at Saratoga,* English translation. New York, G. & C. Carvill, 1827.

Epping, Charlotte S. J. (trans.), *Journal of Du Roi the Elder.* New York, D. Appleton & Co., 1911.

Garden, Alexander, *Anecdotes of the American Revolution,* 2 vols. Brooklyn, The Union Press, 1865.

Grant, Anne, *Memoirs of An American Lady,* 2 vols. New York, Dodd, Mead & Co., 1901.

Lamb, Roger, *Memoir of His Own Life, by R. Lamb.* Dublin, Printed by J. Jones, 1811.

Moore, Frank (comp.), *The Diary of the Revolution, 1775-1781.* Hartford, J. B. Burr Publishing Co., 1876.

Reid, Arthur, *Reminiscences of the Revolution, or, Le Loup's Bloody Trail from Salem to Fort Edward.* Utica, Roberts, Book & Job Printer, 1859.

Rogers, Horatio (ed.), *Hadden's Journal and Orderly Books.* Albany, Joel Munsell's Sons, 1886.

Sabine, William H. W. (ed.), *Historical Memoirs of William Smith: 1763-1778,* 2 vols. New York, Colburn and Tegg, 1956-1958.

Sizer, Theodore (ed.), *The Autobiography of Colonel John Trumbull.* New Haven, Yale University Press, 1953.

Stark, Caleb, *Memoir and Official Correspondence of Gen. John Stark.* Concord, G. Parker Lyon, 1860.

Stone, William L. (trans. & ed.), *Journal of Captain (George) Pausch.* Albany, Joel Munsell's Sons, 1886.

Stone, William L. (trans.), *Letters of Brunswick and Hessian Officers During The American Revolution.* Albany, Joel Munsell's Sons, 1891.

Stone, William L. (trans.), *Memoirs, and Letters and Journals, of Major General Riedesel During His Residence in America,* 3 vols. Albany, J. Munsell, 1868.

Thacher, James, *A Military Journal During The American Revolution.* Boston, Richardson and Lord, 1823.

Watson, Winslow C. (ed.), *Men and Times of the Revolution or Memoirs of Elkanah Watson,* 2d. ed. New York, Dana & Co., 1856.

Wilkinson, James, *Memoirs of My Own Times,* 3 vols. Philadelphia, A. Small, 1816.

Willcox, William B. (ed.), The American Rebellion, *Sir Henry Clinton's Narrative of His Campaigns, 1775-1782, with an Appendix of Original Documents.* New Haven, Yale University Press, 1954.

NEWSPAPERS

The Pennsylvania Gazette.
The New-York Mercury.

SECONDARY SOURCES

BIOGRAPHIES

Alden, John Richard, *General Charles Lee, Traitor or Patriot?* Baton Rouge, Louisiana State University Press, 1951.

Alexander, Edward P., *A Revolutionary Conservative: James Duane of New York.* New York, Columbia University Press, 1938.

Freeman, Douglas Southall, *George Washington: A Biography,* 5 vols. New York, Charles Scribner's Sons, 1948-1952.

Gerlach, Don R., *Philip Schuyler and the American Revolution in New York, 1733-1777.* Lincoln, University of Nebraska Press, 1964.

Hamilton, John C., *The Life of Alexander Hamilton,* 2 vols. New York, Halsted & Voorhis, D. Appleton & Co., 1834-1840.

Huddleston, Francis J., *Gentleman John Burgoyne*. London, J. Cope, 1928.
Humphreys, Mary Gay, *Catherine Schuyler*. New York, Charles Scribner's Sons, 1897.
Jay, William, *The Life of John Jay*, 2 vols. New York, J. & J. Harper, 1833.
Leake, Isaac Q., *Memoir of the Life and Times of General John Lamb*. Albany, Joel Munsell, 1850.
Leonard, Lewis A., *Life of Charles Carroll of Carrollton*. New York, Moffat, Yard & Co., 1918.
Lossing, Benson J., *The Life and Times of Philip Schuyler*, 2 vols. New York, Sheldon & Company, 1760-73.
Mitchell, Broadus, *Alexander Hamilton: Youth to Maturity, 1755-1788*. New York, Macmillan Co., 1957.
Monaghan, Frank, *John Jay*. New York, Bobbs-Merrill, 1935.
Patterson, Samuel W., *Horatio Gates*. New York, Columbia University Press, 1941.
Pell, John, *Ethan Allen*. London, Constable & Co., Ltd., 1930.
Schachner, Nathan, *Alexander Hamilton*. New York, D. Appleton-Century Co., Inc., 1946.
Smith, William Henry, *The Life and Public Services of Arthur St. Clair*, 2 vols. Cincinnati, Robert Clarke & Co., 1882.
Sparks, Jared, *The Life of Gouverneur Morris*, 3 vols. Boston, Gray & Bowen, 1832.
Spaulding, E. Wilder, *His Excellency George Clinton: Critic of the Constitution*. New York, Macmillan Co., 1838.
Tuckerman, Bayard, *Life of General Philip Schuyler, 1733-1804*. New York, Dodd, Mead & Co., 1903.
Valentine, Alan Chester, *Lord George Germain*. London, Oxford University Press, 1962.
Van Schaak, Henry C., *The Life of Peter Van Schaak, LL.D.* New York, D. Appleton & Co., 1842.
Ver Steeg, Clarence L., *Robert Morris: Revolutionary Financier*. Philadelphia, University of Pennsylvania Press, 1954.
Wallace, Willard M., *Traitorous Hero, The Life and Fortunes of Benedict Arnold*. New York, Harper & Brothers, 1954.
Wilson, David, *The Life of Jane McCrea*. New York, Baker, Goodwin & Co., 1853.

GENERAL WORKS

Alden, John Richard, *The American Revolution, 1775-1783*. New York, Harper & Brothers, 1954.
Alexander, De Alva Stanwood, *A Political History of the State of New York*, 3 vols. New York, Henry Holt & Co., 1906-1909.
Anderson, Troyer Steele, *The Command of the Howe Brothers During the American Revolution*. New York, Oxford University Press, 1936.
Bancroft, George, *History of the United States*, 6 vols. New York, Appleton, 1888.
Barck, Oscar Theodore, Jr., *New York City During the War For Independence*. New York, Columbia University Press, 1931.

Bascom, Robert O., *The Fort Edward Book*. Fort Edward, James D. Keating, 1903.

Baxter, James Phinney, *The British Invasion from the North, the Campaigns of Generals Carleton and Burgoyne from Canada, 1776-1777, with the Journal of Lieut. William Digby, of the 53d, or Shropshire Regiment of Foot*. Albany, Joel Munsell's Sons, 1887.

Becker, Carl Lotus, *The History of Political Parties in the Province of New York, 1760-1776*. Madison, University of Wisconsin Press, 1960.

Bennett, Clarence E., *Advance and Retreat to Saratoga in The American Revolution*. Schenectady, Robson & Adee, 1927.

Bird, Harrison, *March to Saratoga*. New York, Oxford University Press, 1963.

Bonney, Mrs. Catharina V.R. (comp.), *A Legacy of Historical Gleanings*, 2d. ed., 2 vols. Albany, J. Munsell, 1875.

Burnett, Edmund Cody, *The Continental Congress*. New York, Macmillan Co., 1941.

Carrington, Henry B., *Battles of the American Revolution, 1775-1781*. New York, A. S. Barnes & Co., 1876.

Cunningham, Anna K., *Schuyler Mansion, a Critical Catalogue of the Furnishings & Decorations*. Albany, New York State Education Department, 1955.

Dangerfield, George, *Chancellor Robert R. Livingston of New York, 1746-1813*. New York, Harcourt, Brace & World Co., 1960.

De Peyster, John Watts, *Major General Philip Schuyler and the Burgoyne Campaign in the Summer of 1777*. New York, Holt Brothers, 1877.

Dillon, Dorothy Rita, *The New York Triumvirate*. New York, Columbia University Press, 1949.

Drake, Samuel Adams, *Burgoyne's Invasion of 1777*. Boston, Lee and Shepard, 1889.

Fiske, John, *The American Revolution*, 2 vols. Boston, Houghton, Mifflin & Co., 1891.

Flick, Alexander (ed.), *History of the State of New York*, 10 vols: New York, Columbia University Press, 1933-1937.

(Flick, Alexander), *The American Revolution in New York*. Albany, University of the State of New York, 1926.

Gipson, Lawrence Henry, *The Coming of the Revolution, 1763-1775*. London, Hamish Hamilton, 1954.

Greene, Francis Vinton, *The Revolutionary War and the Military Policy of the United States*. New York, Charles Scribner's Sons, 1911.

Hatch, Louis Clinton, *The Administration of the American Revolutionary Army*. New York, Longmans, Green and Co., 1904.

Howell, George R., and Jonathan Tenney (ed.), *Bi-Centennial History of Albany: History of the County of Albany, N.Y., From 1609 to 1886*. New York, W. W. Munsell & Co., 1886.

Jones, Charles Henry, *History of the Campaign for the Conquest of Canada in 1776*. Philadelphia, Porter & Coates, 1882.

Knollenberg, Bernhard, *Washington and the Revolution: A Reappraisal*. New York, Macmillan, 1940.

Lossing, Benson J., *The Pictorial Field. Book of the Revolution*, 2 vols. New York, Harper and Brothers, 1860.

MacMillan, Margaret Burnham, *The War Governors in the American Revolution*. New York, Columbia University Press, 1943.

Miller, John C., *Origins of the American Revolution*. Boston, Little, Brown & Co., 1943.

Moore, Frank (ed.), *Songs and Ballads of the American Revolution*. New York, D. Appleton & Co., 1855.

Neilson, Charles, *An Original, Compiled, and Corrected Account of Burgoyne's Campaign*. Albany, J. Munsell, 1844.

Nickerson, Hoffman, *The Turning Point of the Revolution, Or Burgoyne in America*. Boston, Houghton, Mifflin Co., 1928.

Schachner, Nathan, *The Founding Fathers*. New York, G. P. Putnam's Sons, 1954.

Scheer, George F. and Ranking, Hugh F., *Rebels and Redcoats*. New York, The New American Library, 1959.

Schuyler, George L., *Correspondence and Remarks Upon Bancroft's History of the Northern Campaign of 1777, and the Character of Major-Gen. Philip Schuyler*. New York, David G. Francis, 1867.

Schuyler, George W., *Colonial New York: Philip Schuyler and His Family*, 2 vols. New York, Charles Scribner's Sons, 1885.

Scott, John Albert, *Fort Stanwix and Oriskany*. Rome, Rome Sentinel Co., 1927.

Spaulding, E. Wilder, *New York in the Critical Period, 1783-1789*. New York, Columbia University Press, 1932.

Stone, William Leete (comp.), *Ballads and Poems Relating to the Burgoyne Campaign*. Albany, J. Munsell's Sons, 1893.

Stone, William Leete, *The Campaign of Lieut. Gen. John Burgoyne, and the Expedition of Lieut. Col. Barry St. Leger*. Albany, J. Munsell, 1877.

Van Doren, Carl, *Secret History of the American Revolution*. New York, The Viking Press, 1941.

Vrooman, John J., *Forts and Firesides of the Mohawk Country New York*. Philadelphia, E. E. Brownell, 1943.

Wallace, Willard M., *A Military History of the American Revolution*. New York, Harper & Brothers, 1951.

Ward, Christopher, *The War of the Revolution*, 2 vols., Edited by John Richard Alden. New York, The Macmillan Co., 1952.

Weise, Arthur J., *The History of the City of Albany, New York*. Albany, E. H. Bender, 1884.

Wright, Esmond, *Fabric of Freedom. 1763-1800*. New York, Hill & Wang, Inc., 1961.

ARTICLES

Becker, Carl Lotus, "The Growth of Revolutionary Parties and Methods in New York Province, 1765-1774." *American Historical Review*, VIII (Oct. 1901).

Clark, Jane, "Responsibility for the Failure of the Burgoyne Campaign." *American Historical Review*, XXXV (April, 1930), p. 542.

Gregg, C. E., "General Philip Schuyler and the Schuyler Mansion." *The Dutch Settlers Society of Albany Yearbook*, XXV-XXVI (Albany, 1949-1951).

Hargreaves, Reginald, "Burgoyne and America's Destiny." *American Heritage*, VII (June, 1956), pp. 4-7, 83-85.

Schuyler, Robert Livingston, "Philip Schuyler." *New York History*, XVIII (April, 1937).

PERIODICALS

The Bulletin of The Fort Ticonderoga Museum.
New Jersey Historical Society — *Proceedings.*

HANDBOOKS AND ENCYCLOPEDIAS

Griffin, Grace G. (ed.), *A Guide to Manuscripts Relating to American History in British Depositories Reproduced for the Division of Manuscripts of the Library of Congress.* Washington, The Library of Congress, 1946.
Guide To The Manuscript Collections of the Historical Society of Pennsylvania. Philadelphia, The Historical Society of Pennsylvania, 1949.
Hamer, Philip M. (ed.), *A Guide to Archives and Manuscripts in the United States.* New Haven, Yale University Press, 1961.
Handbook of Manuscripts in the Library of Congress. U.S. Government Printing Office, 1918.
List of National Archives Microfilm Publications 1961. Washington, National Archives, 1961.
Special Report of the Library of Congress to the Joint Committee of the Library Concerning the Historical Library of Peter Force, esq. Washington, 1867.
Wold, Ansel (comp.), *Biographical Dictionary of the American Congress, 1774-1927.* Washington, Government Printing Office, 1928.

INDEX